100 Walks in
New South Wales

GW00708234

100 Walks in New South Wales

Fourth Edition—Fully Revised

Tyrone T. Thomas

(Features 54 new walks)

HILL OF CONTENT

MELBOURNE

First published in Australia 1977
by Hill of Content Publishing Co Pty Ltd
86 Bourke Street, Melbourne, Australia 3000

© Copyright Tyrone T. Thomas 1994

Reprinted 1980
Second Edition 1983, 1985, 1987
Third Edition 1988, 1991
Fourth Edition 1994

Cover photograph: Lagoon and Mount Eliza
from Lovers Bay, Lord Howe Island
Frontispiece:
Original wood engraving Mt. Kaputah
from "Le Tour du Monde" C. 1860
Illustrated by the author with
photographs from his collection

Typeset by Midland Typesetters, Maryborough, Victoria
Printed by Kyodo Printing (S'pore) Pte Ltd

National Library of Australia
Cataloguing-in-publication data

Thomas, Tyrone T., 1938–
    100 walks in New South Wales

    4th ed.
    Includes index.
    ISBN 0 85572 230 4.

    1. Hiking—New South Wales—Guidebooks.
    2. New South Wales—Guidebooks. 1. Title. II. Title: One hundred walks
in New South Wales.

919.440463

Note: It is imperative that users of this book check time-tables and
transport services before undertaking any walk suggestions requiring
public transport.

By the same author

120 Walks in Victoria
100 Walks in Tasmania
50 Walks in South Australia
50 Walks in the Grampians
50 Walks Coffs Harbour Gold Coast Hinterland
50 Walks in Southern New South Wales and A.C.T.
20 Best Walks in Australia
60 Walks in Central Victoria's Goldfields and Spa Country
Wandern in Australien (German language edition)
Wandern in Tasmanien (German language edition)

CONTENTS

INTRODUCTION

This book contains information about one hundred walks in New South Wales. It recommends walking areas in the state which are generally frequented by bushwalkers. Population centres are taken into account so that the greatest number of walk suggestions occur in beautiful places near the biggest cities and the book is organised so that ready reference can be made to those regions. Within each region walks are graded easy, medium and hard. Most routes are circuits of one day duration, or are planned so that public transport can be used to complete circuits. Nine selected walks are included which are of overnight duration and which the author considers to be the best in the state. They are included for those who want to try camping out.

It is hoped that this book will induce people to go out walking, that it will help them to grow to love the New South Wales bush and to learn to care for it and themselves while walking. Special sections deal with safety, mapping and navigation. The book is designed to suit all grades of walkers and should be a useful addition to other walk books in this series.

A feature of this new edition is the replacement of 54 walks with new walk suggestions. This is mainly to provide new interest to the book but some replacements became necessary due to encroachment of built-up areas.

In all walks times taken will vary greatly, depending upon the experience of individual walkers, so track notes are provided with references that give both exact distances and variable times, exclusive of lunch and other significant breaks. As a rough guide the actual walking time taken by the author is doubled.

Generally speaking, walk venues in New South Wales are in rugged country, often with sandstone cliffs and therefore distances that can be covered in a day are relatively short.

All routes in the book have been personally walked

by the author between January 1992 and November 1992 except the two walks at Lord Howe Island which were last walked in May 1987 and one walk at Mount Kaputah last fully walked in April 1986 and (partially) walked August 1992.

Track notes were simultaneously compared with the field checking and updated. However it must be expected that changes will occur in some places with the passing of time. Every care has been taken in notes compilation, but no responsibility will be accepted for any inaccuracies or for any mishap that might arise out of the use of this book. The author and publisher welcome advice of any errors or desirable changes to bring future editions of the book up to date.

Tyrone T. Thomas
1994

EPACRIS

WALKS LOCATION MAP

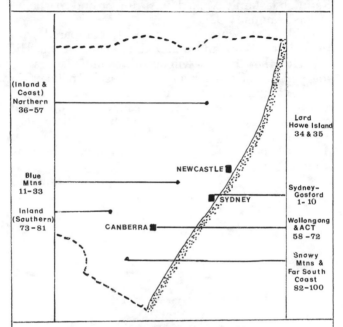

(Inland & Coast) Northern 36-57

Lord Howe Island 34 & 35

Blue Mtns 11-33

NEWCASTLE

Sydney-Gosford 1-10

SYDNEY

Inland (Southern) 73-81

CANBERRA

Wollongong & ACT 58-72

Snowy Mtns & Far South Coast 82-100

GRADINGS

EASY	MEDIUM	HARD
1 2 4 5 6 7 9	10 15 17 18 20 27 29	3 8 34 39 65 68 81
11 12 13 14 16 19 21	35 37 51 53 56 69 76	94
23 24 25 26 28 30 31	77 79 84 86 87 93 96	
32 33 36 38 42 43 44	97	
45 46 48 49 50 52 54		
55 57 58 59 60 61 62		
63 64 66 67 71 72 73		
74 75 78 80 85 88 89		
91 92 95 98		
OVERNIGHT 82 100	OVERNIGHT 22 40 41 47 70 83 90 99	OVERNIGHT -

INDEX TO WALK SUGGESTIONS

10

BANKSIA

SAFETY AND COMMONSENSE IN THE BUSH

Bushwalking is a very enjoyable recreation, and commonsense safety precautions will keep it that way. Be prepared for any problem that may arise.

1 Plan your trip and leave details of your route in writing with some responsible person and report back to them on return. Always carry maps, compass, mirror, first-aid kit, plenty of paper, warm, bright-coloured, waterproof clothing, whistle, matches in a waterproof container, candle, small sharp knife, torch and emergency rations of food. It is of the utmost importance that you should be able to read maps and use a compass.

2 Never try to rush a trip. Think before you act, watch your route on a map and recognise your limitations, especially with distance. A good walker can cover three to five kilometres each hour, and in dense bush perhaps only two kilometres each hour. Always keep together when walking in a group and never walk in a party of less than three.

3 If lost, STOP! Only move once you have very carefully thought things through. Remember that any movement is best made on ridges and spurs, not in scrub-choked gullies. You should be absolutely sure of directions and should leave a prominent note indicating your intentions and time of leaving. You should put on bright-coloured and warm clothing. Once moving, constantly watch the compass, remain on as straight a line as possible and leave notes along the route. If you become tired, stop and rest. Do not over-exert yourself. Remember that severe physical and mental strain, plus cold, can mean death by exposure. Over the years far too many people have died unnecessarily, or suffered serious injuries, mainly because they have not understood the seriousness of being caught unprepared in the bush, and then have not been able to cope with the

situation. The accepted distress signal is three long whistles, cooees, mirror flashes, or any other signal repeated in threes every minute. Do not force yourself physically; rather, do things objectively and calmly, with plenty of rest.

4 When following suggested walk routes, ensure that you obtain and use the recommended maps so that the maximum amount of information is available to you. Where more than one map of an area is available, it is advisable to use both. Maps frequently become outdated. The maps included in this book should be used in conjunction with other maps wherever possible.

5 Remember that care of the bushland itself is very important. Many walk routes are in declared National Parks and commonsense regulations must be respected. The bush and the life within it is often in a delicate state of ecological balance. Make sure your camp fire is completely extinguished. Remember the slogan, 'The bigger the fire—the bigger the fool', and on no account light a fire on a high fire-danger day.

6 The camp fire is ideal for the disposal of the majority of waste, but silver paper and other foils and cans will not destruct so readily. Wash all cans, remove both ends, flatten them, and carry them, along with any foil or glass, in a plastic bag to the nearest garbage bin. Many walking areas are frequented far more than you may realise and burial of rubbish will eventually create problems. Human waste should always be buried properly away from streams and drinking water. Always wash downstream from the camp site and collect drinking water upstream from the camp site. Remember other people do not appreciate drinking your bath water.

Most walkers like to pitch their tents around a central camp fire but bad weather can drastically change the preference and when this happens an available hut or rock shelter in the sandstone country can provide a welcome shelter in surroundings just as congenial. It is most important that huts used are respected, in return for the generosity of the owners in allowing bush-walkers to use them freely. They should always be left clean and with a good supply of firewood. Walkers who reach a hut or shelter first should not assume that they will be the only occupants for the night. Another party may come along later, probably feeling more tired than you through walking further, so you should move over, sleep on the floor, or do the best possible to share accommodation. It is always wise to carry your tent every trip you intend stopping overnight and not to rely on huts or rock shelters. It is best to carry a small stove for cooking in any environmentally sensitive areas.

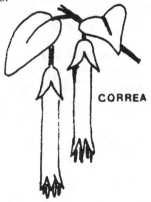

CORREA

Camping in National Parks is frequently confined to certain areas and walkers should ensure that they are aware of those regulations. Some parks charge camping fees.

7 Flooding of streams, even days after heavy rains, can cause delays and even prevent walkers from continuing along their intended route. Some areas mentioned in these track notes are subject to flooding and walkers' discretion should be used.

8 In the Snowy Mountains, Cooleman Caves and occasionally in other districts suggested as walk venues in this publication, snow falls in winter. The

Snowy Mountains, being Australia's highest, become completely snowbound and walks cannot be undertaken for a number of months of the year. This applies to a lesser extent in the Cooleman Caves area.

9 If you should be unlucky enough to be threatened by bushfire while walking do not panic. Do not run uphill, or run to try and outstrip a fire without giving some thought to the situation. Consider the area, the approach direction of the fire and the wind direction and velocity. In taking action remember that northern slopes are usually hot and dry and therefore a greater risk area. Fire tends to burn uphill and is usually most fierce on spurs and ridges. Choose the nearest open clear space, then quickly clean away all inflammable material, leaves etc. Cover the body fully with clothing, preferably wool and wet, if possible, even to the point of using urine to wet clothing if nothing else is available. Wear proper footwear, not thongs. Wet any towels and lie face down in the clearing. Cover all exposed skin surfaces as radiant heat from fire kills, as well as the flame. Do not be tempted to lift your head too much and so inhale smoke or get smoke in your eyes. The freshest air is right next to the ground surface.

Do not try to run through a fire front unless it is no wider than 3 m and no higher than 1.5 m. If you have a car parked *in an open spot* get in it and shut all windows, then lie low on the floor away from radiant heat. If possible clear all inflammable material from under and near the car, especially near the tyres. Do not chance driving in dense smoke.

If near a dam or deep flowing stream get right into the water. Avoid getting into shallow pools or water storages. Remember that concrete water tanks can explode and iron water tanks might buckle and break open. Also, their water contents tend to boil in great heat. It is safer to use available water from shallow pools or doubtful storages to wet a clear patch of ground and clothing and then lie down as instructed above.

FIRST AID AT A GLANCE

It is essential that any emergency can be dealt with adequately. The St John Ambulance Association *First Aid Book* or an equivalent book should be carried by at least one member of every walking party.

The most likely troubles to be encountered are listed here for rapid reference as in many cases there is no time to do research in a full first-aid book. In virtually all serious situations the patient needs to be rested and reassured, often while some other person obtains medical assistance. For this reason walk parties should never be less than three in number in any remote place. One person should stay with the patient while the other goes for aid.

EUCALYPT

COMPLAINT	TREATMENT
BLISTERS	Apply an adhesive foam patch; wear extra socks; if possible, do not break the blister, which increases the risk of infection.
HEAT EXHAUSTION	Replenish body fluids with plenty of drinks of water or fruit juice and take a little salt if badly dehydrated. Rest in a cool place and fan the patient. Remove excess clothing from the patient.
ABDOMINAL DISORDERS, FEVERS	Rest is essential. Give plenty of liquid to patient.

BURNS

Immediately immerse burn area in cold water to chill. Clean burn thoroughly, despite the pain, and apply a clean bandage. Immobilise the burn area.

SPRAINS

Immobilise the area of the sprain and rest it. Immerse in cold water (stream etc.).

EXPOSURE TO COLD

Do not rub the skin, apply direct heat, or give alcohol as all cause blood to come to the skin surface, then return to the heart, cooler. The body trunk and brain must be warmed. Insulate the entire body. Assuming the patient is conscious, give sugar in easily digested form, (e.g. sweetened condensed milk). Put patient in a sleeping bag, preferably with a warm person; cover bag with insulation, provide a wind break and pitch a tent over the patient. If breathing stops, apply mouth-to-mouth resuscitation. Only move to a warmer place if in doing so the patient is in no way physically exerted. Avoid patient standing as fainting will follow. The recognisable signs of the onset of exposure are: pallor and shivering, listlessness, slurred speech, poor vision, irrational and violent behaviour, collapse. *It is wet cold particularly that kills.*

SNAKEBITE

Most bites are of a minor nature and not all snakes are venomous. It is, however, wise to treat all bites as if dangerous. Many people have a disproportionate fear of snakebite so need reassurance and rest. The majority of bites are to the limbs rather than the body trunk so first aid is easier. The need is to restrict venom movement in the body, therefore a broad bandage should be firmly applied to any limb bite area or pressure kept on bites to the body trunk. The bite area should be kept immobilised with pressure applied to bandage or pad until antivenene is received from a doctor.

Immobilisation can best be achieved by binding a splint to any limb bite area. Old first aid methods of cutting the bite and of washing venom off skin are no longer recommended. Cutting upsets the patient and venom retained on the skin can be tested to identify a snake species. Bring transport to the patient, or carry the person to maximise rest. If the patient deteriorates to unconsciousness, apply mouth-to-mouth resuscitation and artificial respiration until medical aid is given.

EQUIPMENT AND FOOD SUGGESTIONS FOR WALKS

SAFETY EQUIPMENT
Maps, compass, small mirror, paper, whistle, matches in a waterproof container, sharp knife, small candle, small torch, textacolour or similar marker, first-aid reference book, first-aid kit containing bandages, Bandaids, adhesive foam, antiseptic, aspirin, safety pins, safety clothing consisting of warm pullover, thick wool socks, bright-coloured shirt and bright-coloured parka, and safety food rations such as nourishing concentrated foods plus a little bulky food like dried fruits, chocolate, nuts, fruit and seed bars and brown rice.

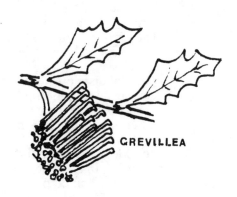

GREVILLEA

OTHER EQUIPMENT
Overnight walks: tent, tent pegs, tent guys, good quality sleeping bag, plastic groundsheet, a newspaper, toilet items, a billy and preferably a small stove.
All walks: shirt or blouse (wool for winter), shorts, jeans, handkerchief, walking or gym-boots, mug, bowl, cutlery, small towel, lightweight bathers for summer, waterbag (canvas type with zip top), water bottle (aluminium or plastic), can opener and pack.

FOOD

In addition to emergency rations which should be used *only* in an emergency, the following foods should be carried in quantities dictated by the number of days that the walk will occupy: nuts, dried fruits, chocolate, fruit and seed bars, hard-boiled eggs, packet or cube soups, fruit drink powders, brown rice and packet rice preparations, fresh fruit, honey, wholemeal bread, Vegemite, salami, fruit cake, coffee, tea or other hot drink, bacon, carrot, packet mashed potato and some muesli or porridge. Cans should only be carried by persons accustomed to carrying heavy packs, and empty cans should be washed and carried out of walk areas to garbage disposal bins.

HAKEA

WEIGHT

The most important consideration when carrying an overnight pack is the combined weight of the contents, and if you carry no more than stated in this list of equipment and food suggestions then you should not encounter trouble. However, far too many people include that little extra item or two, or overestimate the quantity of food that they can possibly eat and so suffer the consequences when they have to climb a hill bearing 'a ton of bricks'.

MAPPING AND NAVIGATION

Navigation procedures are best learned from experience in the field using map and compass. This is sometimes difficult to arrange if one does not have a friend who can teach in the field.

There are excellent opportunities to learn navigation when walking with a bushwalking club. Clubs help walkers gain safety, advice, experience and companionship. Usually, their organised walks are led by experienced leaders, often with transport arranged. Inquiries of a general nature and those concerning the various clubs can be best made through the Federation of Walking Clubs based in Sydney.

This publication provides a map of the immediate area of every walk suggestion and to some extent these maps should assist with navigation. To rely upon these maps entirely would be unwise; for example, the walker might travel off the map coverage if lost. It is strongly recommended therefore that every endeavour be made to purchase government or other maps before setting out on these trips.

One important point with which all walkers should be familiar is that magnetic north is presently twelve degrees east of true north in New South Wales.

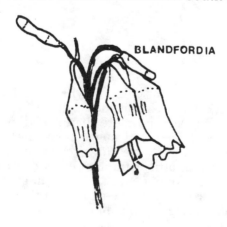

BLANDFORDIA

FAMILY WALKS ADVICE

Some walks that cater especially for families have been included in this book. It is stressed that parents or party leaders attempting these trips should at no time leave the children unattended as becoming lost is a very unhappy experience for a child. Emphasise that any walking along roads should be done facing oncoming traffic, and instruct children not to wander away from the party. Tell them that if they do become separated or lost, to wait where they are until help arrives. It is also important to tell children not to drink from streams without supervision and not to eat tempting looking berries in the bush. Many leaves, fruits, berries and fungi, if not actually poisonous, can cause acute discomfort.

The areas selected are in the more commonly frequented places where usually tracks and signs are quite clear. This is not to be taken as an indication that adult supervision can be relaxed or that walkers can dispense with recommended maps. It is unwise to take babies on walks, especially if it will expose them to the hot sun and wind.

By using a little extra care and avoiding placing children in dangerous situations, you can enjoy great family outings. What better way is there to give children fresh air, exercise and a first-hand knowledge of the wonder that is the Australian bush?

HOVEA

MAP LEGEND

ALL MEASUREMENTS METRIC

MAIN ROAD	═══
MINOR ROAD	≈≈≈≈
JEEP TRACK	4wd
FOOT TRACK	– – – –
ROUTE	·······
RAILWAY	+++++
MAJOR SUMMIT	▲
CONTOUR	—50—
CLIFFS & QUARRY	⊤⊤⊤⊤ ◌
STREAM & WATERFALL	◄
WATER FOR DRINKING	w
BUILDING	■
LAVATORY	wc
BRIDGE	br
LOOKOUT	L'out
BARRIER OR GATE	bar =‡=
PICNIC AREA	PG
BARE ROCK AREA	▨▨▨
CAVE ENTRY	o
RIDGE / SADDLE / KNOB	··‖···o····

SYDNEY–GOSFORD REGION

1   CLIFTON GARDENS— BRADLEYS HEAD

A number of headlands around Sydney Harbour, including Bradleys Head, are incorporated into the Sydney Harbour National Park. Bradleys Head area is particularly suited to a day's walking. It is close to the city, has harbour views and a variety of natural and historical attractions. It is practical to walk through pleasant residential streets in Mosman to make the walk into a circuit. The circuit can be joined at the Taronga Park Zoo wharf after a ferry trip from Circular Quay as an alternative to car or bus to the Bradleys Head Road area of Mosman. Bus routes service Clifton Gardens, Bradleys Head Road and the Zoo.

Start your circuit at the intersection of Bradleys Head Road and Thompson Street, Mosman. Walk the three blocks east on Thompson Street to its end, turn left into Burrawong Avenue which leads to Morella Street via some steps, then head down Morella Street to Clifton Gardens. There is bushland on the north side of the street as the descent is made. Clifton Gardens has a fine beach, park and full picnic facilities. A short zig-zag road and a path leads into the parkland. At the south end of the small bay is the start of a path near the water's edge. Follow the path and climb some steps which soon divide. Keep left. Then, where the steps start to rise away from the shoreline, diverge left again on to a small foot pad. This pad leads into native bushland near a rock outcrop and above low cliffs along the water's edge. It remains close to the clifftops in scrub as a minor track. There are periodic views of the harbour. Avoid several pads which lead off inland away from the

¹ Bradleys Head

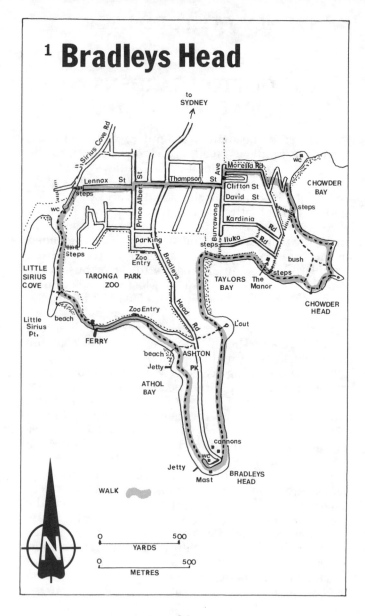

to SYDNEY

Sirius Cove Rd

Lennox St

Thompson St

Prince Albert St

Morella Rd

wc

CHOWDER BAY

Clifton St

David St

Kardinia Rd

Burrawong Ave

Iluka Rd

steps

steps

bush

steps

parking

Zoo Entry

steps

TARONGA PARK ZOO

Bradleys Head Rd

TAYLORS BAY

The Manor

CHOWDER HEAD

LITTLE SIRIUS COVE

beach

Zoo Entry

Little Sirius Pt.

FERRY

L'out

beach

ASHTON PK

Jetty

ATHOL BAY

cannons

wc

Jetty

Mast

BRADLEYS HEAD

WALK

N

0   500
YARDS

0   500
METRES

cliffs. The bush hosts a remarkable number of birds in spite of the suburban location. Currawongs seem especially prevalent. Keep going to Chowder Head then turn westwards to Taylor Bay. The pad remains fairly close to the water's edge and becomes more defined.

As the northern side of Taylor Bay is skirted, large houses facing nearby Iluka Street back on to the track. One house called 'The Manor' is very grand and has a National Trust classification. The pad passes through bush with a variety of native and exotic plants. It then turns south to follow Taylor Bay. Ashton Park covers much of Bradleys Head peninsula and the park is entered as the track turns southwards. Bushland continues in the park. Follow the coast track south to Bradleys Head point to where there are views of the city skyline.

A picnic area, the mast of the old HMAS *Sydney* and a nineteenth-century fortification are at the spot. The fortification dates from 1840, and includes a jetty, cannons and three gunpits with connecting galleries for riflemen. Convict labour was used in some of the construction which was undertaken in stages. The actual sandstone in the locality was hewn out and sandstone blocks were used. The fortification was intended to ward off foreign colonising powers such as the Russians, but no threat eventuated. The complex was part of an overall defence network to protect New South Wales. The gunpits are located up the hill about 200 m from the mast and actual point. They are positioned on the hillside with its aspect towards the heads of Sydney Harbour.

The track continues not far up from the water's edge and should be followed north-west from Bradley's Head around Athol Bay. Views of the city skyline are even better in this region. There is also a naval anchorage in Athol Bay. The pad leads to the rear entrance of the Taronga Park Zoo and the nearby zoo ferry wharf. Beyond the wharf the track is very close to the water's edge at first, then it passes a small point and leads along Little Sirius Cove to the cove head and beach. The *Sirius* was one of the ships of the First Fleet.

Sirius Cove Road leads from the cove head northwards into residential areas containing many historic houses, some with National Trust classifications. There is also a small and pleasant park at the cove head. Walk up Sirius Cove Road to a nearby overhead foot bridge. Climb steps eastwards at the bridge to join Lennox Street which is a beautiful palm-lined residential street. Walk Lennox Street east up to its end, turn left into Prince Albert Street and immediately right back into Thompson Street to reach Bradleys Head Road and the end of the walk circuit. The zoo front entrance is just two blocks south along Bradleys Head Road and some walkers may then wish to extend the day's activities by visiting the zoo.

MAP: Sydney street directories and Map 1.
WALK: One day, 6 km, easy grade, last reviewed July 1992, allow 2½ hours.

2   BUNDEENA—LITTLE MARLEY BEACH

There are very few beaches close to Sydney which are not crowded at weekends and on public holidays in summer. Little Marley is almost on the suburban doorstep. It is a beautiful, quiet beach reached by a short ferry trip from Cronulla to Bundeena and a 5 km walk through the Royal National Park. The beaches at Bundeena and at Marley are passed on the way. Marley Beach surf can be dangerous when rough however, so you should continue the short extra distance to Little Marley with its grassy slopes and good swimming.

Ferries operate regularly from Cronulla Station

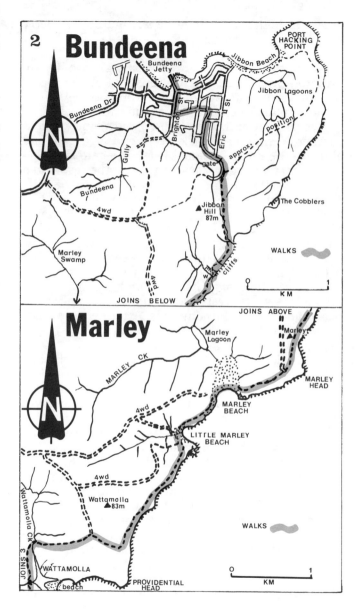

2

Bundeena

PORT HACKING POINT

Jibbon Beach

Bundeena Jetty

Jibbon Lagoons

Bundeena Dr

Brighton St

Eric St

position

approx.

gate

Gully

Bundeena

The Cobblers

4wd

Jibbon Hill 87m

Marley Swamp

cliffs

4wd

WALKS

0 ——— 1
KM

JOINS BELOW

Marley

JOINS ABOVE

Marley

Marley Lagoon

MARLEY CK

MARLEY HEAD

4wd

MARLEY BEACH

LITTLE MARLEY BEACH

4wd

Wattamolla ▲83m

WALKS

Wattamolla Ck

JOINS 3

WATTAMOLLA

beach

PROVIDENTIAL HEAD

0 ——— 1
KM

29

wharf. In high season they depart hourly. The ferry trip across Port Hacking to Bundeena takes about 25 minutes.

From Bundeena jetty, walk straight south up Brighton Street past a few shops and at the top of the rise turn left (east) up Scarborough Street which is the second street on the left from the jetty.

Two streets east, turn right (south) into Beach-comber Avenue and walk to its end at a gate and entry to the Royal National Park. The gate is 1.4 km approximately from the jetty and the asphalted roadway, although unused, does extend into the park. About 200 m south on the roadway continuation two tracks fork off left. Take the right-fork track towards Marley Beach which leads off south in sandy country and heathland to reach the ocean cliffs within 1.5 km. A small stream enters the sea at the spot and drinking water is usually available there. The track can then be followed on along the fairly high sandstone cliff tops till it swings westwards and descends to Marley Beach another 2.4 km onwards. A former jeep track links in from the right before you reach the beach. Marley is about 500 m long.

To continue, walk the length of the beach then follow a track from its south end through scrub just above the rocky shoreline to nearby Little Marley Beach. Two pads lead off inland between the coves and should be avoided.

The southern end of Little Marley Beach is usually sheltered and there are adjacent grassy areas. The sea is usually good for swimming too at the south end. The spot is some 800 m from the south end of Marley Beach. Water supply for drinking is usually a problem, but have lunch and a long break before retracing the same tracks back to Bundeena jetty.

MAP: Lands, 1:30,000 Royal National Park and Map 2.
WALK: One day, 13.6 km, easy grade, last reviewed November 1992, allow 4 hours.

3   BUNDEENA—MARLEY—
GARIE—OTFORD

One of the main features of the Royal National Park just south of Sydney is the long and magnificent coastline. There are a number of fine, white sand beaches and quite spectacular clifflines along much of the distance. As well, several waterfalls spill over the cliffs and plunge into the sea. From August to November there are very good displays of wildflowers and in the south there is a virtual jungle, with palms being one of the main species.

It is quite feasible to walk the entire length of the coast in the park in one day, starting at Bundeena and finishing at Otford, but first you should check timetables for the Cronulla to Bundeena ferry and the train times from Otford back via Sutherland to Cronulla. Naturally, the walk length means you must not spend too much time at any one point but it is not necessary to rush the trip. It is essential to start the day early though.

Start off with the leisurely 25-minute ferry cruise across Port Hacking. Then, from Bundeena wharf, walk south straight up Brighton Street past the shops and turn east up the second street on the left (Scarborough Street near the top of the hill). Two streets east, turn south on Beachcomber Avenue and walk to its end at a gate and entry to Royal National Park. The gate is some 1.4 km from the jetty and the asphalted road, although unused, extends into the park. About 200 m south via the road extension, two tracks fork off left. Take the right-fork track towards Marley Beach that leads off south in heathland country to reach the ocean cliffs within 1.5 km. A small stream which usually provides drinking water enters the sea at the spot. The track can then be followed for some 2.4 km near the sandstone cliff tops until Marley Beach is reached. An old jeep track links in from the right before you

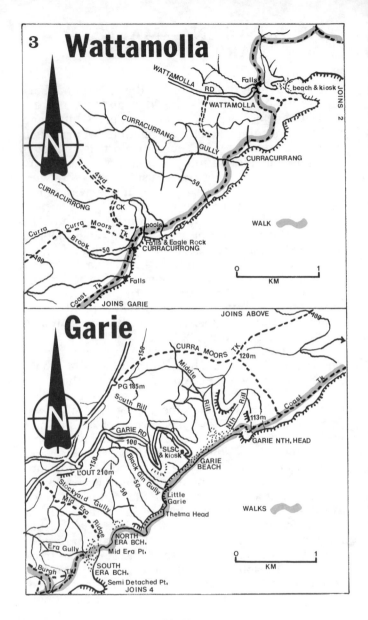

Wattamolla

3

WATTAMOLLA RD

Falls

beach & kiosk

JOINS 2

WATTAMOLLA

CURRACURRANG

GULLY

CURRACURRANG

4wd

CURRACURRONG

CK

Curra Moors Tk

pools

Curra

Curra Brook

Falls & Eagle Rock

CURRACURRONG

50

100

Falls

Coast Tk

JOINS GARIE

WALK

0 ———— KM ———— 1

Garie

JOINS ABOVE

100

CURRA MOORS TK

150

120m

Middle Rill

Nth Rill

Coast Tk

PG 185m

South Rill

113m

GARIE RD

100

GARIE NTH. HEAD

SLSC & kiosk

GARIE BEACH

150

L'OUT 210m

Black Gin Gully

Stockyard Gully

Mid Era Ridge

50

Little Garie

Thelma Head

NORTH ERA BCH.

Mid Era Pt.

Era Gully

SOUTH ERA BCH.

Burgh Tk

Semi Detached Pt.

JOINS 4

WALKS

0 ———— KM ———— 1

32

reach 900 m long Marley Beach. The surf at this spot can be dangerous for swimmers, especially in rough weather.

Walk the length of the beach, then follow a track from its south end through scrub just above the rocky shoreline to nearby Little Marley Beach. Two pads lead off inland between the coves and should be avoided. The southern end of Little Marley Beach is usually sheltered and there are adjacent grassy areas. The sea is usually good for swimming too at the south end. The spot is some 800 m from the south end of Marley Beach and 6.8 km from the walk start.

Next, follow the cliff tops south towards Wattamolla 3 km south-west. About half way the track turns inland amid a lot of prickly hakea then crosses Wattamolla Creek at waterfalls. It then heads down the west bank of the creek to emerge at the head of another waterfall at the Wattamolla picnic ground and car park. At this point, there are complete facilities including kiosk, although the kiosk may not be open at off-peak times.

After a break, walk to the upper level of the car park from where a service road leads south. Walk this road until some 200 m from the kiosk, at an old tank, then head south up a sandy foot track so as to reach cliff tops within 50 m. Thereafter, follow the cliffs south again and soon you should see your next goal—Curracurrang. The track leads down to the head of this small bay 1.4 km from Wattamolla, crosses a small creek then leads on south uphill. There are lovely grassy slopes at this spot. The next section is about 2 km long and leads to Curracurrong via the cliff rim. At Curracurrong there are three waterfalls dropping into the sea. Between the first and second falls a pad forks off west to Stevens Drive but that route should be ignored and the Garie pad, 4.3 km long, should be followed right along the cliff rim to Garie North Head where there are spectacular views southwards from the high headland.

The track descends abruptly through rock outcrops

to Garie Beach, which is perhaps the most popular beach along the park coast. Again there are picnic facilities including a kiosk and there is a surf life saving club.

Next, go along the cliff base south, below Little Garie Head. The track is above the rocks along the shore and there are good views back north to North Garie Head. Cross Little Garie Beach and continue around the cliff base of Thelma Head to North Era Beach and South Era Beach, 2 km from Garie Beach.

HOVEA

About mid-way around South Era Beach, a spur heads off uphill due south and a good track leads up it on to the Burgh Ridge. It should be followed up the grassy slopes, past some small huts, then, when a main east–west spur is reached, 500 m from the beach, keep left and sidle the slopes south a little. Then follow a rough pad down among some trees and beach shacks on to Burning Palms Beach some 500 m from the east–west spur.

Walk to the south end of 300 m long Burning Palms Beach, climb a few steps up on to grassy slopes and within 200 m a ranger's hut should be seen. The pad passes it and then contours through an area which has, in the past, been cleared but is now being re-vegetated.

There are good coast views and views up the slopes in the Palm Jungle vicinity. Suddenly you leave the open slopes and enter the jungle. It is shady and beautiful and, as the name suggests, palms are one of the most common plant varieties. Vines are also numerous. You soon begin to climb up steeper and steeper then, suddenly, you emerge from the jungle into dry forest and arrive at a spectacular rock outcrop at the top of a cliffline which you have skirted around. The view is southwards over Werrong Beach in the foreground and right along the south coast. The spot is called Werrong Point and is 3.2 km from Burning Palms Beach. The track then leads west through scrub for 400 m to an intersection with a north–south aligned jeep track called the Cliff Track. It leads south 1.8 km to Otford Gap.

Follow the jeep track south-west. It soon becomes a good foot track. After crossing a saddle it climbs slightly southwards over a rocky knob, then descends steeply southwards to Otford Gap, initially by sidling down the western side of the spur then actually following the crest of the spur. A track from Werrong Beach joins in from the left just before the gap.

At Otford Gap there are open grassy slopes, a car park, the Lady Wakehurst Drive and an excellent south coast view. Cross the main road at the gap, walk west down Fanshawe Road which becomes a minor road then swings south, then back east. Where it turns east a foot track descends sharply by way of many steps to Otford station and the end of the walk, 800 m from Otford Gap.

MAP: Lands, 1:30,000 Royal National Park and Maps 2, 3 and 4.
WALK: One day, 27 km, hard grade (by reason of length), last reviewed November 1992, allow 8½ hours plus ferry and train travel of about 2 hours.

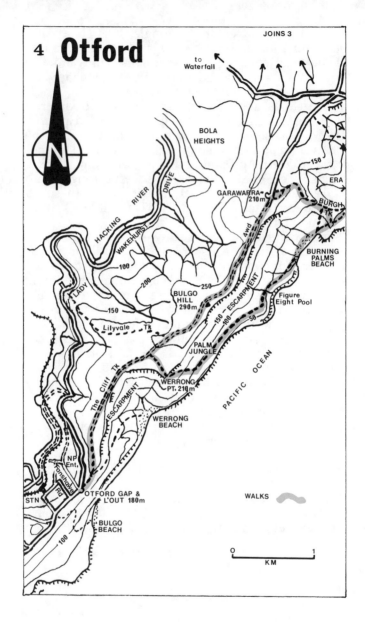

4 Otford

N

to
Waterfall

BOLA
HEIGHTS

HACKING RIVER

WAKEHURST DRIVE

GARAWARRA
210m

ERA

BURGH TK

100

200

250

LADY

150

BULGO
HILL
290m

4wd

BURNING
PALMS
BEACH

Lilyvale Tk

150 ESCARPMENT

Figure
Eight Pool

100

50

PALM
JUNGLE

The Cliff Tk

ESCARPMENT

WERRONG
PT. 210m

PACIFIC OCEAN

WERRONG
BEACH

NP
Ent.

Hensshaws Rd

STN

OTFORD GAP &
L'OUT 180m

BULGO
BEACH

100

WALKS

0   1
KM

4 OTFORD—BURNING PALMS—GARAWARRA

Burning Palms is a small beach locality in the southern part of the Royal National Park south of Sydney. It is a pleasant, remote beach which cannot be reached by car. To reach it the walker must either descend what is known as The Burgh Ridge or sidle down through Palm Jungle. This walk suggestion includes both these access routes and permits the walker to see wonderful beaches, views, palms and jungle.

Travel by car to Otford Gap, or catch a train to Otford. Check train times though, as few stops are made at this little station. If the station is your start, climb up a foot track to the east. Shortly, the track forms a T shape with a minor road. Turn left and follow the road uphill until it emerges via Fanshawe Road on to Lady Wakehurst Drive at Otford Gap. The gap provides superb views south to Wollongong and beyond.

From the gap, a foot track leads north up a main grassy spur. Head up the spur and after just 200 m fork left rather than take the pad to Werrong Beach. The spur is on a rocky ridge with reasonable views to east and west. Some 800 m from Otford Gap a hilltop should be reached. Next head 1 km north-east along the pad which broadens into a jeep track. Turn right (east) when a cross foot pad is intersected. The pad leads to Werrong Point, initially, for spectacular views of Werrong Beach below. Werrong Point is a rock outcrop right on a coastal escarpment. From the point head down around the slopes, sidling below the escarpment into Palm Jungle. In the jungle there is virtually no plant understorey, so the pad is open and easy to follow. The palms and vines of the jungle extend for about 2 km. You should then emerge from the jungle on to steep slopes which are grassy, open and give good views along the nearby coast. A ranger's hut should be passed just before descending on to the south end of Burning Palms Beach. At this point you are about 5.4 km from Otford Gap. The beach is 300 m long and picturesque and a break for swimming and lunch is recommended.

There are a number of huts on the slopes from the beach and a foot pad leads between the huts, climbing steeply up a small gully to a saddle 600 m northwards on the Burgh Ridge. This ridge is aligned east–west. Once at this grassy saddle, turn west uphill on a well defined foot track which soon leads up through forest to Garawarra picnic area and car park on the hilltop, 900 m away. The pad divides as it nears the car park so that there are the two alternative tracks to take. At the top, turn left and go south-south-west along the jeep track known as Cliff Track. After walking it for 2.5 km, the outward walk route should be rejoined. Cliff Track is mainly in forest and affords fast, fairly level walking. A track veers off right to Lilyvale at one stage, but it should be ignored. Once you rejoin the outward route, retrace the same tracks and roads to Otford.

MAP: Lands, 1:30,000 Royal National Park and Map 4. WALK: One day, 11.5 km (from Otford Gap), easy grade, last reviewed November 1992, allow 4 hours.

5   THE BASIN

Along the western margins of the Watagan Range, Wollombi Brook has eroded a deep valley as it flows towards the Hunter Valley. The upper reaches of Wollombi Brook are especially rugged and include a spot known as The Basin within which there is a circuit walking track.

Access is easiest from Sydney north via Peats Ridge and Kulnura, then along Walkers Ridge Road for

The Basin

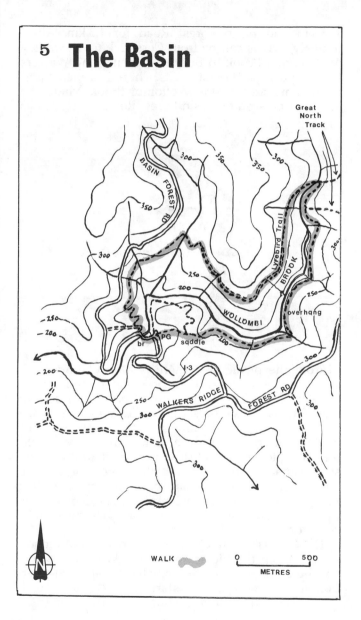

Great
North
Track

BASIN FOREST RD

Lyrebird Trail

BROOK

WOLLOMBI

overhang

PG   saddle

br

·3

WALKERS RIDGE   FOREST RD

WALK

0   500
METRES

N

16.5 km and Basin Forest Road for 1.3 km. Alternatively, access can be from Cessnock up the valley of Wollombi Brook to Bucketty, then along Walkers Ridge and Basin Forest roads. There is a picnic and bush camp area beside Wollombi Brook where the stream is crossed by Basin Forest Road.

HARDENBERGIA

From the picnic area there is a very short Rock Lily Trail and also the recommended and longer Lyrebird Trail. This longer circuit basically leads up one side of the rainforest-clad valley and back down the other side, but at one spot the track rises out of the rainforest high on a spur slope. Here an old jeep track forms part of the circuit as it contours the steep slopes of the spur end. Hardwood forest trees such as turpentine, oak and blue gum grow on this higher section. As the name implies the valley is home to many lyrebirds; native orchids are also fairly common.

The walk is described here as a clockwise-direction circuit. From the picnic spot, cross Wollombi Brook on the roadway and immediately veer right then double back west up the start of a steep jeep track on an east–west aligned spur. Take the foot track northwards within the next few metres to enter dense forest. The pad should then be climbed to gain significant height as it crosses several gullies. The foot track then links on to the contouring old jeep track 1 km from the walk start. Head around the southern end of the high spur for another 1 km; then the jeep track reverts to foot pad. A steep descent follows to cross Wollombi Brook within 600 m. The circuit then starts the 2.4 km return route. Within about 50 m the Great North Walk track system temporarily links into the circuit only to leave it again within 300 m. Keep to Lyrebird Trail near the creek to pass rock overhangs and native orchids. Over the last 500 m of the walk, the pad rises to a saddle away from the creek to where the Rock Lily Trail forks off to the right (north). The walk finishes with a short descent past a grassy slope back into the picnic area.

MAP: Lands, 1:25,000 Murrays Run and Map 5. Note that the Lands map shows the track routing quite incorrectly.
WALK: One day, 5 km, easy grade, last reviewed July 1992, allow 2 hours.

6   DORA CREEK

Deep within the Watagan Range south of the Hunter Valley there is a fine circuit walk in the headwaters of Dora Creek. This former logging area is now the site of three picnic grounds and large bush camping places. The steep gully of Dora Creek is clothed with rainforest and the stream cascades over Abbotts Falls. The picnic and camp facilities are situated on drier sandstone tops, while Dora Creek has eroded through the upper strata into the underlying stone. Diverse vegetation is the result of the variation in soil fertility

⁶ Dora Creek

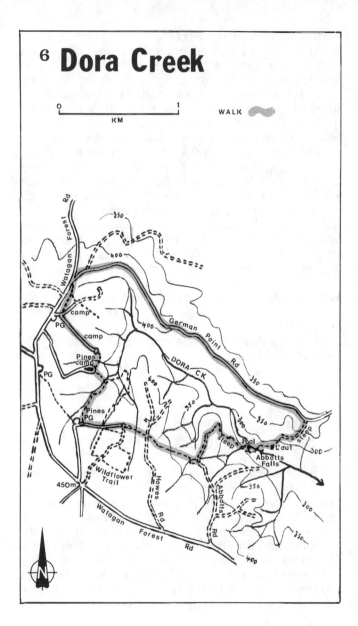

WALK

KM

and the tops feature a special wildflower walking trail.

Access to the walk start is easiest from Cessnock south up and along the Watagan Forest Road to the Old Mill picnic ground just north of the road junction with Wollombi Forest Road.

From Sydney it is better to use the freeway to the Morisset exit, then travel north-west to Martinsville and up Martinsville Hill Road to Watagan Forest Road which leads to the Old Mill picnic ground.

Once walking, keep a close watch on the map as there are many track alternatives in the camping and picnic ground vicinity. Wear stout footwear because the descent to Abbotts Falls is very steep. On a hot day a rock pool just upstream of Abbotts Falls could be attractive for a cool-off.

Head out from Old Mill picnic ground south-east on a road through camping areas to the road end 600 m away. Then cross a small creek southwards by foot pad into the adjacent Pines camping ground. Next go south-east on a foot pad 200 m, to cross another tiny creek by bridge and join what is known as the Pines Walking Track loop. Follow this track upstream south-west into the Pines picnic ground which is under an old plantation of slash pines. This spot is 1.2 km from the walk start and is serviced by a road which turns to lead east. Walk 400 m east along this road to pass the track head of the wildflower walking trail and reach the start of the Abbotts Falls Trail.

Continue on as the track leads across the head of four gullies, crossing minor Howes Road and joining on to Abbotts Road 1.4 km from Pines picnic ground. At Abbotts Road the walk circuit turns left and uses the minor road for 300 m to gain a small hilltop. The way then is by foot track which leaves the drier tops and descends steeply north-east then south-east down deep into rainforest and to Dora Creek in 600 m. Just short of the creek crossing there is a very short side pad to a small rock pool. Take care near slippery rocks in this area.

Cross Dora Creek via the main pad at a point some 50 m upstream of Abbotts Falls. Stay on the track; approaching the top of the falls could prove dangerous. The track climbs a little to a platform lookout with a poor view of the falls. (This is the best vantage point available.) Uphill from the lookout the pad soon links on to the end of an old logging track. A very steep climb then follows, to rise from the rainforest and gorge and to gain German Point Road on a ridge top about 500 m from Dora Creek crossing. German Point Road should then be walked north-west along the tops 2.7 km to Watagan Forest Road. A further 300 m of walking south on this more major road completes the walk at the picnic spot.

MAP: Lands, 1:25,000 Morisset and Map 6.
WALK: One day, 7 km, easy grade, last reviewed July 1992, allow 3 hours.

7   HEATON

Newcastle and Hunter Valley bushwalkers would recognise the Watagan Range as offering many walking opportunities. The range separates the Hunter River catchment from the Macquarie and Tuggerah Lakes system and rises abruptly as a heavily forested backdrop to the region. Relatively high rainfall over millennia has assisted erosion of deep gullies in the range. In these humid spots rainforest is the main form of vegetation. There are numerous cliffs and lookout points, and many old logging roads give good access to walkers.

One excellent walk is the Heaton Circuit Trail near the north-east end of the range and quite close to both Newcastle and Cessnock. Roads provide access to Heaton Lookout and picnic area where the walk starts. Best access is south from Cessnock via Watagan

7 Heaton

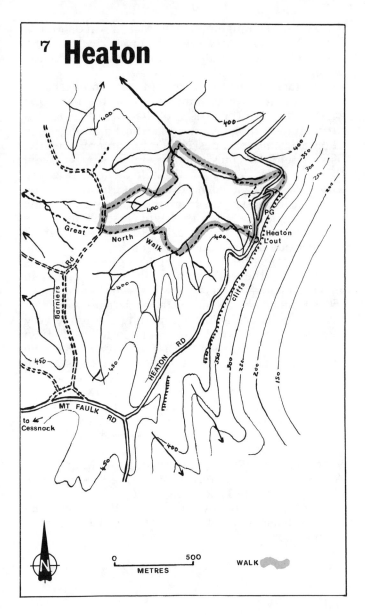

Great North Walk

Barniers Rd

WC

PG

Heaton L'out

Cliffs

HEATON RD

MT FAULK RD

to Cessnock

400 400 400 400 400 350 300 250 200 450 450 350 300 250 200 150 450

0   500
METRES

WALK

Road on to the rangetops, then east 1.7 km on Mount Faulk Road and north-east 1.6 km on Heaton Road. A picnic at the lookout could be an added attraction before or after the short walk.

The track begins to the left of toilets and descends westwards into forest immediately at the head of a gully. The forest consists of hardwoods such as turpentine, mahogany, oak, blackbutt and blue gum. The track sidles and descends into rainforest and the usual attendant vines: Soon the gully is crossed and the pad rises steeply north-west on to a ridge, to lead back into mixed hardwood forest and to gain Barniers Road, 1.3 km from the walk start. Follow this old logging road north (right) just 200 m on the ridge, then diverge north-east on to another foot track which leads down a spur into rainforest again. The track descends quite steeply into a gully then turns north down the gully to a confluence of gullies in an area of moss-covered boulders and small cliffs, 750 m from Barniers Road. Take special care near these slippery boulders, as the steep gully can prove very treacherous when wet. The route to follow is then by track for 750 m south-east, upstream, near the north side of the creek, still within rainforest, until a saddle is gained at Heaton Road. Finally, turn south to walk 500 m up and over a small grassy hill in the Heaton Lookout picnic area. Heaton Road skirts the west side of the picnic ground for the 500 m but is best avoided so as to enjoy views from the hill.

MAP: Lands, 1:25,000 Quorrobolong and Map 7.
WALK: One day, 3.5 km, easy grade family suitability, last reviewed July 1992, allow 1½ hours.
Warning: Watch any children in the group—the bush is dense and rocks and tracks can be slippery at times.

8   SOMERSBY

This circuit walk in the Gosford district includes four well-known attractions—Girrakool, Mooney Mooney Creek, Somersby Falls and Old Sydney Town. The latter is a possible addition to the actual walk. The walk starts at the public car park at the reconstruction of Sydney *circa* 1810. Access is thus very easy from the Gosford–Somersby exit of the Sydney–Newcastle freeway, the car park being within 1.5 km of the freeway exit. To make a circuit, Myoora Road and other short nearby roads need to be walked.

The sandstone country around Gosford is very old, dissected and eroded. Shallow soils on the tops make good wildflower habitats, while in the humid, more fertile gullies, plant species are very different and forest predominates. On this walk, therefore, a vast array of plant species is to be seen. They include large numbers of giant Gymea lilies west of Somersby Falls.

Initially, the aim is to walk from Old Sydney Town car park to Girrakool picnic ground in the Brisbane Water National Park. Go south past the Old Sydney Town entrance and for 700 m to the Pacific Highway. Follow it west 400 m, then walk south 600 m under the freeway and into the picnic spot. The route is by sealed roads but the road bash is softened by plantings of many fine native plants along the way.

Next, take the walking track south-west down a short spur to a lookout overlooking 12 m Cascade Waterfall and the pool at its base. The falls are at the confluence of Pile Creek and Leasks Creek, just 400 m from Girrakool picnic ground. Ahead there are two tracks, one leading down each side of the gully of Pile Creek to where they rejoin about 2 km away.

The southern route is perhaps more appealing for its wildflowers but bridges over Pile Creek have been washed away, so that occasionally stream crossing can prove difficult. If fording above the waterfall is easily achieved then use the southern route. The downstream crossing is just above the upper tidal

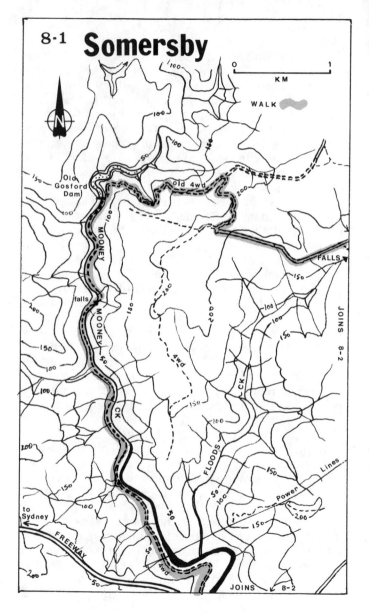

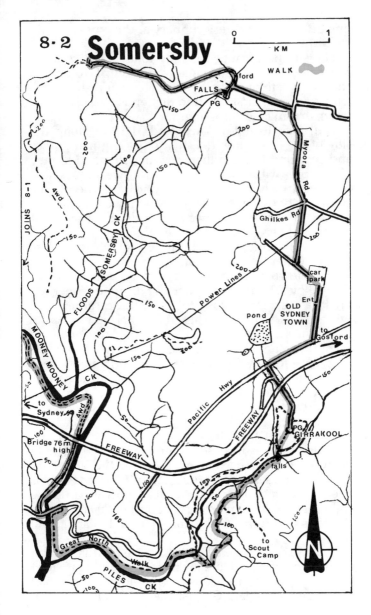

8·2 Somersby

0   1
KM

WALK

ford

FALLS
PG

150

200

200

150

100

JOINS 8-1

4wd

200

150

Myoora Rd

Ghilkes Rd

200

SOMERSBY CK

Power Lines

200

car park

150

FLOODS

150

200

100

Ent

OLD SYDNEY TOWN

to Gosford

150

MOONEY

pond

MOONEY

CK

50

50

Pacific Hwy

FREEWAY

150

to Sydney

4wd

FREEWAY

Bridge 76m high

FREEWAY

PG
GIRRAKOOL

50

150

falls

50

50

100

150

Great North

Walk

100

to Scout Camp

PILES

50

CK

100

N

limit. Rocks can be very slippery at the crossings and care is needed.

The southern route basically follows the contour, and there is a lot of boronia to be seen. Two branch tracks off left need to be avoided before the track leaves the higher slopes and descends sharply to the downstream creek crossing.

The track to follow then leads 1.5 km along the side of the creek and its estuary, passing mangroves and reaching the confluence with Mooney Mooney Creek. Still within forest and at the stream junction, turn north and walk 500 m north to the Pacific Highway bridge over Mooney Mooney Creek. Go 150 m east to gain the roadway, then double back west for 250 m to cross the bridge and its approaches.

Across the bridge, turn north on a gravel road close to the water. Walk 800 m on the road to see the incredible 76 m high freeway bridge which crosses the valley. Then, once under the structure, veer left on to a jeep track close to the hillside rather than on the creek flats. Walk this creekside jeep track until it becomes a foot pad, then go further until you are 4 km from the freeway bridge, where the track fords Mooney Mooney Creek. The ford is on smooth rock above small falls and the creek is within a narrow forested gorge. This crossing would be a good spot for a break.

Continue upstream 1 km on the east bank track to reach the dam wall of the Old Gosford Reservoir. A disused and badly eroded jeep track leads generally eastwards from the dam wall out of the valley on to the drier sandstone tops. After 1.5 km, there is a jeep track junction. Double back south-west up the right fork and climb further for another 700 m to gain the tops and to reach the end of a road near several houses.

This road can then be walked eastwards 1.8 km to Somersby Falls. Floods Creek is forded just short of the falls car park. Along both sides of the road there are many giant Gymea lilies (*Doryanthes*) which in winter have flower stalks up to 4 m long and large red blooms. Steps take you to the top and bottom of Somersby Falls and time should be spent enjoying the locality.

Lastly, walk along Somersby Falls Road east, uphill for 800 m to Myoora Road where you need to turn south (right). Walk Myoora Road then for 2 km to the Old Sydney Town car park. Regrettably this section of road walking passes an industrial estate and is rather unappealing.

The day's walk is relatively long, but some may enjoy entering Old Sydney Town to cap off a memorable day.

MAP: Lands, 1:25,000 Gosford and Gunderman sheets and Map 8.
WALK: One day, 19.5 km, hard grade, last reviewed July 1992, allow 7 hours.

9   BOUDDI NATIONAL PARK

Bouddi is a narrow coastal National Park situated on the northern entrance to Broken Bay and some 20 km south-east of progressive Gosford. Access to the park from the Gosford direction is via the Scenic Road.

The park features coastal elevated heathlands and dry sclerophyll forest and in gullies and the Bouddi Deep behind Maitland Bay there is coastal rainforest with palms, coachwood, cabbage tree and the lovely smooth-barked angophora tree.

The park is on horizontally bedded sandstone shales and conglomerates. Extensive rock platforms, including 'tesselated pavements' offshore, support a large variety of marine life. The park thus has a marine extension to its boundaries. Maitland Bay is perhaps the most beautiful of the bays, so that a walk to it

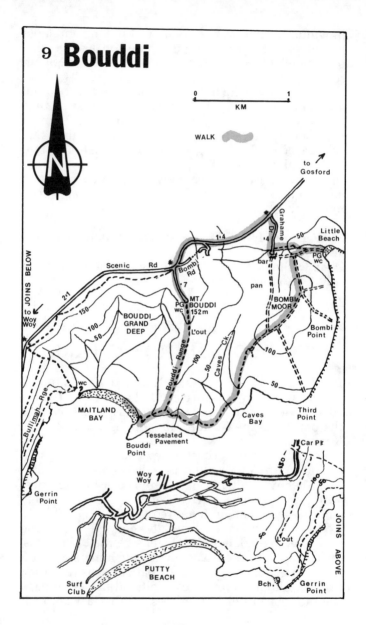

9 Bouddi

from the northern part of the park would be most rewarding.

Start walking at the eastern end of sealed Grahame Drive beyond McMasters Beach via the Scenic Road. First walk 100 m back from the road end to a gully and foot track off east to Little Beach 700 m away. Descend to Little Beach through rainforest in a gully via the foot pad at first, then on a jeep track. The jeep track links the end of Grahame Drive with Little Beach direct. As the little cove is neared the vegetation suddenly changes to exposed coastal stunted vegetation. There are camping and picnic facilities at the cove.

After seeing Little Beach, return back up the jeep track for 400 m then turn left up another track which ascends to the Bombi Moors. The climb is steep, but soon the tops are gained along with good views south towards Sydney. As the tops are reached, avoid two left-fork tracks to Bombi Point and Third Point. These are at the 400 m and 900 m stages from the Little Beach jeep track junction. Just 200 m after the Third Point track is passed, on a hill crest another track joins in from the right. It leads directly from the east end of Grahame Drive up and across the moors.

Next, descend south to where the wide track ends and a narrow pad continues. The pad to follow veers to the right from the end of the broad (former jeep track) route. It then leads down to Caves Creek and Caves Bay some 1.2 km from the Third Point track junction. Rock overhangs near the pad appear to be the reason for the name of the creek and small rocky bay. The pad should then be followed as it leads on around the coast for 1 km to be joined by a more pronounced track from Mount Bouddi. Shortly afterwards on the coast track there is a grassy saddle near tesselated pavement formations at the water's edge. From the saddle, descend steps west on to the end of Maitland Bay Beach. Lunch is suggested at the 700 m long beach. Note that nude bathing is common here. For those who would rather not descend to the beach, the grassy saddle is an appropriate alternative lunch venue, 4.8 km from the walk start.

After lunch, retrace the pad from the east end of the beach for 500 m, then diverge left and climb the track to Mount Bouddi. The summit is 152 m above sea level and 2.2 km from Maitland Bay via the foot tracks. On the ascent there are excellent coast views and at the peak there is a picnic area. A sealed road should then be followed for 700 m to Scenic Road. Turn right on to Scenic Road and follow it east 1.4 km to turn right down Grahame Drive for a final 400 m walk to complete the day's outing. The road walking required towards the end of the day is beside fairly busy roads, but mostly through bushland rather than residential areas.

MAP: Lands, 1:25,000 Broken Bay and Map 9.
WALK: One day, 9.5 km, easy grade, last reviewed July 1992, allow 3½ hours.

10   DHARUG NATIONAL PARK

The Hawkesbury River country around Wisemans Ferry consists of Hawkesbury sandstone deposits eroded by the river to form a huge valley. The Hawkesbury's erosive power has been such that it has left steep slopes on both sides of the valley. This in turn has caused side streams to descend very rapidly from the heights, making the countryside quite rugged.

Dharug is the name of an Aboriginal tribe that once inhabited the district. Dharug National Park covers part of this craggy tract on the north side of the river and it is because of the ruggedness that there is such a wide variety of birds and animals to be seen,

10 Dharug

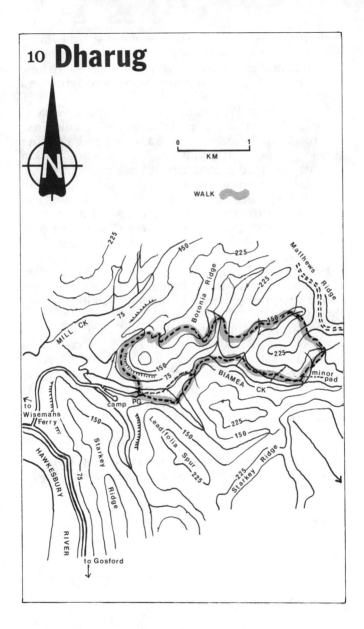

N

0   1
KM

WALK

225
150
225
Botonia Ridge
225
Matthews Ridge
75
MILL CK
150
75
150
225
BIAMEA CK
minor pad
camp PG
75
to Wisemans Ferry
150
Starkey Ridge
Leadfolia Spur
150
225
150
225
225 Starkey Ridge
HAWKESBURY RIVER
75
to Gosford

including lyrebirds. The creek valleys have fairly dense forest which includes vines, epiphytes, sassafras and coachwood, while the high sandstone outcrops and peaks support many eucalypts and angophoras.

South-east of Wisemans Ferry, along the Gosford Road and about 1 km past Hazel Dell picnic area, is a road which leads into a camp area and a further picnic ground in the Mill Creek area. Some 2.3 km up this side road a good circuit walk route has been established to show features of the park. The circuit is only 8 km long, but is through hilly terrain. The two ends of the circuit walk are just 50 m apart at the rear of the grassed picnic area. The return pad, however, is a little hard to see due to scrub along the creek.

Head off on the anti-clockwise circuit up the valley of Biamea Creek. Almost immediately take the right fork of two tracks which divide and rejoin 1 km up the valley.

Grasstrees will become quite evident as the track leads on through lovely forest. The track continues to climb past a number of bluffs and spurs, arcing around on to ridgetops with typical, dry, sandstone vegetation. Good views will be encountered at times before a final sharp descent down a 'hanging valley' formation, and across Biamea Creek and to the walk end.

MAP: Lands, 1:25,000 Gunderman and Map 10.
WALK: One day, 8 km, medium grade, last reviewed July 1992, allow 3 hours.

BLUE MOUNTAINS REGION

11 NEPEAN LOOKDOWN— ERSKINE CREEK

The Blue Mountains National Park has some quite remote sections where the walker can be far removed from life's rush and bustle. Surprisingly, one of the closest parts of the park to Sydney is one of the most isolated. It is the Nepean Lookdown area and is ideally suited to walking in hot weather as the route is along a creek side with white sand beaches, rock swimming pools and abundant shady trees.

Travel to Glenbrook and turn south into the National Park where there is a visitors centre. Go on down the hill across pretty Glenbrook Creek Causeway and drive on 11.5 km via the gravelled Oaks fire trail to Nepean Lookdown. There are several forks in the road on the way but the area is well signposted.

Have a look at the Nepean River far below, then walk back 600 m to a car park and start of the Jack Evans Walking Trail.

Walk south along this good track and, within 100 m, turn right to a superb view down on to Erskine Creek from a rock ledge known as Erskine Lookdown. Return the 20 m to the main track and descend via steps and the well-graded track to a saddle then fork right (west) down to the creekside beach. The left fork at the saddle is the return route and should be noted. The total distance from the carpark to Erskine Creek is only a kilometre. The creek forms a loop southwards called Platypus Loops so it is best to wander south then east, following the stream bank and wading where necessary until you choose a sandy beach for lunch. Take your time walking as rock scrambling is required and it can be rather tiring if you rush. Perhaps some sun basking and swimming would be good, too. Just to sit and listen to the myriad

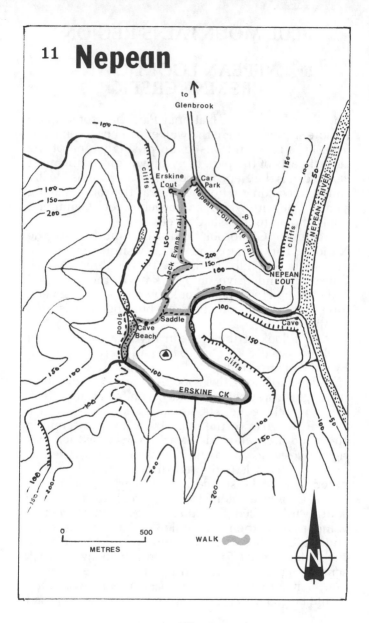

11 Nepean

to
Glenbrook

—100

cliffs

Erskine
L'out

—100
—150
—200

Car
Park

—150
100
50

NEPEAN RIVER

Nepean L'out Fire Trail

Jack Evans Trail

.6

150

200
150
100

50

NEPEAN
L'OUT

cliffs

50

pools

Saddle

100

Cave

Cave
Beach

150

150
100

▲

100

cliffs

ERSKINE CK

100

100
50

150
100

200

200

150

100

0   500

METRES

WALK

N

58

birds, or to gaze up the towering cliffs would be enjoyable.

The walk continues on downstream, swinging north-west then east again until you reach the junction of the Nepean River. Have a rest by the river then retrace 600 m back to where Erskine Creek bends south. At this spot an almost obscured, small, foot track leads west directly up to a saddle only 250 m from the stream. Head up this small track, then turn north back up the well-graded, short track to the car park. Finally, retrace the 600 m along the road to Nepean Lookdown for another look down on where you have been.

MAP: Lands, 1:25,000 Penrith and Map 11.
WALK: One day, 6 km, easy grade, last reviewed July 1992, allow 3 hours.

12 SPRINGWOOD—MAGDALA CREEK—SASSAFRAS CREEK

Much of the walking in the Blue Mountains becomes difficult once you try to descend into the deep forested areas of the valleys and gorges. The structure of the mountains is such that the further west you go towards the Blackheath area, the more rugged the sandstone country.

At Springwood you are still well east and any walking is relatively easy, yet you can see gullies equally as beautiful. Magdala Creek, south of the town, is especially good and cascades over two pleasant waterfalls as well.

Start and finish this walk at Springwood Railway Station. A restored 1880s track, Fairy Dell, can then be followed south from the shops on the south side of the railway. The track is best accessed by walking

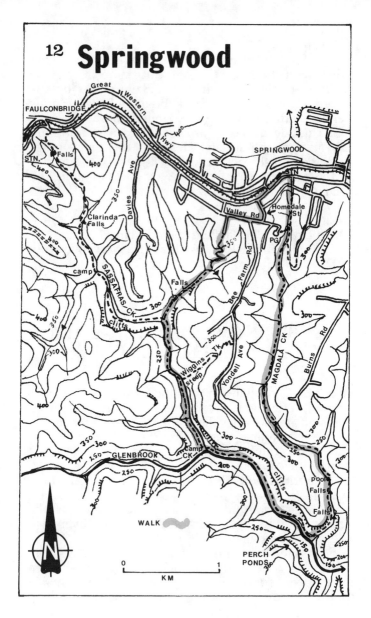

12 **Springwood**

one block south from opposite the car park east of the station entrance. It is signposted and is in effect just at the back of the shops. It leads south into the headwaters of Magdala Creek, then links on to a network of tracks which have long been in use by walkers based in Picnic Point.

The short track from Picnic Point and the restored Fairy Dell track unite only 500 m south of the railway station area then follow Magdala Creek. In 200 m veer right rather than take the Lawsons Lookout track. Cross from one side of the creek to the other a number of times as you descend south through fine forest.

After 2 km, rock outcrops become bold and, 500 m later, a very minor track joins in from the north as you cross to the east bank after having swung east for a few hundred metres. It is then a 600 m walk south down to Magdala Falls and Blue Pool. The track crosses to the west bank on the way to the 10 m high falls. There is a small gorge in the area downstream from the falls. Rock overhangs and cascades make a perfect setting. It is only about 400 m south down to Martins Falls, which drop 10 m. A further 500 m walk brings you to the junction of Magdala Creek and Glenbrook Creek for a lunch break at Perch Ponds, 5.5 km from the walk start.

At this confluence, a track branches off south-east to Martins Lookout and should be avoided. Instead, turn north-west and follow the north-east slopes of Glenbrook Creek for 1.8 km to the confluence of Sassafras Creek and Glenbrook Creek. There is a good swimming hole and camp area, and the track crosses to the west bank of Sassafras Creek. Follow it northwards 750 m, to the junction of a track via Bee Farm Road to Springwood where you should stay on the west bank of Sassafras Creek and continue north. In 350 m you must cross to the east bank and in a further 400 m meet a further track junction.

The left fork leads to Faulconbridge. Follow the right fork north-east on a well-trodden pad up a side valley past rock overhangs and small falls. Continue on to a spur to zig-zag up to Sassafras Gully Road, Springwood, about 1.5 km from Sassafras Creek. Finally, walk north 250 m along the road, turn right into Valley Road, walk 400 m east, turn north up Homedale Street 150 m, then north-east 400 m on Macquarie Road to Springwood station.

MAP: Lands, 1:25,000 Springwood and Map 12.
WALK: One day, 11.5 km, easy grade, last reviewed July 1992, allow 4 hours.

13   DARWINS WALK

In January 1836 noted English naturalist Charles Darwin arrived in Sydney aboard the Beagle and made a journey across the Blue Mountains to Bathurst. He spent time at Wentworth Falls township (formerly Weatherboard) and at Blackheath, visiting both Wentworth Falls and Govetts Leap. He was in fact far from complimentary and described the bushland as having a desolate and untidy appearance. He thought that the massive clifflines may once have been sea cliffs. He formed his theory of evolution while in South America and the Galapagos Islands but what he saw in New South Wales undoubtedly helped him confirm his ideas.

The route taken by Darwin at Wentworth Falls is today the site of a walking track known as Darwins Walk. It follows Jamison Creek closely to the head of the massive waterfall. This recommendation is to retrace the steps of Charles Darwin.

The walk starts in Wilson Park, which is on the south side of the Great Western Highway near the town centre. Jamison Creek flows under the highway and through the park. Falls Road skirts the west side of the park. There are tennis courts between Falls

13 **Darwins Walk**

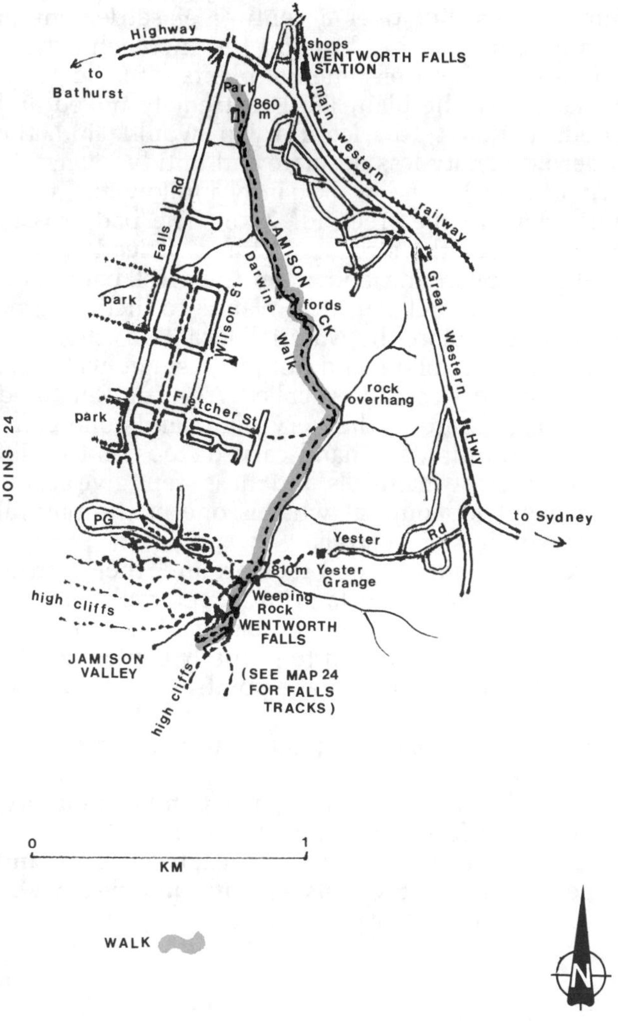

Highway

to Bathurst

shops
WENTWORTH FALLS
STATION

Park
860 m

main western

railway

Falls Rd

JAMISON CK

Darwins Walk

Wilson St

fords

park

rock overhang

Great Western Hwy

park

Fletcher St

JOINS 24

to Sydney

PG

Yester Rd

810m Yester Grange

high cliffs

Weeping Rock
WENTWORTH FALLS

JAMISON VALLEY

high cliffs

(SEE MAP 24 FOR FALLS TRACKS)

0   1
KM

WALK

N

Road and Jamison Creek. Between the tennis courts and the creek there are signposts and the official track head. The Jamison Creek valley has relatively cool climate vegetation, including many fern and native plant species. But over a century of settlement in the adjacent town has brought the encroachment of myriad exotic and ornamental plants into the gully, so that today the plant life is extremely mixed and varied. Perhaps Charles Darwin would find the modern diversity less desolate and untidy.

To undertake the walk, simply follow the track south close to the creek for 2 km. The pad crosses and re-crosses the stream six times. It leads past a small rock overhang and is on the west bank as it nears the waterfall. An ideal plan is to include time to properly explore the waterfall locality as there are many tracks to follow and not just a single waterfall. The uppermost cascade is called Weeping Rock and the main falls are at the very high sandstone cliffs. There are hundreds of hand-carved steps on the cliff face south of the main falls, and these steps give access to excellent lookouts at what is one of the natural scenic wonders of Australia.

One could, after a good look around, then retrace the 2 km back up the Jamison Creek valley to the Great Western Highway. Probably 1 km of extra walking would be needed to properly explore all the waterfalls, tracks and vantage points.

MAP: Lands, 1:25,000 Katoomba (track not shown) and Map 13.
WALK: One day, 5 km, easy grade, family suitability, last reviewed July 1992, allow 2¼ hours.
Warning: Keep well clear of exposed cliffs and slippery rocks in the falls vicinity and watch any children in the party carefully.

14   LOCKLEY PYLON

Much of the walking in the Blue Mountains is along clifflines and streams, often within timbered areas. This suggested walk route at about 900 m elevation takes the walker across open tops with virtually no trees and with some sub-alpine vegetation.

Access to the area is via Mount Hay Road from Leura. The road is quite rough in several places, even in dry weather. After or during wet weather, access could only be achieved by four-wheel-drive vehicles or by walking.

The suggested walk starting point is 8.9 km north of the Great Western Highway at the Fortress Ridge jeep track turnoff. The planned walk distance is 9.6 km return, but if the Mount Hay Road is impassable the 9.6 km walk could be as much as 17 km. The resulting road bash would probably spoil the trip. The first 5 km out of Leura usually offers reasonable motoring.

The Mount Hay Road continues north-east around the western slopes of Flat Top then on to Mount Hay, in extremely wild country. Leave transport at the small car park at the Fortress Ridge turnoff and walk the Mount Hay Road for 1.3 km past interesting and rocky Flat Top. Next, leave the road and head north for 3.5 km on the Lockley Track, which is closed to vehicles. It leads past The Pinnacles and Lockley Pylon then down to the Grose River, Bluegum Forest and Acacia Flat.

Continue on the track through open country, along the western slopes of the three Pinnacles (small rocky knobs), then north-west across two saddles and up through some small trees on insignificant Mount Stead. In this area honeyflower (*Lambertia*) and banksia grow in profusion. Once past Mount Stead the views so characteristic of the whole walk become even more expansive. Lockley Pylon can be seen as an obvious conical treeless hill just near the cliffline of the Grose Valley. The main track descends around the eastern slopes of Lockley Pylon, then descends dramatically

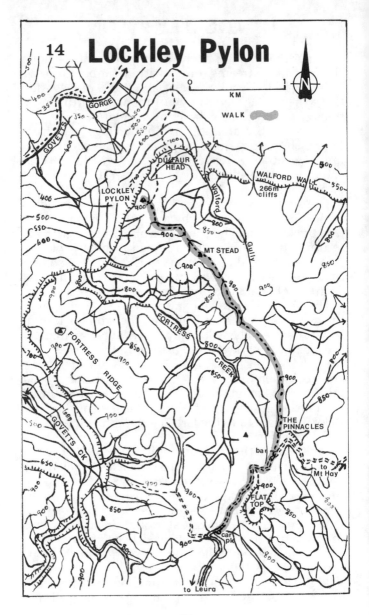

Lockley Pylon

14

0   KM   1

WALK

GOVETTS GORGE

DU FAUR HEAD

LOCKLEY PYLON

WALFORD WALL
266m cliffs

Walford Gully

MT STEAD

FORTRESS

FORTRESS RIDGE

CREEK

FORTRESS RIDGE

GOVETTS CK

THE PINNACLES

bar

to Mt Hay

FLAT TOP

car pk

to Leura

to the Grose. You should see the short summit access track directly ahead as you approach. The view from Lockley Pylon is indeed superb but, before you leave, walk 100 m down the slopes westwards to the cliff rim for an even better view of the valley straight below. Do not go too close to the rim though, especially on a windy day.

There is no drinking water near Lockley Pylon but the peak would be a good lunch spot, after which you should retrace your outward route.

MAP: Lands, 1:25,000 Katoomba and Map 14.
WALK: One day, 9.6 km, easy grade, last reviewed July 1992, allow 3½ hours.

15   MOUNT HAY

Geologically, much of the Blue Mountains consists of eroded sandstone with shallow soils on the tops, massive clifflines and lush vegetation only in the gullies and ravines. Some of the highest summits are, however, still capped with the basalt which once overlaid much of the region. The rich basalt soils support luxuriant vegetation of sturdy eucalypts, blackwoods and ferns with lyrebirds and parrots among the fauna.

Mount Tomah and Mount Wilson are perhaps the two best known basalt-capped peaks, but others include Mount Irvine, Mount Banks, Mount Caley, Mount Bell and Mount Hay. They are all relatively close to each other and only Mount Hay is south of the tremendous gorge of the Grose River. On some of the tops cool climate ornamental gardens including the Mount Tomah Botanic Garden have been established. At Mount Wilson and Mount Irvine, last century, substantial houses were built by the wealthy as retreats. Mount Hay (once called Round Hill) has

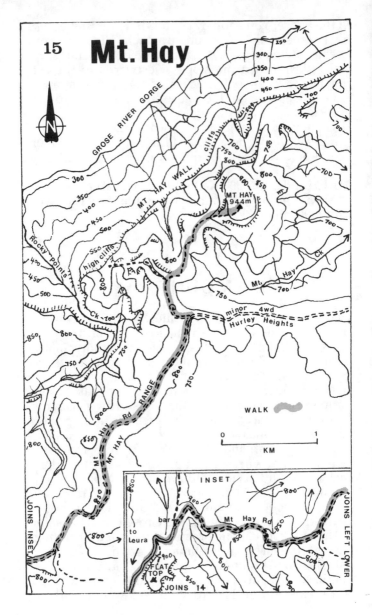

15 Mt. Hay

N

GROSE RIVER GORGE

MT HAY WALL   cliffs

MT HAY 944m

Rocky Points

high cliffs

Ck

Mt Hay Ck

Mt Hay

minor 4wd
Hurley Heights

WALK

0   1
KM

MT HAY RANGE

Mt Hay Rd

JOINS INSET

INSET

to Leura

bar

Mt Hay Rd

FLAT TOP

JOINS 14

JOINS LEFT LOWER

68

remained isolated and is now part of the Blue Mountains National Park.

This walk to Mount Hay involves crossing dry sandstone tops at about 850 m above sea level near some of the highest cliffs in the Blue Mountains and ascending the 944 m summit—into dramatically different vegetation.

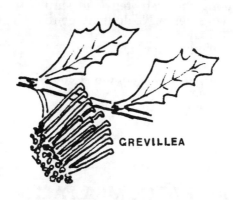

GREVILLEA

Because of its isolation the walk should not be attempted during or after wet weather. The road access is poor and the rocks could prove slippery. Access is from the Great Western Highway at Leura, via Mount Hay Road for 8.9 km to a car park at the Fortress Ridge jeep track turnoff. The rough road continues towards Mount Hay and can be accessed by four-wheel-drive vehicle to a point 15.8 km from the highway. The recommendation is that the road be walked for the latter 6.9 km, then that a foot track be walked for a further 1.6 km to the hilltop. This results in a 17 km return walk. The road walking is pleasant except on very hot days, and features broad views and many wildflowers. Just 300 m before the walking track starts, Mount Hay Road divides. Avoid the Hurley Heights route and turn left (west) on to a small hillcrest. The walking track ahead is pronounced and much of the route is visible from the start of the pad. However, it also divides after 400 m, with the left fork leading out to nearby precipitous Butterbox Point. The track to follow leads north then curves to ascend between rocks and approach the summit from the west. There is no view from the top but the approach route is quite dramatic. The view is chiefly into the Grose River Gorge, 670 m lower than Mount Hay. On the top there are some grassy areas among the lush trees and shrubs, and lunch could be considered. No doubt lyrebirds will be heard during the stay.

Return via the same track routing.

MAP: Lands, 1:25,000 Katoomba and Mount Wilson sheets and Map 15.
WALK: One day, 17 km, medium grade, last reviewed July 1992, allow 5½ hours.

16   KATOOMBA FALLS— ECHO POINT—THREE SISTERS

Katoomba must surely rate as the most famous of Australian mountain resorts. Before people used cars so much, walking was one of the more popular leisure activities and facilities for walkers around Katoomba were accordingly installed on a grand scale. It is a pity some tracks, signs, seats, handrails and other facilities have been allowed to fall into disrepair but what remains is good and such magnificent places as Katoomba Falls, Echo Point and the Three Sisters are well serviced. Currently many steps and ladders are being replaced.

It is possible to spend a whole day ambling around on the numerous old tracks as well as the three main points of interest, and yet be no more than 2 km from Echo Point at any one time. The scenic railway, said to be the steepest incline railway in the world, can

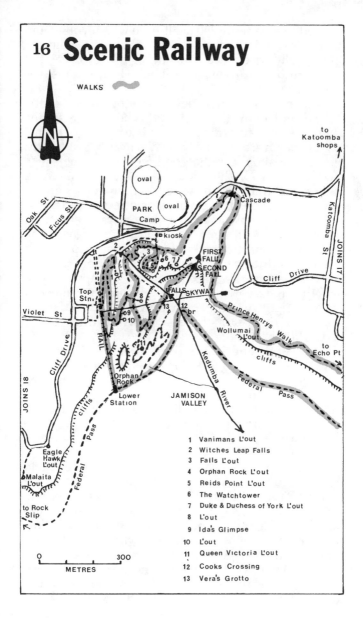

16 Scenic Railway

WALKS

1. Vanimans L'out
2. Witches Leap Falls
3. Falls L'out
4. Orphan Rock L'out
5. Reids Point L'out
6. The Watchtower
7. Duke & Duchess of York L'out
8. L'out
9. Ida's Glimpse
10. L'out
11. Queen Victoria L'out
12. Cooks Crossing
13. Vera's Grotto

71

be used to regain the 250 m altitude which you would have descended during the day. The railway, incidentally, rises at an incline of up to 52° and it passes through a 75 m long tunnel. The last car leaves at 4.55 p.m.

Start this walk suggestion at the top station of the railway and follow the maps in this book very closely. There are so many tracks that it is easy to go wrong.

Walk north around the railway winding-gear sheds, where you should find a good foot track. The sheds are just north of the station, kiosk and restaurant. Follow the track as it contours, then turn right at the first junction. This track leads directly south-east to Vanimans Lookout for a good general view. Next, retrace a few metres and turn left down the continuation of the track which descends to a point due east of the scenic railway's top station. Orphan Rock is just nearby. Next, see Ida's Glimpse as you pass through a narrow gap. It is another small lookout to your right. Continue on downhill and take the first turn right straight east down a track called Federal Pass.

Turn south and descend via Juliets Balcony and Furbers Steps to left fork north-east down to another fork, creek, small waterfall and bridge. Cross the bridge and walk generally north-east to the top of the Second Katoomba Fall. This is a magnificent place for a pause. Rainforest and ferns predominate in the area and there is little undergrowth. Rosellas seem common.

Next, retrace your route back across the bridge and up past Juliets Balcony to the junction with the Federal Pass pad. At this point turn right (north) and walk up to the base of Witches Leap Falls. These falls only have a 20 m drop but are quite beautiful. Follow the track uphill more steeply and within about 250 m you should emerge at the steps on to Reids Plateau. Four tracks join at the steps. The north track leads to a kiosk nearby should you want a short break for a few minutes. To the south, Reids Plateau provides good views of Witches Leap Falls, Orphan Rock, a general view, and a view of Katoomba Falls as you walk anti-clockwise around the oval-shaped track which returns you to the steps. The track should next be taken east 100 m past the Watchtower Lookout and on another 100 m to the Duke and Duchess of York Lookout. It gives good views southwards over Katoomba Falls area. Next, head north along the west bank of Kedumba Creek to some cascades just near Cliff Drive. Cross the creek at the cascades and follow the track back south on the eastern slopes of Kedumba Creek. The track, incidentally, is called Prince Henrys Walk. It leads underneath the Katoomba Skyway cables where there is a good view south, then it heads east round the cliff rim, under small rock overhangs and past two minor lookouts to Lady Darleys Lookout near the south end of Katoomba Street (Katoomba's main street). Continue south-east and very shortly you should arrive at Echo Point where all facilities exist and where there is, of course, the famous broad view of the Jamison Valley, Mount Solitary and the Three Sisters. Perhaps this lookout is the most famous in Australia. It is known as Queen Elizabeth Lookout.

Two concrete paths lead from beside the north end of the tourist information office at Echo Point. They lead to the Three Sisters and either path could be taken. The lower path passes a lookout then rejoins the more important higher path. From the Three Sisters Lookout turn down the Giants Staircase. It leads to Honeymoon Point (which is actually on one of the Three Sisters) then past Eves Lookout and down 900 steps to join a contouring track called the Dardanelles Pass. Turn right (south) and follow the Dardanelles Pass pad around below the Three Sisters. It is joined by the Federal Pass Track from your left as you turn north. Keep walking roughly north-west through magnificent forests to cross Kedumba Creek again. The bridge at the creek is a favourite vantage point from which to view Katoomba Falls above. Next, swing south-west and climb slightly past a track coming in from the right, then in 200 m arrive at the foot of the scenic railway. A hair-raising ride by rail ends the day. Lunch could be enjoyed just about anywhere along the way, but it is best to carry available water as the water, below the cliffline especially, is badly polluted.

MAP: Lands, 1:25,000 Katoomba and Maps 16 and 17.
WALK: One day, 7 km, easy grade, last reviewed July 1992, allow 3 hours.
Note: This walk includes a great number of steps and slippery places where care is needed.

17   KATOOMBA CLIFFTOPS— FEDERAL PASS

This walk recommendation basically follows the route of the Katoomba Falls, Echo Point and Three Sisters suggestion in this book, but an extension is included to raise the grading and to create added interest by having some of the walk route in quieter, less frequented places.

Follow instructions as for walk number 16, but once at the Three Sisters do not descend the Giants Staircase but follow the contouring track around the cliff rim as it swings north. Within 200 m you reach Lady Carrington Lookout, and as the track continues north for 1.5 km, other minor lookouts will be encountered. After 1.5 km a track forks left up to Cliff Drive, but you should continue to contour around the head of a small gully to Jamison Lookout. From this point a steep descent down the gully's east bank starts. It is ferny, has rock overhangs and generally is very pleasant. Shortly, Lila Falls should be seen as the track crosses to the west bank and descends

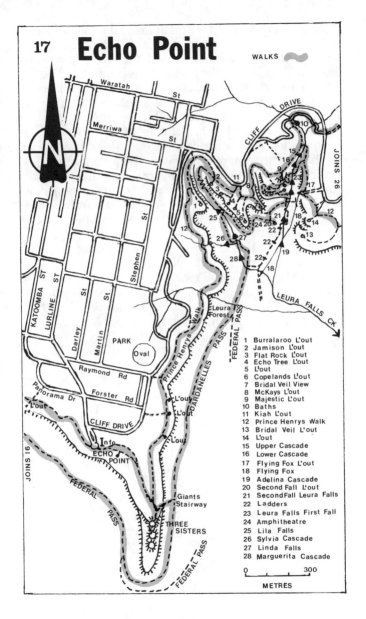

Echo Point

WALKS

1 Burralaroo L'out
2 Jamison L'out
3 Flat Rock L'out
4 Echo Tree L'out
5 L'out
6 Copelands L'out
7 Bridal Veil View
8 McKays L'out
9 Majestic L'out
10 Baths
11 Kiah L'out
12 Prince Henrys Walk
13 Bridal Veil L'out
14 L'out
15 Upper Cascade
16 Lower Cascade
17 Flying Fox L'out
18 Flying Fox
19 Adelina Cascade
20 Second Fall L'out
21 SecondFall Leura Falls
22 Ladders
23 Leura Falls First Fall
24 Amphitheatre
25 Lila Falls
26 Sylvia Cascade
27 Linda Falls
28 Marguerita Cascade

0   300

METRES

through Fairy Dell. A turnoff at Lila Falls east to Leura Falls should be avoided. Further down the gully, Linda Falls should be seen and the track crosses to the east bank below the falls. At this point, head down further, fork right (south), cross to the west bank again and soon you will be amid magnificent rain forest at Leura Forest rotunda and the junction of the Federal Pass and the Dardanelles Pass. Fork right up Dardanelles Pass and in 1 km you should arrive at the base of the Giants Stairway. Keep on contouring around below the Three Sisters and head north, ignoring the Federal Pass Track joining on the left. The track swings north-west, crosses Kedumba Creek and climbs slightly up to the lower station of the scenic railway. A track joins in from the right, 200 m before the station. It is the main walking track to the cliff tops and would only be needed should you miss the last car at 4.55 p.m.

Carry water for lunch, as the water, especially below the cliffline, is polluted. Lunch could be taken just about anywhere along the way.

MAP: Lands, 1:25,000 Katoomba and Maps 16 and 17.
WALK: One day, 10.5 km, medium grade, last reviewed July 1992, allow 4 hours.
Note: This walk includes a great number of steps and slippery spots where care is needed.

HOVEA

18   GOLDEN STAIRS— MOUNT SOLITARY

One of the main features seen from Echo Point and other vantage points at Katoomba in the Blue Mountains, is Mount Solitary. It stands out alone and imposing above the Jamison Valley so that its name seems very fitting, and walkers are attracted simply because of its isolation.

Narrow Neck Road leaves Cliff Drive west of the Katoomba scenic railway and other attractions. Travel Narrow Neck Road to a car park at the top of the Golden Stairs, where this walk suggestion starts. The track down the Golden Stairs starts about 100 m north of where you reach the steep incline and guard-railing. The spot is some 2 km from Cliff Drive.

The walk basically involves a descent from Narrow Neck Road to the main contouring access track, a long fairly level walk and then an ascent up Mount Solitary itself. The Golden Stairs descent is steep but relatively short and formed steps make the going easier. There are two steel ladders to negotiate and at the bottom of the descent at a T junction you should turn right along the contouring track to the Ruined Castle. This track is through rainforest and is very beautiful. It is also virtually flat walking as the route was once a busy coal miners' access route between the pits and the now touristic Katoomba scenic railway. Once, the railway hauled coal. After about 2.5 km there is a branch track to the Ruined Castle. At this point it is well worth diverging right and climbing on to a saddle then up a ridge to the Ruined Castle. Make sure you scramble on to these natural rock stacks to get the best views. Next, continue south-east steeply off the Ruined Castle via a pad off a southern spur. It leads back to the main contouring track near a saddle called Cedar Gap.

From this point on, climbing starts and first you need to climb up and over three knobs, keeping to

77

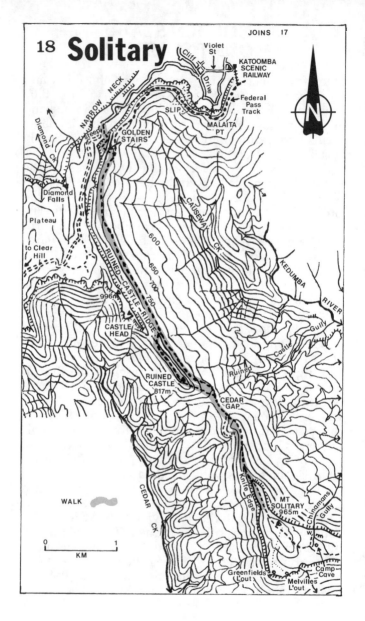

18 **Solitary**

Violet St

Cliff Drive

KATOOMBA
SCENIC
RAILWAY

N

NARROW NECK

steep

SLIP

Federal
Pass
Track

MALAITA
PT

Diamond Ck

GOLDEN
STAIRS

Diamond
Falls

Plateau

to Clear
Hill

CAUSEWAY CK

600

650

700

750

KEDUMBA RIVER

RUINED CASTLE RIDGE

996m

CASTLE
HEAD

RUINED
CASTLE
817m

Castle Gully

Ruined

CEDAR
GAP

WALK

CEDAR CK

Knife Edge

MT
SOLITARY
965m

Chinamans Gully

0   1
KM

Greenfields
L'out

Melvilles
L'out

Camp
Cave

the crest of the ridge and avoiding a right fork near the base of the first knob. In 300 m this side pad leads to a fern gully where water is sometimes available.

The steep ascent of Mount Solitary involves two 'steps' each some 75 m high and up a knife-edge formation. The track is not dangerous or even really awkward but requires use of hands as well as feet. It is suggested that you stop at the extreme western end of the mountain's plateau and have lunch on the rocks overlooking the views to the north, west and south. There is little point in going further along the plateau unless you walk a long way. The tops are thickly covered with dry vegetation and offer views only if you scrub-bash. From the lunch spot (no water available) you will be astounded how insignificant the Ruined Castle appears, considering the effort in climbing it earlier. It is suggested that you retrace your outward route after lunch. You could however omit the Ruined Castle deviation by remaining on the main track along the castle's eastern slopes.

MAP: Lands, 1:25,000 Katoomba and Jamison and Map 18.
WALK: One day, 14 km, medium grade, last reviewed July 1992, allow 5 hours.

19 BLACKHEATH—
GOVETTS LEAP—BRAESIDE

Govetts Leap, just east of Blackheath is a spectacular lookout point and there is a good tourist road to it and all amenities at the lookout. Starting and finishing at Blackheath station, it is possible to have a very enjoyable day's walk with Govetts Leap as the main attraction. Two beautiful gully walks lead to and from the lookout.

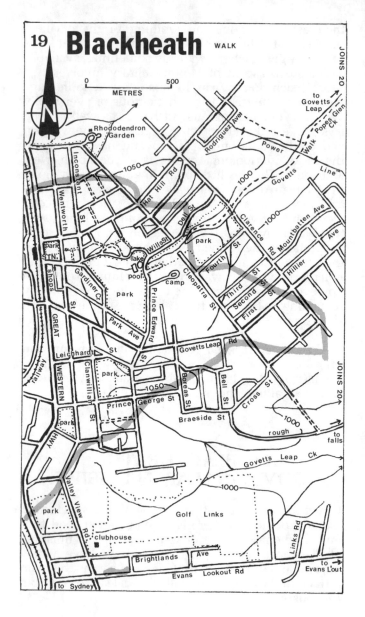

Opposite the east side of the railway station Gardiners Crescent should be followed east. It leads down to Memorial Park. Walk east down through the park to emerge at Wills Street, a gravelled road near a gully 500 m from the station. Walk east along Wills Street for 300 m to a foot track turnoff on the right hand side of the road. This is the start of Govetts Walk along Popes Glen. After walking 600 m along the north-west bank you should cross a bridge to the south-east side. There the valley is fairly open and descends gently. Hat Hill Road track joins in from the west at power transmission lines. About 1.6 km from the start of Govetts Walk a rock overhang can be seen some 300 m after crossing to the north bank as the stream turns east. Only 100 m more to the east you should recross to the south bank. Almost immediately a track leads off to the left to Boyds Beach. This short detour should be taken, as it is only 50 m to the beach beside the creek. Tea tree and honeyflower are both especially beautiful in the area. The stream water is not suited to drinking. A minor waterfall is to the left of the beach.

Next, walk 300 m south to the Pulpit Rock Track turnoff which leads left (east) across the stream. You should, however, go southwards and it is at this point that Popes Glen reaches a cliffline and the creek spills over lovely Horseshoe Falls down into the Grose Valley. Four lookouts are on your left once you reach the cliff rim.

The falls no doubt were named from the horse-shoe-shaped cliffline. The track ascends steps past banksias and coral ferns and, in 200 m, forks. Take the left fork nearest the cliff rim for 200 m up the slopes to Govetts Leap Lookout and car park. This is the suggested lunch place. There are all facilities. The view from the lookout is one of the best in New South Wales.

After lunch, follow a clifftop track from Govetts Leap Lookout southwards. In 750 m, and after having descended to Govetts Creek, you should be at the head of Govetts Leap Falls.* Like Horseshoe Falls, it is one of the biggest and best falls in the Blue Mountains and would have a vertical drop of well over 100 m. You should then turn south away from the cliffs along Braeside Walk.

The track follows the east bank of Govetts Leap Brook through areas renowned for hakea and wild-flowers. The valley is fairly open and at the end of the track, some 1.4 km from the falls, there is a small picnic area. It is then 2.5 km back to Blackheath station and you must use roads for the remainder of the walk. It is suggested you follow the gravelled road uphill, south-east from the picnic area for 1 km then join into Braeside Street which heads west. Next, turn north along Boreas Street at the end of Braeside Street, and then west again along Govetts Leap Road which leads back to the Great Western Highway. It is then only 200 m north back to the station via the highway.

MAP: Lands, 1:25,000 Katoomba and Maps 19 and 20.
WALK: One day, 8 km, easy grade, last reviewed July 1992, allow 3 hours.

20 GOVETTS LEAP—EVANS LOOKOUT—GRAND CANYON

Govetts Leap, Evans Lookout and the Grand Canyon are undoubtedly the three major attractions of Black-heath district in the Blue Mountains. All three features are the result of tremendous erosion of sandstone and the valleys north-east of the two lookouts are some 600 m deep. The Grand Canyon is really a

*National Park literature and signs have recently used the name Bridal Veil Falls for these falls, which for over a century have been known as Govetts Leap Falls.

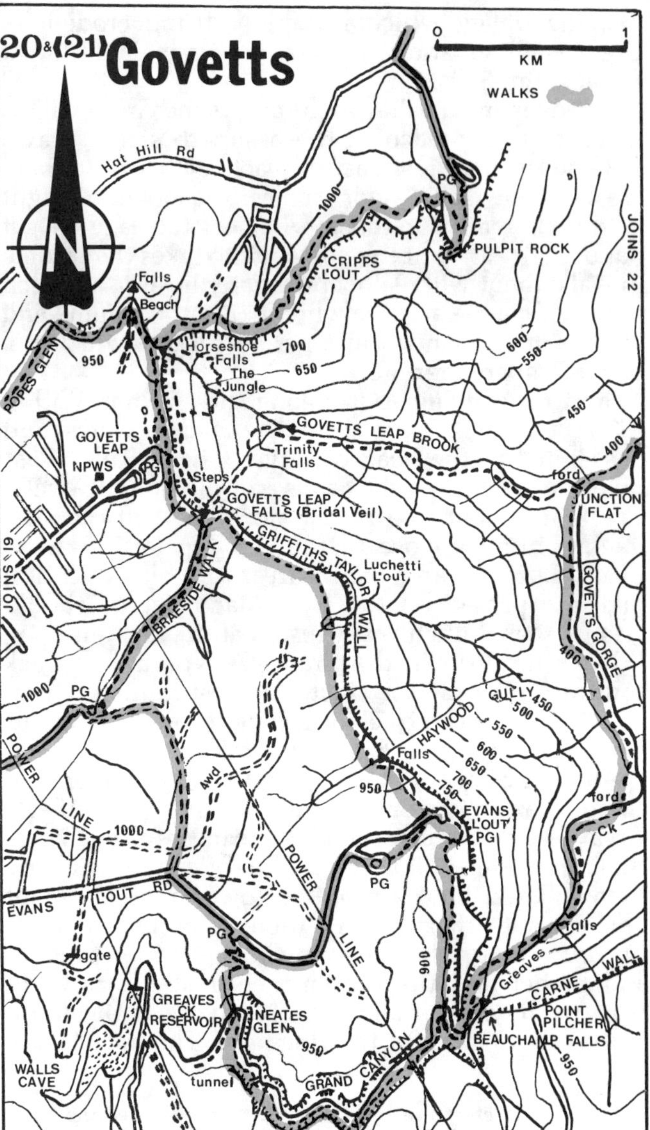
20&(21) Govetts
0
1
KM
WALKS
Hat Hill Rd
PG
PULPIT ROCK
JOINS 22
CRIPPS L'OUT
1000
Falls
Beach
Horseshoe Falls
The Jungle
700
650
600
550
450
400
950
POPES GLEN
GOVETTS LEAP BROOK
GOVETTS LEAP
NPWS
PG
Trinity Falls
Steps
ford
JUNCTION FLAT
GOVETTS LEAP FALLS (Bridal Veil)
GRIFFITHS TAYLOR WALL
Luchetti L'out
JOINS 19
BRAESIDE WALK
GOVETTS GORGE
400
1000
PG
GULLY
450
500
HAYWOOD
550
600
650
700
750
Falls
POWER LINE
4wd
950
EVANS L'OUT PG
ford
Ck
1000
POWER LINE
PG
EVANS L'OUT RD
PG
falls
gate
900
Greaves
CARNE WALL
GREAVES CK RESERVOIR
NEATES GLEN
POINT PILCHER
BEAUCHAMP FALLS
950
950
WALLS CAVE
tunnel
GRAND CANYON

hanging valley which is rapidly being eroded by Greaves Creek and it plunges into a main valley at Beauchamp Falls.

The deep main valley of the area is the Grose Valley. In order to see each of these superb sights, travel to Govetts Leap just east of Blackheath where there are complete facilities for picnics. The lookout is right at the car park for those who feel too lazy to get out of their cars, but the person who takes the trouble to walk about will really appreciate the area so much more. Of course anyone who follows the cliffline and walks some distance will experience sights which will be remembered for life.

Start off walking south along the cliff top. Within 750 m you will have seen the valley views and descended to the head of Govetts Leap Falls.* Pass Braeside Walk which heads south along Govetts Creek and climb south-east along the cliff rim. The track continues close to the cliff top for 2.5 km to Evans Lookout and picnic area. Ant hills over 1 m high are passed on the way. Many lizards should also be seen. Lunch is suggested at the lookout.

Next, head down the Grand Canyon access track south from beside the shelter nearest to the eastern-most lookout. The track descends through a cliffline, via many steps, then heads down a ferny gully.

About 1.2 km south of Evans Lookout you should come to an intersection where the side gully meets Greaves Creek. Turn right upstream into the Grand Canyon at this point. Some 2 km of canyon walking then follows. Look up at the towering cliffs about you. Despite their beauty there is better to come. As you walk up the canyon floor the cliffs get higher and higher and the canyon gets really narrow. In parts the daylight is all but excluded due to the depth of the canyon and the thriving ferns. The track leaves

*National Park literature and signs have recently used the name Bridal Veil Falls for these falls, which for over a century have been known as Govetts Leap Falls.

the canyon floor on two occasions to avoid waterfalls and cliffs, and in both cases you must climb steps up the southern sandstone walls. At one point the track passes through a 10 m long tunnel.

You should be really impressed by the Grand Canyon. It is of course not as grand as its counterpart in America but its sandstone overhangs, waterfalls and underground section of river all make it a most remarkable place. At the upper end of the canyon and at a sharp bend the track crosses the stream and ascends steeply up ferny Neates Glen for 700 m to meet the Evans Lookout road. Above the clifftops, dry bushland commences. At the road there is a small picnic area and tap.

HAKEA

Turn left along the road and within 600 m the road bends west. At the bend double back north-east (hard right) on to a lesser road, then follow that road 1.4 km to Govetts Creek and Braeside Walk. The road has a couple of minor jeep tracks forking off it as it leads north for about 900 m then west down to Govetts Creek. Head off to the right down the pad called Braeside Walk until the cliff rim at Govetts Leap Falls is rejoined in 1.4 km. Braeside Walk provides easy walking in open scrubland along the creek's east bank. Once at the falls go left back up the hill for 750 m to return to Govetts Leap Lookout and the end of the circuit.

MAP: Lands, 1:25,000 Katoomba and Map 20.
WALK: One day, 10.3 km, medium grade, last reviewed July 1992, allow 4¼ hours.

21   NEATES GLEN—GRAND CANYON—EVANS LOOKOUT

One of the more interesting places in the Blue Mountains is the Grand Canyon near Blackheath. The canyon is, of course, nothing like its famous counterpart in the United States, but it is quite deep in relation to its width and is about 2 km long. Greaves Creek flows through it, eroding the sandstone formations into incredible shapes, and in places one cannot see the bottom from the track because of the narrowness and darkness. Ferns, rock overhangs, a tunnel and the constant sound of rushing water all contribute to making it an excellent walk venue.

It is better to walk downhill through the canyon so that you can really appreciate it and not think about the difficulties encountered in climbing up the other way. Also at two points the track descends from the south side on to the canyon floor and if walking uphill, one tends to miss the lower turnoff and to walk into the section of the canyon floor from which the only exit is a retrace of your route.

Take the Evans Lookout Road east off the Great Western Highway just 2 km south of Blackheath station and proceed to a small car park about 2.8 km east of the highway. It is at the head of Neates Glen and the Grand Canyon, on the south side of the road.

To start the walk itself, descend the zig-zag foot track south into Neates Glen which is a very ferny and pretty gully leading into, and providing access to, the deeper Grand Canyon. Steps assist in the descent but in places they are slippery with constant running water.

It is only about 700 m to the Grand Canyon junction where you must cross Greaves Creek and commence a 2 km walk down the canyon. At first the canyon is relatively dry and even scrubby as you contour above the stream on the south side. Many species of lizards live here in the drier conditions. Then the track leads down into much damper terrain. You need to pass through a 10 m long tunnel at a spot where the stream goes underground temporarily.

Continue downstream on the south bank through fern glades and rock overhangs. The track is well formed and has hand rails for safety over most of its length. Eventually you will find that the stream is descending more rapidly than the track and you come across drier vegetation on the higher slopes. Again you must suddenly descend to the canyon floor, this time via a side gully and the descent is quite steep. It is then a matter of following the bed quite closely, crossing and re-crossing to then reach a junction.

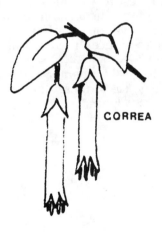

CORREA

Fork right downstream at this intersection for a side trip. Follow the track near the creek as it swings south then back north to near the top of Beauchamp Falls 300 m away. This pad is the Rodriguez Pass Track. Continue down the pad another 300 m to the base of the falls which is a good spot for a lunch break. As you descend there are good views of towering cliffs and the more distant peaks and valley vistas.

Return the 600 m up the Grand Canyon then turn right up the Evans Lookout track. It ascends through extremely beautiful ferns and in places the only vegetation is tree and ground ferns.

There are many steps to climb as the 1.2 km long pad leads up to Evans Lookout shelter sheds, water tanks and picnic area. Evans Lookout is a well-known vantage point for views of the Grose and Govetts Creek valleys. The cliffs are extremely high and the valley floor is about 600 m lower than the lookout. After a good rest and look at the view, walk back along the tourist road for 1.3 km to the walk starting point.

Alternatively use a short foot track from Evans Lookout south-west to a picnic area, then follow the road out from the picnic area on to the main tourist road. This alternative route is of similar total distance (1.3 km) but does reduce the road walking a little.

MAP: Lands, 1:25,000 Katoomba and Map 21.
WALK: One day, 6.4 km, easy grade, last reviewed July 1992, allow 2½ hours.

HARDENBERGIA

22 BLUE GUM FOREST

Blue Gum Forest is a name which many Sydney district bushwalkers seem to immediately associate with great beauty, serenity and relative isolation. The forest is at the junction of Govetts Creek and the Grose River, way down in the Grose Valley out from Blackheath. It is a perfect place to get away from the rush and bustle of the city. On a hot day the forest is especially attractive due to shady trees, park-like grassy flats, swimming spots and views up to the towering cliffs all around the valley.

Acacia Flat, adjacent, is an excellent large bush camp and ideal for an overnight stop. (To help blue gum seedlings to grow on the forest floor and so maintain the present forest, camping in the valley is restricted to Acacia Flat.)

Access to the valley is difficult from any direction. The shortest route is from the end of the road at Perrys Lookdown, but there is a 600 m difference in elevation between the valley floor and Perrys Look-down or other access points.

The suggestion is that walkers undertake a two day circuit from Govetts Leap picnic ground and car park. The walk is medium grade due to the fairly short distances travelled each day, but participants should realise that the climb back out of the valley up the 600 m rise is very steep and hard.

Those who use public transport could go by train to Blackheath station then walk the extra distance to Govetts Leap. The one-way distance thus added is 3 km via Govetts Leap Road or 3.5 km via Popes Glen walking track.

It is best to carry some water for drinking as Govetts Creek and streams descending from the Blackheath area tend to be polluted. The quality of water in the Grose River upstream of Govetts Creek is better. Carrying a small fuel or gas stove for cooking is a good idea. In some sections the tracks can be slippery and rocky underfoot so wear sturdy footwear. Care

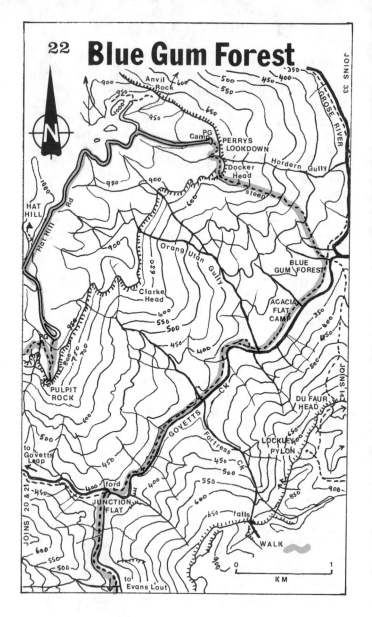

Blue Gum Forest

22

is essential for a good walk.

To start the walk, follow the cliff rim foot track from Govetts Leap car park south, uphill a little then down, to the top of Govetts Leap Falls 750 m away. (In recent years these falls have been signposted as Bridal Veil Falls but all available information including literature over a century old refers to Govetts Leap Falls. The author has noted many such changes by National Park authorities throughout New South Wales of late, together with anomalies in the spelling of the names.)

Govetts Leap Falls was visited by the noted naturalist Charles Darwin during his historic crossing of the Blue Mountains. The falls have about the biggest single drop in the Blue Mountains.

Continue up the cliff rim track from the falls for another 3.25 km to gain Evans Lookout. Like Govetts Leap, this lookout is a popular tourist attraction with broad vistas to Grose and Govetts gorges. It also has picnic facilities.

The long descent to the valley floor then begins. Take the Grand Canyon track from the lookout, south, down steeply through the cliffline to the very ferny canyon, 1.2 km away. Greaves Creek flows through the canyon and as you reach the creek crossing there is a track junction.

Most walkers turn upstream to see the main part of the Grand Canyon but the plan here is to turn downstream to enter the wild remote region below. A break at the junction and short look at the upstream features could be an added attraction to some walkers.

Some 300 m downstream of the track junction, Beauchamp Falls tumble away out of the canyon into the broad valley below. Geologically, the spot is not unlike a glacial hanging valley formation. The track is known as Rodriguez Pass and can then be descended steeply past very high cliffs to the base of Beauchamp Falls. Take special care with slippery rocks in this locality. Some people may like to stop near the falls for a lunch break before descending further into the damp flourishing forests.

The pad leads down past more waterfalls, crosses Greaves Creek twice and then passes near the confluence of Greaves Creek and Govetts Creek. The way is then roughly north near the west bank of Govetts Creek, to Junction Rock 5.1 km from Evans Lookout.

At this point Govetts Creek joins Govetts Leap Brook and the brook has to be crossed on boulders. Thereafter, the rest of the day's walk is basically along the valley floor, following the west bank of the stream north-east on a reasonable track for 2.9 km to the Acacia Flat camp. At times the track climbs a little to skirt creekside bluffs and scrub overhangs the pad somewhat and is annoying when dripping wet. Most walkers should be at camp reasonably early where time can be spent relaxing and enjoying this little bit of bushland paradise.

Next day, the climb to Perrys Lookdown comes early in the walk. The climb is 2.6 km long and the rise 600 m. There are hundreds of steps to be negotiated. If the day is hot, wet a towel in the stream and use it to mop your brow as you climb. And, on hot days start off early to avoid the worst heat of the day.

Proceed from camp 600 m in the Blue Gum Forest downstream, then turn uphill for the main climb north-west. (If the forest was not explored the previous day then walk to the confluence of the Grose River nearby and spend a little time there before the big climb.) The ascent is via Dockers Buttress to Dockers Head. Then the track skirts around Hordern Gully and up to the lookout, picnic and camp areas at Perrys Lookdown.

After a well-earned rest at the lookout and road end the next stage is to follow quiet Hat Hill Road for 3.5 km towards Blackheath. Anvil Rock Road links in from the right at the 900 m stage. Turn left on to Pulpit Rock Road and descend to its end and a picnic area 800 m away. A short foot track then leads to Pulpit Rock Lookout. It has particular fascination in that it juts well beyond the huge cliff tops surrounding the Grose Valley and Govetts Gorge. The view is excellent towards the tourist lookouts at Govetts Leap and Evans Lookout. It is unwise to go too close to the cliff rim, especially on a windy day. The sweeping vista includes the now familiar valley floor you walked the previous day. Pulpit Rock would make a suitable spot for a lunch break.

On again; follow the cliff top foot track for 2.5 km as it winds in and out at minor gullies and past Cripps Lookout to a track junction near the head of impressive Horseshoe Falls at Popes Glen Creek. The falls clearly take their name from their shape. From the track junction across the creek, fork left up the track for 500 m, past several good lookouts to reach Govetts Leap car park.

MAP: Lands, 1:25,000 Katoomba and Mount Wilson sheets and Maps 21 and 22.
WALK: Two days, 22.25 km (day one 11.25 km, day two 11 km), medium grade, last reviewed July 1992, allow day one 5 hours and day two 6 hours.

23 PULPIT ROCK

From Govetts Leap Lookout near Blackheath, a most enjoyable walk can be taken to Pulpit Rock and return. Pulpit Rock has a particular fascination in that it extends well beyond the main cliffline surrounding the Grose Valley and enables walkers to see truly spectacular views across the valley to Griffiths Taylor Wall and the main tourist spots at Evans Lookout and Govetts Leap.

After a look at the valley and cliffs from Govetts Leap Lookout and car park, head off to the left, downhill along the foot track which leads close to

Pulpit Rock

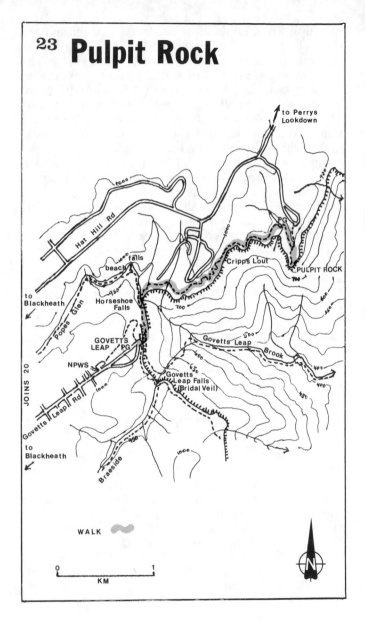

to Perrys
Lookdown

Hat Hill Rd

PG

Cripps Lout

PULPIT ROCK

falls

beach

to
Blackheath

Horseshoe
Falls

Popes Glen

GOVETTS
LEAP PG

Govetts Leap

Brook

NPWS

JOINS 20

Govetts Leap Rd

Govetts
Leap Falls
(Bridal Veil)

to
Blackheath

Braeside

WALK

0   1
KM

N

the cliffline. Within 400 m the lovely Horseshoe Falls crest is gained at the spot where Popes Glen Creek reaches the cliff tops. Some steps need to be descended to reach the creek area and a track fork. Turn right to cross the creek then simply continue on the good foot track as it leads east and north-east near the cliff rim, past Cripps Lookout and to Pulpit Rock. The last 300 m involves walking southwards after crossing a gully. As the rock lookout area is neared, a track from the nearby car park joins in from the left. The lookout is tremendously exposed, especially on a windy day. The cliffs in the locality are about 250 m high. A sweeping panorama includes much of Govetts Gorge and the Grose Valley, so that the lookout is a good venue to enjoy lunch before retracing the route back to Govetts Leap.

MAP: Lands, 1:25,000 Katoomba, Mount Wilson and Map 23.
WALK: One day, 6 km, easy grade, last reviewed July 1992, allow 2¼ hours.
Warning: Keep clear of the edge of the very exposed cliff tops at Pulpit Rock.

24   VALLEY OF THE WATERS— NATIONAL PASS

The cliffline walks at Katoomba in the Blue Mountains are both popular and scenic, but nearby at Wentworth Falls, the scenery is even better and goes largely unnoticed. At Katoomba, the tracks are at the top and at the base of the cliffs. But at Wentworth Falls the track is cut into the cliffs halfway up, so the views are uninterrupted and really spectacular and cliff overhangs are seen to their fullest advantage. So, next time you visit the Blue Mountains area, travel along the Great Western Highway to a point near Went-

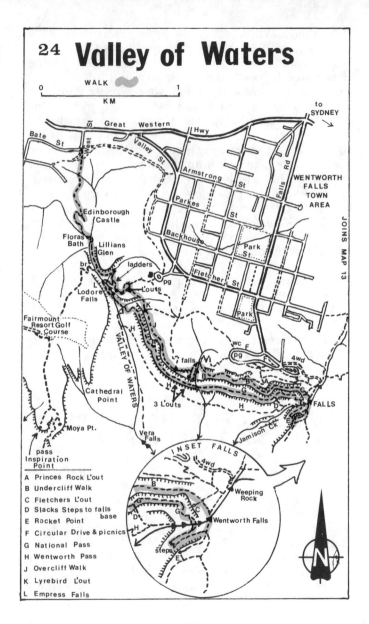

WALK

0 ————————————— 1
KM

Great Western Hwy
to SYDNEY

Bate St
West St
Valley St
Armstrong St
Parkes St
Backhouse St
Fletcher St
Park St
Park St

WENTWORTH FALLS TOWN AREA

JOINS MAP 13

Edinborough Castle
Floras Bath
Lillians Glen
ladders
pg
br
L'outs
L
K
J
Lodore Falls

Fairmount Resort Golf Course

VALLEY OF WATERS

H
falls
M
B
B
wc F
pg
4wd
G
G

Cathedral Point
H
H
D
FALLS
3 L'outs
E

Moya Pt.
Vera Falls
Jamison Ck.

pass
Inspiration Point

A Princes Rock L'out
B Undercliff Walk
C Fletchers L'out
D Slacks Steps to falls base
E Rocket Point
F Circular Drive & picnics
G National Pass
H Wentworth Pass
J Overcliff Walk
K Lyrebird L'out
L Empress Falls

INSET FALLS

4wd
B
Weeping Rock
G
C
D
Wentworth Falls
H
steps
E

N

worth Falls 100 km from Sydney. There are some big pine trees at the corner of West Street at the spot. It is the suggested starting point for this walk.

First walk 100 m south on West Street. Then where the road turns west walk to the road edge and you should see jeep tracks and adjacent foot pad leading downhill, south. Do not take the jeep tracks diverging left and right. Follow the foot track down across a small gully and up on to Edinburgh Castle Rock. Then descend around the rock's western edge, below its cliffs and on down into the Valley of the Waters. A short creekside walk and climb follow to meet a bridge to the west bank and Leura at a track junction. The spot is called Lillians Glen.

Remain on the east bank and within 200 m you will be at a track intersection. This junction is just 20 m past a small waterfall.

Follow the National Pass Track which is the one leading down the valley. It leads to the top of lovely Lodore Falls, then descends to their base via magnificent rock overhangs, swimming holes and ferny glades. Just below the falls, take the left-fork track rather than the right fork to Vera Falls. National Pass Track, the one you should follow, then continues for nearly 2 km on what surely is the most spectacular cliff walk in Australia and about the best overall walk in the Blue Mountains. The sandstone cliffs are in horizontal beds and this remarkable track follows around the contour of the bedding on a tiny ledge. In places the cliffs have been carved out to permit a through walk, and for most of the way you are under cliff overhangs and even walking behind waterfalls. The views of the Jamison Valley are spectacular as there is little foreground vegetation to block the view. Eventually you should arrive at Wentworth Falls which descend in two stages. National Pass Track crosses the stream amid spray between the two drops. (If there have been recent heavy rains a raincoat would be advisable.) The track then climbs up stairs cut out of the sandstone, to the head of the upper fall. Lunch is suggested here.

At this point a number of foot tracks begin, as the area is a picnic reserve. Stay as close to the cliff rim as possible, diverging left at each junction. The aim is to follow the Undercliff and Overcliff Walking Tracks which, like National Pass, follow cliff overhangs along sandstone bedding, but well above National Pass.

Keep heading west. At two points tracks lead off left. At the first the side route leads to a small waterfall and then on to a lookout, and in the second case the side route leads to a minor lookout. Take both these side trips. Some six tracks lead off to the right from the cliff rim area and all should be ignored in favour of the cliff edge route. Always diverge left at each junction. At the fifth branch off to the right, double back left down to Queen Victoria Lookout. After the lookout this track leads back down ladders to the head of Lodore Falls and from that point on you should retrace your outward route back to West Street.

MAP: Lands, 1:25,000 Katoomba and Map 24.
WALK: One day, 6 km, easy grade, last reviewed July 1992, allow 2¾ hours.

25 LAWSON—LUCY'S GLEN— DANTES GLEN

In the Blue Mountains there is a good, easy walk from Lawson station. A circuit walk is feasible and it includes several waterfalls and a lot of cool ferny gully walking. The circuit is within North Lawson Park with an extension into the Blue Mountains National Park.

From Lawson railway station go to the north side of the rail line and on to Loftus Street. Turn east,

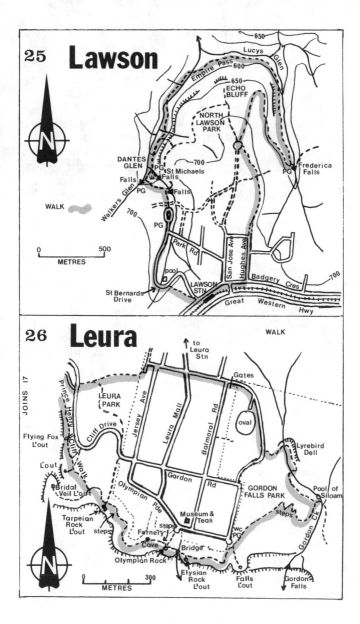

25 Lawson

650
Lucys Glen
Empire Pass 600
ECHO BLUFF
650
NORTH LAWSON PARK
N
700
DANTES GLEN
PG
St Michaels Falls
Falls
PG
Frederica Falls
Falls
PG
WALK
700
PG
0 500 METRES
Park Rd
San Jose Ave
Hughes Ave
pool
Badgery Cres
700
St Bernards Drive
LAWSON STN
Great Western Hwy

26 Leura

WALK
to Leura Stn
Gates
JOINS 17
Prince Henry Cliff Walk
LEURA PARK
Cliff Drive
Jersey Ave
Leura Mall
Balmoral Rd
oval
Flying Fox L'out
L'out
Lyrebird Dell
Bridal Veil L'out
Olympian Pde
Gordon Rd
GORDON FALLS PARK
Pool of Siloam
Tarpeian Rock L'out
steps
Museum & Teas
wc PG
steps
Gordon Ck
N
Ferney
steps
Cave
Bridge
0 300 METRES
Olympian Rock
Elysian Rock L'out
Falls L'out
Gordon Falls

99

following the line so that Badgery Crescent is entered east of the road bridge across the line just east of the station. Turn north along Hughes Street one block later and walk to the end. Power lines then cross a track which continues north as an extension of Hughes Street. The spot is about 600 m from Lawson station. Just north of the electricity line, the pad leads off north into scrub and intersects more power lines and tracks under the lines. Within 900 m it reaches an intersection of tracks on a ridge. From this high point, diverge right to descend north-east at first then back south to Frederica Falls within 1.1 km. This locality is good wildflower territory, given the drier northerly aspect and shallow soils. The Falls are small but have a pleasant pool at their base and a rock overhang into the pool. There is a fireplace at the base of the falls.

Turn downstream next on the pad, continuing into damper vegetation along Lucy's Glen. After 1.4 km, the track leads west past the confluence of the two main valleys of the locality. Thereafter, follow Dantes Glen upstream southwards 300 m on the track to a rock pool and to where the pad crosses the stream to the west bank. Then enter a more pronounced gorge formation, with steps and dripping moss-covered rocks. After 400 m the pad returns to the east bank then climbs to be close to the gorge rim for 400 m. A pad to Fairy Falls and Echo Point then forks off left uphill and should be bypassed. Stay near the ferny creek, heading south for 400 m to the confluence of creeks. There is a picnic table and a left fork pad side trip of just 100 m to the base of St Michaels Falls. After inspecting these falls retrace the 100 m and head on upstream 150 m to more waterfalls on the Walkers Glen stream branch. Again, there is a picnic table near the base of the falls. A lunch break could be considered before climbing out of the gully system.

The track crosses to the east bank below the falls then ascends rocky bluffs eastwards via a number of sandstone steps. Then, within 400 m, it divides again. The left branch leads 100 m to Fairy Falls then continues. Take the 100 m walk as a side trip to see the falls then return to traverse the right fork, diverging right again almost immediately. Within 250 m, enter a large grassy picnic area and road end. Follow the road south up a valley past the Lawson swimming pool and 1.3 km towards the town. The road, St Bernards Drive, curves and ascends to join Loftus Street just beside the Lawson station. There is a short-cut foot pad connecting the swimming pool and station and bypassing the bend in St Bernards Drive. That short-cut could be used to complete the walk circuit.

MAP: Lands, 1:25,000 Katoomba and Map 25.
WALK: One day, 8 km, easy grade, last reviewed July 1992, allow 2¾ hours.

26   LEURA CLIFFS—LYREBIRD DELL

The Leura Falls area has a multitude of foot tracks, mostly installed in the days before cars. There are, of course, so many interesting little glens, falls, overhangs and other features to see that the number of tracks is indeed necessary. Sometimes it is rather pleasant just to wander round every little track seeing the attractions along each.

This suggestion is based upon the Leura Falls map included in this book and the map should assist greatly. In order to make the trip one which involves a day's activity rather than an hour or two, the adjoining Leura cliffline walk is included. People without transport could easily start and finish this walk at Leura station and simply add the short distance along Leura Mall.

Start the walk at the intersection of Leura Mall and Malvern Road, Leura. Leura Mall is the town's main street and Malvern Road is the fourth east-west cross street southwards from the railway line. First, walk west to the end of Malvern Road, turn south for 50 m, then veer right down a rough foot track which joins sealed Cliff Drive within 300 m. There are shelter sheds, and a picnic area across a bridge just west of the spot. Also Leura Falls Creek flows through south and a track leads down its west bank. Follow this track, then diverge right (rather than cross a bridge) and continue to Majestic Lookout. It provides a reasonable view of the valley. Continue west and at the next junction keep going along Prince Henry's Walk.

Cross the head of a stream, turn south and pass a rock overhang amid beautiful ferns. Then at the next fork, shortly afterwards, take a minor side trip to lovely Bridal Veil View. It is perhaps the best view in the area. Return to the main track, bypass the Copeland Lookout track (next on the left) and another viewpoint off left soon after. Turn right and climb a few steps north to the restaurant at Kiah Lookout on Cliff Drive, then walk just 50 m west on Cliff Drive and join another trail, an alternative route to Federal Pass via Lila Falls. Just 10 m south, turn west and walk to Jamison Lookout. Have a look at the view, then fork left and start the long descent through a magnificent gully down many steps along the east bank of the gully. You should then arrive at Lila Falls. The falls are small but pretty. Stay on the east bank rather than cross near the falls base, then walk around below the cliffline through The Amphitheatre with its magnificent ferns and overhang. Take a very short side trip to the right, to the lookout overlooking the second Leura Fall. Then continue to the intersection of four tracks at Leura Falls Creek, just at the base of Weeping Rock. Turn north uphill to the base of First Leura Fall (or Bridal Veil) which from this position is very pleasing. Then swing back west then east up many steps until you arrive near the top of First Leura Fall. On the way, ignore a turnoff to the left and stop for a look at the fine views at each of the two lookouts. Once above the falls, walk north along the stream's east bank past pleasant little cascades.

Not far upstream at a bridge, Prince Henry's Cliff Walk doubles back to your right and contours southwards. Follow it past Flying Fox Lookout and another unnamed lookout soon after (a rock overhang with a seat under it), and past the turnoff to Bridal Veil Lookout on your right. The cliff walk turns north-east temporarily then continues on past interesting Tarpeian Rock with its strange sandstone bedding ridges, Fernery Cave, Olympian Rock, Buttenshaw Bridge, and Elysian Rock to Gordon Falls Lookout car park.

At the car park there are drinking water and picnic facilities. It would be a good place for lunch before continuing on down a track to the Pool of Siloam, a lovely, cool swimming hole on Gordon Creek. The pool is just 40 m east of the main Lyrebird Dell Track, which should next be followed north. There are three remarkable rock overhangs and a waterfall along Lyrebird Dell. The track then swings west up to a gravelled road. Turn right (north) and walk up the road out through the reserve Memorial Gates into Malvern Road. It is then only 300 m back west to the walk starting point.

MAP: Lands, 1:25,000 Katoomba and Maps 17 and 26.
WALK: One day, 6 km, easy grade, last reviewed July 1992, allow 2¾ hours.
Note: This walk includes a great number of steps. Care is needed in numerous slippery spots.

27   MOUNT YORK

In 1813 the Blue Mountains were finally crossed from Sydney by Blaxland, Lawson and Wentworth, the now famous explorers who began the opening up of Australia's interior. By 1815, Cox's Road was opened up to descend the western escarpments to the interior plains. This first road was very steep and therefore was replaced by Lawsons Long Alley Road built by 1822-23. But it too had a very short steep incline so further routes were built. These included Lockyers Road 1828-29 (never completed), Mitchells Road and the present Victoria Pass. These earlier roads were too steep for the first motor vehicles to use nearly one hundred years later. Berghofers Pass, opened in 1912, was the first road built to overcome the motor vehicle difficulty.

In recent years these historic roads (all in the Mount York vicinity), have been reopened for walkers and linked by extra walking tracks to permit circuit walks of historic and natural interest. One interesting loop day walk leads down Lawsons Long Alley and back up Cox's Road. It passes over historic Mount York. The walk starts in a saddle 2 km from Mount Victoria via Mount York Road. One option would be to walk the route as an easy overnight trip, and camp at Hartley Vale. Another option is to access the walk start by rail to Mount Victoria station.

To start off, head down from the saddle northwards on the restored historic Lawsons Long Alley. It was originally built by Lieutenant William Lawson, one of the explorers. The road soon leads steeply down into the valley of Kerosene Creek where its alignment becomes indistinct. It also crosses private land. As a result, a track has been constructed to lead past the western boundaries of the private land and join back on to the north-bound road further down the valley. Some of the indistinct section is aligned across swampy land and corduroy was originally laid there. A disused oil shale works is passed as you approach

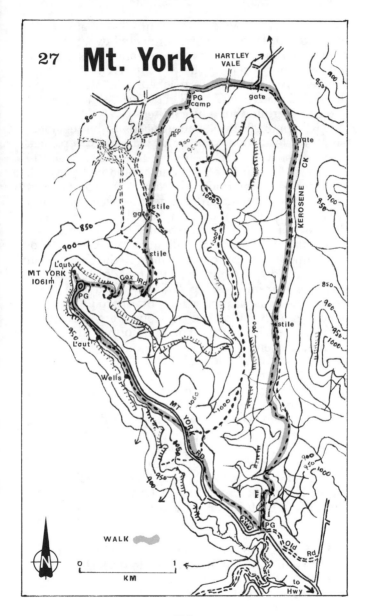

27 **Mt. York**

HARTLEY VALE

PG camp

gate

gate

KEROSENE CK

stile

gate

stile

MT YORK 1061m

L'out

Cox Rd

PG

L'out

Wells

stile

MT YORK RD

PG

Old Rd

to Hwy

WALK

N

0   1

KM

850
900
950
1000
1050

the tiny Hartley Vale settlement. The shale works were built in 1865 and were connected by a funicular railway to the main rail line on the range tops. Hartley Vale is some 5 km from the walk start. Once through a gate, as the hamlet is reached, walk west along the sealed road for 600 m to Lockyers Roadhead picnic and camp ground for a lunch break.

Next, some 250 m elevation needs to be regained. The track leads over a stile and via an old jeep track into forest westwards at first then turns south. Lockyers Road forks off left and should be bypassed. Walk south on the track, adjacent to a fenceline, past some pines. Then via an easement between farmland cross a fairly broad gully. Forest is then entered near the base of Mount York. About 2 km out from the lunch spot you reach the alignment of Cox's Road. Thereafter it can be ascended through the cliffs 1.9 km to Mount York summit. This, the most historic of the roads, is extremely steep and rough. At one point near some cliffs, it divides temporarily to give choice of routes. As soon as the cliff tops are gained there is an impressive natural rock platform with a view of the afternoon's route so far. Mount York summit is just westwards up the old road.

On the summit there are four commemorative monuments, indicating the mountain's importance in Australian history. There are also picnic facilities. From the peak, sealed Mount York Road leads along a high ridge to Mount Victoria. The alignment basically coincides with the old Cox's Road. A walking track has been formed adjacent for most of the way. This 4 km long track leads south-east back to the saddle and walk circuit end at Lawsons Long Alley. During this last stretch you pass Bardens Lookout.

MAP: Lands, 1:25,000 Hartley and Map 27.
WALK: One day, 13 km, medium grade, last reviewed July 1992, allow 5 hours.
Note: Water is best carried for the day.

28   JENOLAN CAVES

Walking underground can be just as rewarding as beach or mountain walking. Jenolan Caves must surely rate as the best in Australia and are quite a good location to spend a day walking. There are surface trails in the reserve to familiarise walkers with the area and the tracks pass several interesting arches and external limestone formations such as the Grand Arch and the Devils Coachhouse, the Peephole and Carlotta Arch. Some considerable time should be spent seeing the wonderful underground caverns in the company of a guide and the usual tourist groups.

Basically, the area consists of a broad band of limestone with three streams descending to it, sinking and running through the caves and emerging as the Jenolan River on the lower side of the Grand Arch which is so large that even the main access road passes through it. The caves are said to be of outstanding quality and there are innumerable caves which can be inspected so the choice of which ones to enter is difficult.

First, it is suggested that you start outside Caves House, a large guesthouse, and walk down the main road past the guides' office, kiosk, and bus parking bay, then pass through the Grand Arch and the entry points to a number of the caves. As soon as you emerge from under the Grand Arch, start the ascent up a left fork path into and through the Devils Coachhouse. Like the Grand Arch it is huge inside and very interesting. At the top end of the Devils Coachhouse the path leads along the banks of the Jenolan River a short distance then crosses it and ascends via many steps and hairpin bends to the Peephole. This is a small hole which enables you to view the Devils Coachhouse from above.

Continue on uphill to join a main track coming from a car park (No. 2 car park). Pass on to a ridge top and arrive at Carlotta Arch which gives a lovely view down on to the lower Jenolan River and the

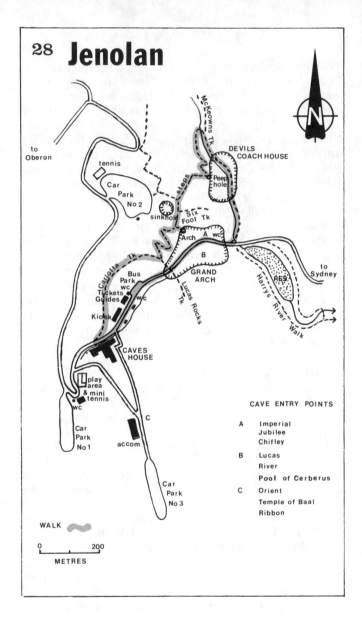

28 Jenolan

N

to Oberon

tennis

Car Park No 2

sinkhole

McKeowns Tk

DEVILS COACH HOUSE

steps

Peep hole

Six Foot Tk

Arch A wc

B

GRAND ARCH

Carlotta Tk

Bus Park wc

Tickets Guides

wc

Kiosk

Lucas Rocks

Lucas Tk

RES

to Sydney

Harrys River Walk

CAVES HOUSE

play area & mini tennis

wc

C

Car Park No 1

accom

Car Park No 3

CAVE ENTRY POINTS

A   Imperial
       Jubilee
       Chifley

B   Lucas
       River
       Pool of Cerberus

C   Orient
       Temple of Baal
       Ribbon

WALK

0   200

METRES

small reservoir downstream from the Grand Arch. Keep going downhill via hairpin bends then sidle back down to the roadway outside Caves House to finish the 1.3 km long circuit.

The ticket box for cave inspections is to the left just down the road and the choice is yours about which caves to visit. Some of the better-known formations are in the Lucas Cave which is also the longest cave. Baal, Orient and Pool of Cerberus Caves are relatively short, especially Pool of Cerberus Cave, and the River Cave is quite pretty. Obviously cost must be considered as tickets are far from cheap, but you should visit at least two caves. Official advice is to avoid choosing two of River, Baal and Orient if you want to see variety and to avoid seeing both Imperial and Jubilee. Lucas, Pool of Cerberus and Chifley can be grouped with any others.

	Cave walking metres	Total tour metres
Lucas Cave	527	861
Jubilee Cave	302	1574
River Cave	402	1271
Pool of Cerberus Cave	133	1016
Imperial Cave	494	1069
Chifley Cave	465	692
Temple of Baal Cave	151	363
Orient Cave	175	470
Ribbon (includes Orient)		560

(The first six caves listed have access from the Grand Arch and the latter three from near the rear of Caves House but with assembly near the guides' office.)

MAP: Map 28.
WALK: One day, 1.3 km surface walking plus caves distance, easy grade, last reviewed July 1992. No specific time.

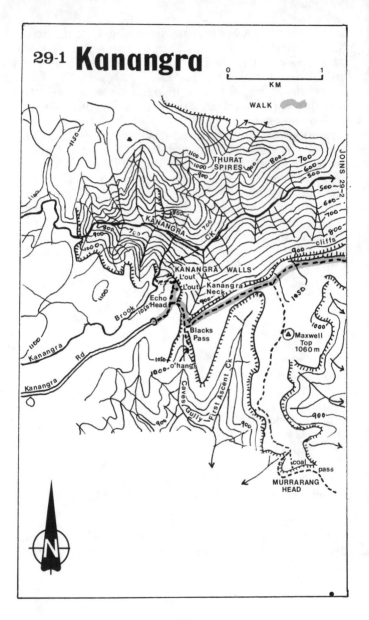

29-1 **Kanangra**

WALK

THURAT
SPIRES

KANANGRA CK

JOINS 29-2

cliffs

KANANGRA WALLS
L'out
L'out Kanangra
Neck
Echo
Head
Brook
Blacks
Pass

Maxwell
Top
1060 m

Kanangra Rd

Kanangra

o'hangs

Caves Gully

First Ascent Ck

coal pass
MURRARANG
HEAD

N

110

29 KANANGRA WALLS— CRAFTS WALL

Kanangra Boyd National Park south of Jenolan Caves has as its main attraction an exceptionally deep gorge surrounded by massive clifflines. A tourist road leads south to the focus point at Kanangra Tops. The road ends close to one of several quite high waterfalls and also close to some of the best cliffs which are known as Kanangra Walls.

Kanangra Tops are quite flat and open and, consequently, there are panoramic views—especially from their edges. An unusual feature is that the tops terminate in a peninsula jutting out eastwards from the main plateau. The peninsula itself is almost divided into three sections by some narrow necks. As well, an 'island' known as Crafts Wall is still further east but joined to the peninsula by Kilpatricks Causeway which is somewhat lower than the other necks linking the three peninsula sections. A really magnificent walk is therefore possible. It crosses all the necks out to Crafts Wall.

Make sure you carry some water for lunch which would be best had at Crafts Wall. First, walk from the road end north-east 550 m to two lookouts for a good general view. Retrace 250 m and then turn on to the plateau pad. The track at first leads 300 m down into Blacks Pass, the first neck to be crossed. A 150 m diversion should be made to inspect fine rock overhangs on the side of the gully just south of the saddle.

Next, continue up a ramp on to the westernmost section of the peninsula. The ramp, like much of the track, was used by cattlemen in the past and constant treading by cattle caused bad erosion but left the track clearly defined. The track keeps close to the northern rim of the plateau. Consequently there are good views all the way as you head east-north-east. Some 800 m from Blacks Pass you should arrive at

111

the second neck, known as Kanangra Neck. It is about 400 m long. There is a track fork immediately east of this second neck.

You should keep walking in the same east-north-east direction along the tops. The pad keeps close to the cliff rim for another 1 km, crossing a lesser defined neck in the process and bringing you to the top of a ravine on the north-east corner of Mount Brennan. Small rock cairns are a guide. If you look over the cliff rim in this area you can clearly see the route of the foot track ahead, down on Kilpatricks Causeway some 100 m lower. To reach it you should first get on to the north side of the top of the small ravine. Then in about 25 m start the rocky descent through the ravine. As soon as you are through it, diverge left near the base of the clifflines and head down the pad beside a small scree slope.

The pad leads off the 'rock river' well down the slopes. Once on to the causeway the track is less clearly defined, especially after about 1 km where the ridge becomes rocky. The route of the track is right along the very crest of the rocky section of the causeway. Then you must cross a saddle, after entering dry forest and acacia, and climb to the base of the cliffs 4.2 km from Blacks Pass and at Crafts Wall. Wallabies may be seen in the area if you are quiet. The track at this point divides and one branch skirts each side of Crafts Wall. Then they rejoin at the north-east end to continue along the range. It is suggested that you take the minor, right, branch and follow the cliff base very closely southwards past some rock overhangs. Then swing north-east to more overhangs.

Along this side of Crafts Wall the forest is dense and little sunlight filters through, so it is a cool refreshing place on a hot day. Lunch under one of the overhangs should be most pleasant on a hot day but if it is cooler you should ascend one of the two ramps up on to the summit of Crafts Wall so that you can sit on the cliff tops in the sun, admiring

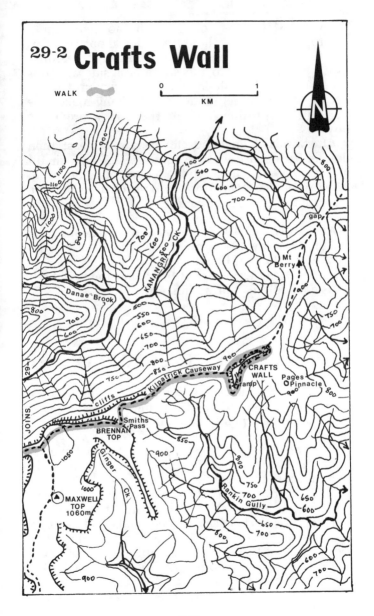

29-2 Crafts Wall

WALK

0 ——————— 1
KM

N

Kanangra Ck

Danae Brook

Kilpatrick Causeway

cliffs

JOINS

Smiths Pass

BRENNAN TOP

Ginger Ck

MAXWELL TOP
1060m

gap

Mt Berry

CRAFTS WALL
ramp

Pages Pinnacle

Rankin Gully

the view. Make sure you go to the northern rim of the tops. Later, you should wander about the tops and see Pages Pinnacle nearby, among other features. You must descend to the south-east side again as access is too difficult from other directions. If you decide to have lunch under an overhang make sure you later visit the summit; the ramps are quite obvious.

Afterwards, follow the cliff base north-east then double back south-west to complete a 1.6 km circuit of Crafts Wall. Then retrace your route down to Kilpatricks Causeway and back up on to Kanangra Plateau, then to the car park.

MAP: Lands, 1:25,000 Kanangra and Map 29.
WALK: One day, 12 km, medium grade, last reviewed July 1992, allow 4½ hours.
Warning: Keep well clear of the rim of the very high cliffs encountered during this walk.

30   MOUNT VICTORIA

Close to Mount Victoria station are escarpments, rock climbers' venues and good walking tracks. One Tree Hill, the highest point in the Blue Mountains is also nearby. The forests of the district are fairly dry, but gullies and cliff bases have damp vegetation. For each of these reasons, an enjoyable day trip is to walk a circuit from the station.

Head south to cross the Great Western Highway into Hooper Street which leads south then becomes Carlisle Street. This sealed street ends and a rough gravel road heads downhill to Mount Piddington lookout, about 1.5 km from the station, where the road forms a small loop around the lookout area set on an outcrop of rock. A track branches off west just as the road divides, to form the northern side of the

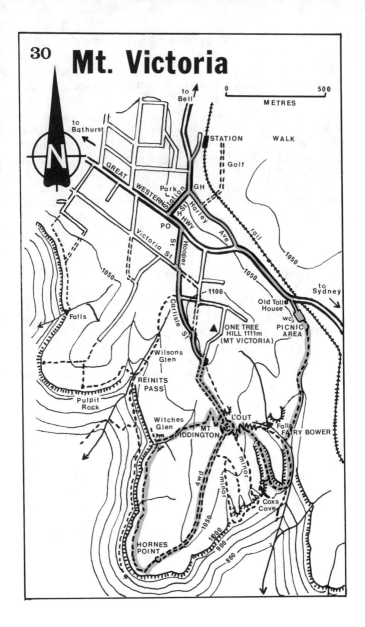

Mt. Victoria

30

to Bell

to Bathurst

N

0   500
METRES

STATION
Golf
WALK

GREAT WESTERN HWY

Park
Station
GH

Harley Ave

PO

Victoria St
St
Hooper

rail

1050

1050

1100

Carlisle St

Falls

1050

to Sydney

Old Toll House
WC
PICNIC AREA

ONE TREE HILL 1111m
(MT VICTORIA)

Wilsons Glen

REINITS PASS

Pulpit Rock

Witches Glen

MT PIDDINGTON

L'OUT

Falls
FAIRY BOWER

4wd

minor

minor

Coxs Cave

HORNES POINT

1050
1000
900
800

road loop. It is just opposite another rock outcrop. Head down the pad which soon turns south-west and descends a small gully known as Witches Glen to reach the main escarpment rim. There are a couple of rock overhangs in Witches Glen. The next stage involves walking south along the cliff tops and via a ledge formation to Hornes Point. The cliffs section is frequented by rock climbers and gives excellent views. At Hornes Point the pad leads uphill, slightly away from the cliffs, to join the end of a jeep track. This jeep track should be followed back north on dry forested tops up to Mount Piddington Lookout. A circuit totalling some 1.7 km is then completed.

Next, take another track south-east from the east side of the lookout road loop. The pad almost immediately divides, so fork left to descend zig-zags to another track fork. Diverge right and descend through a magnificent pass in the escarpment, passing Cox's Cave in the process. The cave is high up the cliffs and accessible by a nineteen-rung ladder.

The descent is by many steps past a lot of ferns. At the cliff base, turn left and follow the base north up a ferny ravine. A short-cut track from Mount Piddington Lookout joins into the ravine via Fairy Bower. Then continue northwards until you emerge at a picnic ground back on the tops. A short road should then be followed out on to the Great Western Highway. The road meets the highway at a rail bridge and an old stone toll house. Lastly, walk up the highway north-west to the station. A foot pad runs alongside the highway for some of the distance of 1 km from the toll house. Harley Avenue could be used instead of Station Street for actual station access.

**MAP: Lands, 1:25,000 Mount Wilson and Map 30.
WALK: One day, 6.4 km, easy grade, last reviewed July 1992, allow 2½ hours.**

31 MOUNT WILSON

Quite a number of Australia's best private gardens are located at Mount Wilson in the Blue Mountains. Many are open to the public, especially in spring and autumn. Small entry fees are charged, often to aid charity. In autumn the colours of the deciduous trees and shrubs create a truly magnificent spectacle.

Mount Wilson is located on a basalt-capped small section of the mainly sandstone Blue Mountains. Its soils, therefore, are more suited to ornamental gardens than are the sandstone regions. It is suggested that a circuit be walked to appreciate the locality and its lovely streets lined with fine deciduous trees and conifers. Any gardens open to the public at the time should be added to the circuit. Walkers should naturally respect private gardens and not intrude in any way.

Start the walk at the corner of Queens Avenue just after the road zig-zag is passed approaching Mount Wilson from the Bells Line of Road direction. For most enjoyment the circuit should be walked anti-clockwise.

Walk east along Queens Avenue past the lovely gardens at Yengo, Cherry Cottage and Windy Ridge to the Wyndham Road corner. Leave the roadway at the corner to cross adjacent Waterfall Creek into a picnic area with toilets and a shelter. Next, walk up the northern section of Queens Avenue for 200 m, then turn right on to a fairly minor foot track opposite the property Rimon. Head east on this pad along the southern boundary of the large property Wynstay to join Davies Lane. This lane can then be followed north to the main road. Turn west (left) along the main road past a small picnic area and into the tiny village with its tea rooms. At the nearby church make sure that a side walk, and return, is taken up Church Lane. This lane has the best collection of gardens at Mount Wilson. The gardens include Withycombe,

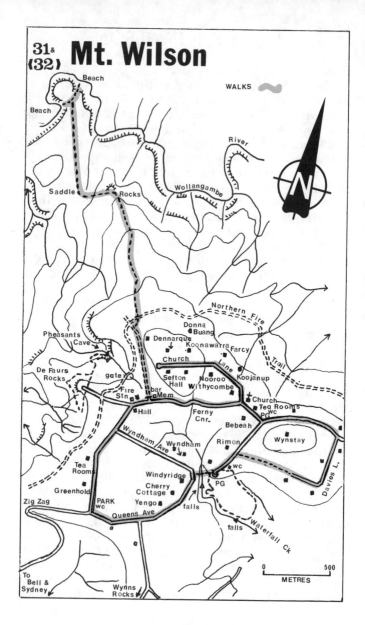

31 & (32) Mt. Wilson

WALKS

Beach

Beach

River

Saddle

Rocks

Wollangambe

Northern Fire

Pheasants Cave

Donna Buang

Dennarque

Koonawarra

Farcy

Church

Lane

Koojanup

Trail

De Faurs Rocks

gate

Sefton Hall

Nooroo

Withycombe

Church

Fire Stn

bar

Mem

Tea Rooms

wc

PG

Hall

Ferny Cnr.

Bebeah

Wyndham Ave

Wyndham

Rimon

Wynstay

Tea Room

Windyridge

wc

Greenhold

Cherry Cottage

PG

Davies L.

Zig Zag

PARK wc

Yengo

falls

Queens Ave

falls

Waterfall Ck

To Bell & Sydney

Wynns Rocks

0   500
METRES

118

Nooroo, Dennarque and Donna Buang, each renowned throughout Australia.

Next, head west along the main road again past Ferny Corner with all its fine tree ferns, past the former school, and then south back to the Queens Avenue corner. Just short of the end of the circuit are more tea rooms. This last stretch of road is very beautiful and lined with fine, young Taxodium trees. Silva Plana Reserve and toilets are each at the Queens Avenue corner.

MAP: Lands, 1:25,000 Mount Wilson and Map 31.
WALK: One day, 6 km, easy grade, last reviewed July 1992, allow 2½ hours.

32 MOUNT WILSON— WOLLANGAMBE RIVER

If you have ever dreamed of secluded white sandy beaches along a river flowing through a rugged gorge where there are plenty of swimming places, then the Wollangambe River is just the place to satisfy your dreams. On a hot day it would be almost heaven to take an air bed and float about on the river.

The area is only 2.8 km from the main road at Mount Wilson in the Blue Mountains so the walk total distance is quite short. The walk starts 200 m east of the local fire brigade station and Du Faurs Road. An earth road barred to traffic leads off north at the spot.

To begin, walk the earth road for 600 m and pass alongside private property to an intersection with a contouring jeep track about 100 m beyond where the private property ends. Turn right (north-east) and walk 50 m to the start of a foot track off left. Alternatively, there is a 100 m long short-cut pad which cuts the corner to lead straight to the contouring jeep track and foot track intersection. This point is within forest in an area with many lyrebirds. Then, turn along the pad. It passes down through fine damp forest with many ground ferns. Then it leaves the basalt-capped mountain top of Mount Wilson and descends a spur on its route to the Wollangambe River. Once well into drier sandstone country there is a fairly large area of rock outcrops. At this point, as the rocks are reached, the track turns sharp left, leaves the spur crest and sidles west around the head of a gully and across a saddle. This places the walker on another spur. The track then sidles along this other spur north-west and drops to a deeper saddle, where it forks. To the west of the fork there are rock outcrops from which the Wollangambe River is seen. Both forks descend sharply to the river just 100–200 m away and near its confluence with the Bell and Du Faur creeks system. The overall difference in elevation between the top of the foot track and the river is 330 m, but in the basaltic upper reaches the track is shaded by fine stands of trees and there are masses of ground ferns. On the lower sandstone stretches, the track has a fairly gradual gradient. Return to Mount Wilson later using the same track.

MAP: Lands, 1:25,000 Mount Wilson and Wollan-gambe and Map 32.
WALK: One day, 5.5 km, easy grade, last reviewed July 1992, allow 2½ hours walking time.

33   MOUNT BANKS

Mount Banks or Mount King George as it is also known is near Bells Line of Road in that part of the Blue Mountains once known as the Carmarthen Hills. The peak was ascended on 15 November 1804 by explorer and botanist George Caley who named the peak after botanist Sir Joseph Banks. Caley was trying to find a route from the infant colony across the rugged Blue Mountains. Sir Joseph Banks of course was the very noted English naturalist on board the *Endeavour* with Cook when Australia was discovered. Banks collected specimens of banksia plants at Botany Bay and was later very influential in England over the decision to establish a colony at Botany Bay. Caley was a good friend of Banks.

Mount Banks and several other nearby peaks are distinguished by a capping of fertile basalt rock on their summits. The basalt once overlaid much of the Blue Mountains but has eroded away leaving most of the mountains with sandstone exposed. Consequently, in climbing Mount Banks one is struck by the diversity and dramatic change in vegetation as sandstone country is left and the basalt encountered. The Mount Banks summit has sturdy tall trees including blackwoods, and lyrebirds frequent the forest. The altitude of 1059 m ensures broad panoramas during the walk.

Access to the walk is from Bells Line of Road about 4 km east of the Mount Wilson road junction. A rough 1.1 km long road leads south off Bells Line of Road to a small picnic area near the base of Mount Banks. This road is normally open to passing traffic but seems to be occasionally closed by road barrier. If closed, the extra 1.1 km distance would need to be added to the recommended day's walk. Adjacent to the picnic area is a commemorative tablet to Caley's ascent. The minor road is closed beyond the picnic spot but continues for many kilometres around the northern side of Mount Banks and out east to Mount Caley. The suggestion is to use this minor road for the return section of the day's walk to create a circuit.

The ascent track starts right behind the commemorative tablet and soon rises sufficiently to permit good views southwards of the Grose Valley. The pad leads up the crest of a defined spur among sandstone dry heathlands and passes some rocky

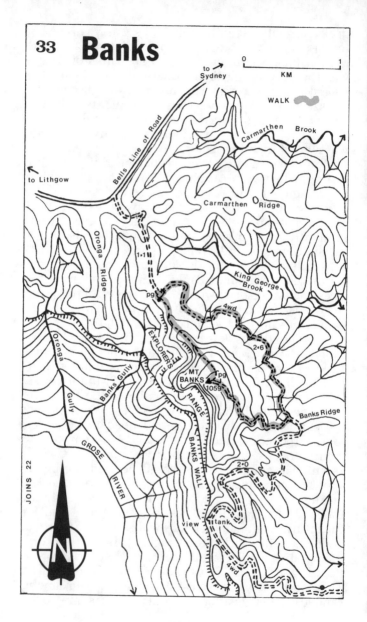

0   KM   1

WALK

to Sydney

to Lithgow

Bells Line of Road

Carmarthen Brook

Carmarthen Ridge

Oronga Ridge

King George Brook

1·1

pg

4wd

2·6

Oronga Gully

Banks Gully

EXPLORERS RANGE

MT BANKS 1059

pg

Banks Ridge

BANKS WALL

GROSE RIVER

JOINS 22

2·0

view

tank

4wd

N

122

bluffs then enters forest. It is only 1 km from the walk start to the summit survey cairn.

A minor jeep track leads off south-east near the cairn and descends about 100 m into a bush picnic area with tables and fireplaces. The spot is ideal for a break.

BANKSIA

The jeep track continues from the picnic ground and descends eastwards. It leaves the basalt tops and winds down to gain the contouring service trail jeep track within 1.2 km. Turn left to then walk this jeep track for 2.6 km back to the end of the walk circuit. The way is across the northern slopes of Mount Banks in sandstone country, with good views and wildflowers in season.

MAP: Lands, 1:25,000 Mount Wilson and Map 33.
WALK: One day, 4.8 km, easy grade family suitability, last reviewed July 1992, allow 2 hours.

34 LORD HOWE ISLAND— MOUNT GOWER

The twin peaks that form the southern end of Lord Howe Island are Mount Gower and Mount Lidgbird. They dominate the whole small island with their massive bulk and cliffs. The cliffs rise sheer from the sea to about 800 m at one spot on Mount Gower, the summit of which attains 875 m.

The ascent of Mount Gower should only be attempted by experienced walkers prepared for a difficult hard climb. The 777 m high Mount Lidgbird is rarely climbed. It is a rock climbers' peak and they too are discouraged due to a lack of full search and rescue facilities on the island. The grey-black volcanic rock of the peaks conveys an awesome, eerie impression, especially near the cliff bases. One wonders, in fact, how Mount Gower could possibly be attained as one approaches southwards along the Far Flats.

Official island advice is that intending climbers of the peaks should use an island guide. This is said to be because of an awkward section known as the Lower Road. It involves negotiating a 500 m long ledge with about 150 m sheer drop to the sea. Clearly there is an advantage in using a guide on any walk in an unfamiliar location, if for no other reason than to ensure the most interesting spots are visited and to have flora and fauna described.

The island park ranger's advice is that although walkers cannot be forced to use a guide, there is a preference that the island registered guides be used. They are islanders and not park staff and they are sometimes very selective about the times when they may be available to lead walks.

On two occasions the author has not used a guide and found the route well defined with a broad pad and track markers. However, the Lower Road and

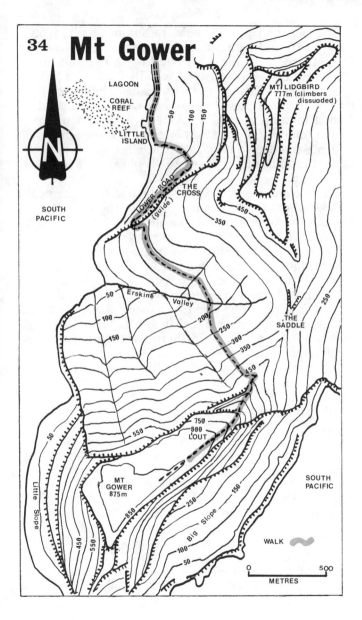

'The Getting Up Place' near the summit both involve very exposed climbing and it would be unwise for most people to climb without a guide. In addition, the rare Lord Howe Island woodhen has the Mount Gower summit as one of its main habitats, so that there is also a need to prevent undue intrusion. The small summit plateau is covered with luxuriant, dripping, mossy rainforest. The tops are often shrouded in mist and on rainy days the whole area appears most forbidding, with waterfalls plunging over huge cliffs into the sea.

There are excellent views to be had from the peak, especially from the knife-edge northern approach spur. The island appears small in a vast expanse of ocean. The colours of the lagoon waters and the coral reef, together with the line of breakers along the outer reef edge, are simply magnificent. Mount Lidgbird's huge bulk dominates the foreground. Closer at hand is a most impressive display of unusual plants and there is a big range of birds, most of them sea birds. The rare woodhen is a flightless bird which displays no fear of man. By 1978 there were said to be just thirty birds in existence, so in 1980 three pairs were taken into captivity and used for raising chicks. By 1984 seventy-nine birds were released and now over two hundred birds live there. One colony at Transit Hill is close to the island settlement. Sea birds are a special feature of Lord Howe Island. They visit each summer in hundreds of thousands, for breeding.

To start this walk to the peak named after John Gower, Rear Admiral and First Captain to Lord Howe, it is best to use bicycle or other transport to reach the south end of sealed Lagoon Road. Rather than walking the road the time would be better spent on the mountain.

The distance from the end of Lagoon Road to Little Island, then up the peak, is only 4.25 km (8.5 km return), but progress will be slow and it is best to allow about seven hours or more. Island advice is to allow eight hours.

From the south end of Lagoon Road a jeep track needs to be walked for 1.2 km to Little Island. The track remains close by the sea. Little Island is the accepted spot to meet guides ready for the climb. The guides, of course, need to be organised well in advance and poor weather can see guides advising against tackling the ascent as rocks can be slippery.

It is suggested that walkers read the track notes for walk No. 35 before setting out on the Mount Gower walk. General background information concerning the Mount Gower area and relating to the island as a whole is included.

After the initial 1.2 km walk to Little Island, rock hop the boulder-strewn beach southwards for about 130 m to locate the indistinct start of the peak's ascent track. The pad leads off immediately adjacent to the southern edge of an old scree. The scree is now partly covered by vines. Palms on the slopes stretch right to the rocky beach immediately north of the scree causing the scree to be more obvious through lack of trees. Once located the pad is easy to discern. The track rises very quickly and perhaps 50 m from the beach there are ropes as an aid to the steep climb. About 150 m elevation is gained in about 300 m distance from the beach to the base of the cliffs.

These cliffs are part of a western buttress of Mount Lidgbird. It is then necessary to begin a contouring walk south at the cliff base. Shortly afterwards ropes are again provided as the pad leads on to a distinct narrow ledge. This ledge (Lower Road) gets quite breathtaking with a 150 m sheer drop to the sea below. Some inexperienced persons could become nervous at this point. Ropes stretch along the side of the track for about 400 m of the 500 m long Lower Road. The pad then turns east around the end of the cliff face and there is a climb up a rocky slope for about 50 m. The way is then via a basically contouring track east into the Erskine Valley for about 600 m to where the creek is forded on flat rocks. The volume of water in the creek varies greatly, depending upon the weather. There is always adequate water for a good drink and at times there can be a real torrent. The whole area is deep within damp forest.

Next, the track swings south-east and climbs steadily for 700 m, gaining 350 m elevation up the crest of a spur to a high ridge linking Mount Lidgbird and Mount Gower. Dense forest, including the usual palms, extends right up to the ridge. The ridge is attained well above and south of the 400 m high Lidgbird–Gower saddle. From this point on there is a very steep ascent of a knife-edge spur and ropes are again provided in the particularly steep section. There is a rise in elevation of about 350 m in about 600 m, so exposure becomes acute as the summit plateau is neared. Sea birds are often seen soaring in the updraughts. Views become spectacular. The vegetation is heavily wind pruned and stunted and the prevailing misty conditions usually mean that great care is needed on slippery rocks.

At the top the main attraction is the view, but the large collection of unusual plants, many of which grow nowhere else in the world, is a great drawcard. The rest of the walk involves a retrace.

After the walk, it is a good idea to take the boat trip around the island which is offered to tourists. The boat passes right alongside both the east- and west-side cliffs of Mount Gower and really highlights how very steep and huge the cliffs are. The eastern face gives an impression of having been subjected to an enormous prehistoric landslide into the sea. Also, as the southern tip of the island is rounded, the famous rock spire, Balls Pyramid, can be seen 17 km southwards. It rises sheer from the sea to a spire 548 m high.

MAP: Lands, 1:15,000 Lord Howe Island and Map 34. WALK: One day, 8.5 km, hard grade, last reviewed May 1987, allow 7 hours.
Note: Refer to walk 35 for information about transport and accommodation for Lord Howe Island.

35   LORD HOWE ISLAND—
MALABAR HILL—KIMS LOOKOUT

Tahiti, Moorea, Bora Bora and Lord Howe Island are all South Pacific tropical islands of incredible beauty. Their magnificence has resulted from the combination of high island, volcanic plug topography surrounded by tropical seas and coral reefs. The author has visited each of these South Pacific islands and now considers Lord Howe equal in scenic and natural attraction to any of the better-known tourist venues of Polynesia. Furthermore, Lord Howe Island is part of New South Wales and unlike the others is relatively close to the Australian east coast. It is also perhaps one of the world's best kept tourist secrets. It does not have the luxury resorts and trappings of tourism and therefore represents a truly natural paradise. In fact a special Act of Parliament protects the people and environment from commercialisation and large scale development. Clearly the aim is to limit the tourist industry, and one gathers that the islanders are intent on keeping their island 'low key'.

There are 600 plant species on Lord Howe Island. Two hundred of these occur nowhere else in the world. There are some 400 fish species and 60 coral species living in the lagoon, reef and surrounding sea. There are 120 species of birds, ranging from large gannets to terns and including the rare Lord Howe woodhen. There is total protection of all plant life, bird life and marine life and the island has United Nations World Heritage classification.

The island lies about 800 km north-east of Sydney and 800 km south-east of Brisbane and is roughly east of Port Macquarie. It is the centrepiece of some 28 islands, islets and rockstacks set on a submarine ridge between Australia and New Zealand. The warm, East Australian sea current ensures that the ocean water temperature remains warm and thereby enables the world's most southerly living coral to flourish. The

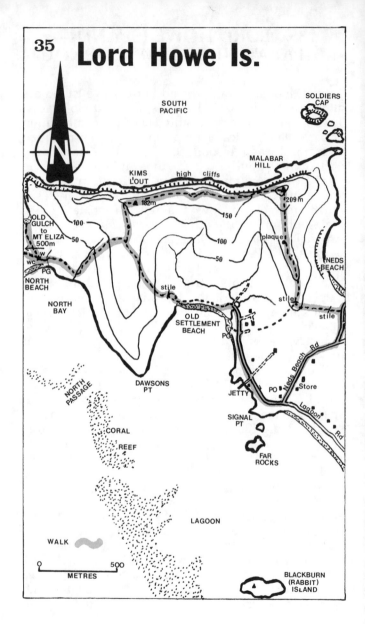

35 Lord Howe Is.

SOUTH PACIFIC

N

SOLDIERS CAP

MALABAR HILL

KIMS L'OUT   high   cliffs

▲182m

▲209m

OLD GULCH to MT ELIZA 500m

100

150

50

plaque

100

NEDS BEACH

wc
w
PG
NORTH BEACH

50

NORTH BAY

stile

stile

stile

NORTH PASSAGE

CORAL REEF

DAWSONS PT

OLD SETTLEMENT BEACH

PG

JETTY

SIGNAL PT

PO

Store

Neds Beach Rd

Lagoon Rd

FAR ROCKS

LAGOON

WALK

0   500
METRES

BLACKBURN (RABBIT) ISLAND

island is about 11 km long, crescent shaped and aligned north–south. Its narrowest point, between Old Gulch and North Beach, is only about 250 m wide. Its widest point is some 2 km and the coastline is readily accessible for only about 8 km. The northern and southern ends of the island are each declared park and the rest is Crown land with perpetual leases. The park was chiefly established to preserve flora and fauna. It is thus not primarily a recreation area. The eastern coastline consists mostly of rugged ocean cliffs with small surf beaches and the west coast is mainly lagoon and coral reef. The lagoon is 6 km long and generally just 1 m to 2 m deep.

The volcanic activity that created the island occurred earlier in the north than in the south where there are massive vertical-sided peaks known as Mount Gower, 875 m, and Mount Lidgbird, 777 m. These two peaks, especially, create the appearance of a typical, South Pacific Bali Hai.

This walk suggestion aims to take the walker to the high points of the northern end of the island, from where there are spectacular views southwards across the coral reef and lagoon, to the cliff faces of the two major peaks. These northern viewpoints can be attained with only moderate effort. The principal lookout en route is 209 m high Malabar Hill. It is one of the most popular island climbs. It was named after a Malabar Indian who fell to his death over the cliffs while trying to catch tropic birds for their long, red tail feathers.

The Lord Howe Island walks, unlike most in this publication, entail a good deal of expense for transport and accommodation. But for the enthusiastic walker the outlay is warranted. Eastern Australian Airlines and Sunstate Airlines fly from Sydney and Brisbane respectively to Lord Howe Island and by Australian standards the fares are very expensive. It should be appreciated that the short island airport runway prevents all but very small aircraft landing and, therefore, each flight can only transport a few people.

131

The use of such light aircraft can often mean delays, and also bumpy rides due to the frequent occurrence of bad weather. Oxley Airlines fly Port Macquarie to Lord Howe with connections to New South Wales coastal towns, and Sydney and Brisbane. A shorter, more direct flight results, but even smaller planes are used.

Accommodation cost is high due to isolation and high transportation costs of supplies. Full-board guest house accommodation or self-contained apartments have to be used. In effect, camping is not permitted. It is limited to islanders and only at North Beach and on the eastern slopes of Mount Gower with the view to facilitating the collection of palm seeds for export. In special cases, permission to camp may be granted to visitors if an island guide is hired to accompany the campers. In such cases North Beach is the venue.

There are four general stores on the island, but merchandise, again, is costly. Excellent restaurants are available and are recommended. The usual mode of transport is by bicycle with a few vehicles being available for hire. Some accommodation operators provide bicycles and operate mini buses for their guests. Otherwise bicycles need to be hired. Walkers, in effect, can reach most parts of the small island and return in a day. There is an extensive walking track network, providing not only for tourists' needs but also for palm seed collection.

The island has a small hospital but limited search and rescue service so walkers should take extra safety measures.

Lord Howe Island has a maritime climate and frosts do not occur. The seas are warm and there is a moderately heavy rainfall spread throughout the year, but heavier in winter. Winter rain and winds cause a definite tourist off season and some accommodation closes during June, July and August. February is the driest month with a minimum monthly average temperature of 23 degrees celsius.

Some special points to remember include the need for a torch as there is very little street lighting. Glass-bottom boat trips are the best way to see the reef and its life. Coral is sharp so do not walk barefoot near it. The island has a very interesting museum. Dress at restaurants is 'smart casual'. Airways luggage limits are very small and there is an airport departure tax. There are no snakes to bite you on the island!

For description purposes this walk begins at the corner of Lagoon Road and Neds Beach Road near the post office. Most accommodation is quite close by.

At first, walk north-east on Neds Beach Road for some 600 m to a small thatch palm forest just 50 m short of the grassy slopes at Neds Beach. A quick look at the beach could be included. Turn west off the road on to a foot pad which leads north-west through palms to a stile and paddock. There are mutton bird burrows under the palms. Head across the paddock (sometimes quite wet underfoot) to rise on to a prominent spur of Malabar Hill, some 300 m from Neds Beach Road. Another pad from the west joins in on the spur at a second stile and here the park is entered. A climb, 800 m long, follows up the spur to the summit of Malabar Hill. At first, the climb is within dense vegetation with a defined pad. Halfway up the hill is a plaque commemorating the 1948 crash of a flying boat and near the summit the vegetation is heavily salt and wind pruned. At several spots during the climb there are excellent views of Neds Beach and the centre of the island. Blackburn Island is prominent in the middle of the lagoon.

On top of Malabar Hill the high basalt sea cliffs of the north coast can be well appreciated, while offshore are the rocky Admiralty Islands. On a clear day most of Balls Pyramid can be seen to the south. Westwards from Malabar Hill there is a high ridge on what is known as the northern hills. A pad leads 800 m along this ridge to Kims Lookout at about 200 m elevation. The cliffs, however, are dangerous, so keep clear of them. The pad is well defined. Sea birds frequent the cliffs and tropic birds can be seen at times soaring in updraughts. Kims Lookout is named after a young islander who liked to visit the beautiful spot. Views to the centre of the island are particularly good at Kims Lookout. By now no doubt you will be familiar with the harmless but big and horrid-looking golden orb spider which has a habit of spinning a strong web across a walking track.

From Kims Lookout the pad leads west another 150 m, then descends south 350 m on the spur towards Dawsons Point to link with Max Nicholls Walking Track. Turn right towards North Beach, then descend a gully among huge banyan trees and palms for some 500 m towards the coast. Still in forest it is then just 400 m west to North Beach. North Beach is a secluded cove to which boats bring people via the lagoon. There are picnic shelters, toilets and tank water at the spot and a fine swimming beach. Lunch is suggested.

From the rear of the picnic shelters, pads lead off to nearby Old Gulch and Mount Eliza. The right fork is a 250 m long level walk to the boulder-strewn Old Gulch cove. In rough weather the sea gets very wild and in calm weather it is good to beachcomb among the rock holes to see the marine life. The left fork is a 700 m long track to the lofty summit of Mount Eliza, 147 m in elevation. The pad at first leads across coral sand amid thatch palms, then climbs to emerge from the palms to windswept tops covered in low scrub. Sheer cliffs surround much of the summit and in summer many birds, especially sooty terns, nest on the top. Some of the best views on Lord Howe are at Mount Eliza.

On return to North Beach the reef could be inspected at the south end of the beach. Being frequently exposed at low tides the coral is mostly dead, but rock pools provide interest.

Retrace the 900 m long pad up on to the Dawson Point Ridge, then keep right to descend to Old

Settlement Beach 600 m away. The ridge crossing is through a mass of banyans, pandanus and palms with many vines. Old Settlement Beach was the site of first settlement in the days of whalers. Lord Howe Island, named after an eighteenth-century admiral in the British Navy, was discovered on 17 February 1788, less than a month after settlement at Sydney Cove. For 100 years, whalers were the main inhabitants.

Having walked the 300 m long Old Settlement Beach (or the line of posts across a paddock behind the beach), the end of Lagoon Road is reached via a bridge and tiny picnic area. It is then just 700 m along the road to the walk end back at Neds Beach Road. The jetty is passed on the way. It is no longer the centre of social activity on the island as it was from 1947 to 1974. That was the era of the flying boat service which operated from Rose Bay in Sydney. Small boats brought people from the plane in the lagoon to the jetty to be welcomed with a lei and South Sea island music. The present airstrip was opened in 1974.

Having completed the walk circuit you, no doubt, will be familiar with the prolific plant symbol of Lord Howe Island—*Howea fosteriana* (the Howea or Kentia palm). It is an endemic plant exported and used round the world as a fine indoor plant specimen. There are four species of Howea on the island all of which are endemic.

MAP: Lands, 1:15,000 Lord Howe Island and Map 35. WALK: One day, 9 km, medium grade, last reviewed May 1987, allow 4 hours.

NORTHERN REGION
(COAST AND INLAND)

36   BELOUGERY SPLIT ROCK

Warrumbungle National Park authorities recommend a walk to Belougery Split Rock which is conveniently located close to the main park access road. This walk suggestion is a variation of their recommendation. The walk is through very rugged terrain but the track system is generally good. To gain the actual southern summit, ladder and chain assistance is provided. The twin summits of the split rock are a favourite among many walk possibilities in the park.

Another great attraction in the locality is the presence of mobs of kangaroos on the grassy flats. It is therefore good to undertake a walk on these flats as well as the more strenuous climb to Belougery Split Rock.

Start at the car park at the park visitor centre and walk west, slightly uphill, on the grassy slopes for 300 m to intersect an old jeep track which is aligned north–south. Turn right (north) and follow this track 1 km across the sealed camp access road and on into the Camp Blackman area.

Locate and walk the foot track which links the western side of the camp to Canyon Camp picnic area. This track leads west, basically following the south side of Wambelong Creek downstream for 1.3 km. It crosses the sealed road midway. Canyon Camp is on the north bank of the creek.

Next, walk the sealed road 500 m west from Canyon Camp picnic area out across Wambelong Creek to the main park access road. Then walk west along this road another 500 m to Camp Wambelong. The traditional Belougery Split Rock Track starts from Camp Wambelong as does Pincham Trail, a jeep track leading south from the main road. Follow Pincham Trail 500 m south from the main road then diverge

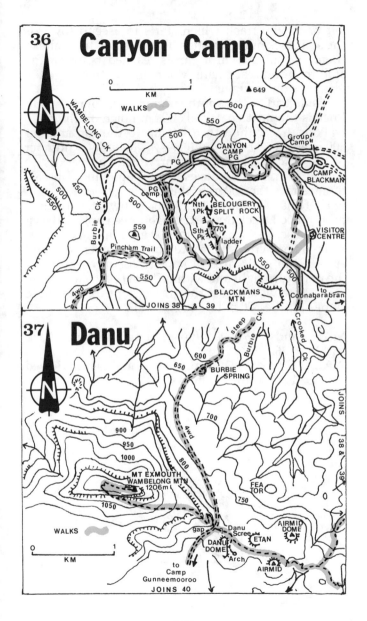

Canyon Camp

36

N

0 — 1
KM

WALKS

WAMBELONG CK

▲649
600
550
500

CANYON
CAMP
PG

Group
Camp

PG

CAMP
BLACKMAN

PG camp

Nth ▲ BELOUGERY
Pk SPLIT ROCK

Sth ▲ 770
Pk ladder

VISITOR
CENTRE

Burbie Ck
500
450
500
559

Pincham Trail

550

550
500

to
Coonabarabran

BLACKMANS
MTN

4wd

JOINS 38 & 39

Danu

37

N

steep

Burbie Ck

Crooked Ck

600
650

BURBIE
SPRING

700

4wd

900
950
1000

MT EXMOUTH
WAMBELONG MTN
▲1206m

800

FEA
TOR

750

JOINS
38 &
39

1050

WALKS

0 — 1
KM

gap

Danu
Scree

DANU
DOME

Arch

ETAN

AIRMID
DOME ▲

AIRMID ▲

to
Camp
Gunneemooroo

JOINS 40

137

left on a jeep track which starts to ascend towards the split rock but soon ends. Take the foot track ahead then, and after 1 km a gap is reached between the split rock and Blackmans Mountain. By this stage the terrain is quite rugged.

A side trip to the south summit of Belougery Split Rock is the next goal. Walk 300 m north on the main walking track, then turn left up to the top another 300 m away. The summit views include a number of the volcanic lava plugs for which the park is so well known. Take a pause and perhaps a lunch break, then retrace the 600 m to the saddle.

There is no official track to follow ahead but a pronounced track does exist. From the gap, head east down in scrub via a gully for 700 m to the road below. Animal pads cross the route but no problems should arise if the gully area is kept to for navigation. At the road, turn right and within 500 m the visitor centre comes into view across the grassy slopes. Cross these slopes for the 300 m to end the walk.

MAP: Lands, 1:30,000 Warrumbungle National Park and Map 36.
WALK: One day, 7.8 km, easy grade, last reviewed August 1992, allow 3½ hours.

EUCALYPT

37   MOUNT EXMOUTH

One of the better walks in the Warrumbungle National Park, west of Coonabarabran, is to Mount Exmouth (Wambelong Mountain). It is the highest point in the park. The walk starts at Camp Pincham, south of the park visitor centre, and leads through relatively arid country. (Drinking water needs to be carried.) The summit view includes most of the volcanic park and surrounding plains.

Next to Camp Pincham there are grassy flats where kangaroos in large numbers can be seen feeding. From the car park there is an excellent walking track leading south.

First, proceed 1.2 km south along the track beside Spirey Creek; then turn right, down and across the creek, on to the 3 km long Ogma Gap track.

Follow the Ogma Gap track south-west along West Spirey Creek valley, through forested areas and past two small caves on your left. Then, after about 2 km, start to ascend steeply up to the gap.

Turn right (west) and gradually ascend the track past Churchill Rock and the Grassy Glades ramp and, in 1 km, meet a track junction. Fork right uphill over a saddle then descend the Danu Scree ramp for 500 m to Danu Gap. The Burbie fire trail crosses this saddle to link Burbie Springs with Camp Gunneemooroo.

A 2.6 km long track to Mount Exmouth lies ahead. Follow it uphill. The climb is quite steep but well worthwhile as the view from the top is superb. Lunch is suggested on the top while you admire the view. But there is no water supply. At this point you are 8.3 km from Camp Pincham and the return trip is simply a retrace of the outward route. The walking however will be mostly downhill.

MAP: Lands, 1:30,000 Warrumbungle National Park and Maps 37 and 38.
WALK: One day, 16.6 km, medium grade, last reviewed August 1992, allow 5½ hours.

38   THE BREADKNIFE

Near Coonabarabran is the Warrumbungle National Park. It is an area of volcanic spires, domes and mesas, the remains of composite volcanic activity about thirteen million years ago. Formations such as the Breadknife are dykes developed along cracks in a volcanic cone. The lava was a viscous, trachyte type containing a lot of silica which caused rapid hardening. In many cases, hardening blocked the throat of volcanic vents and, with the passing of time, the surrounding area was eroded, leaving the lava plugs. Such features as Belougery Spire and Crater Bluff are excellent examples.

The park is noted for a wide variety of flora and fauna. Grey kangaroos, echidnas, wedge-tailed eagles and galahs abound. Cypress pines, grass trees and ironbarks are common. Generally speaking, the park is quite dry and water is often a problem. Any walking on hot summer days is, therefore, not the best. It is a good idea to carry water on all walks in the Warrumbungles.

Near Spirey Creek is the park centre and just north of it is Camp Blackman, the main camping area. There is also accommodation nearby for camping by groups, schools, etc. There are other less developed camps. The park has an excellent system of good tracks, especially those radiating from Camp Pincham. Climbing the Breadknife itself is an offence.

This walk to the Breadknife starts at Camp Pincham and, although it scales the heights above the Breadknife, it is not very hard. Make sure you carry some water when you leave Camp Pincham, heading south along the Spirey Creek valley.

Some 1.2 km south of Camp Pincham car park, fork left, avoiding the West Spirey Creek valley track, then after 500 m, fork right, avoiding Macha Tor track. Continue south and pass the Bress Peak track after 700 m and pass the Macha Tor return track after another 200 m. Some 600 m further south, avoid the

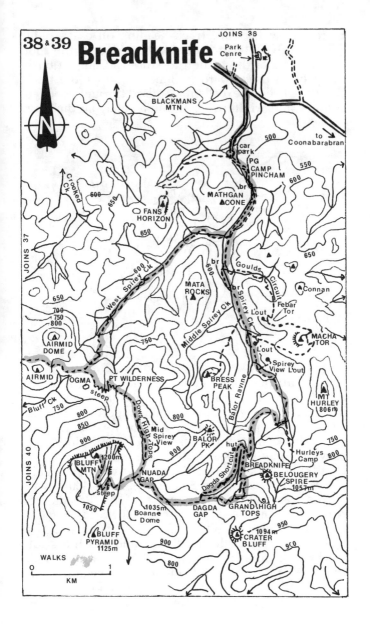

38 & 39 **Breadknife**

Spirey View Lookout track heading off east uphill. After another 800 m you should arrive at the foot of the climb at the turnoff to Hurleys Camp, a bush camp often used by rock climbers. So far the track will have been of excellent standard through wooded country and wildflowers and in a valley all the way.

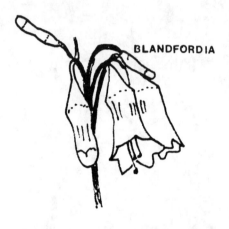

BLANDFORDIA

It is a further 1 km to a track junction at the lower end of the Breadknife but there is a steep climb involved. Excellent views of Belougery Spire and western cliffs plus a seat at Wilsons Rest all help to make this climb more pleasant. Cypress pines also provide some shade. Once at the lower end of the Breadknife, fork left uphill and pass right alongside the eastern base of the Breadknife. After 400 m you should reach the upper end of the Breadknife. However, you need to climb a little further for spectacular views. Follow the track east around the base of another blade parallel to, and south-east of, the Breadknife and, as you reach its top end, walk 10 m west up on to the blade for an excellent view. Next, continue up some rocky slopes following paint marks showing the track route. Within about 300 m, you will arrive at the Grand High Tops. A wonderful view is obtained from the knob at this point. It is about the best view in the park and is particularly good towards the Breadknife. Belougery Spire, of course, is in full view as it has been for much of the ascent. It is suggested that you have lunch (no water supply) at this point, then head 600 m west, at first along the tops, then down to Dagda Gap. From this gap it is 6.2 km back to Camp Pincham (via the Dagda short-cut track). Follow it down as it sidles to the lower end of the Breadknife. There is a locked hut (Balor Hut) and toilets at this point, 1 km from Dagda Gap. The hut can be used as an overnight stop if required and if previously arranged with the park ranger. Drinking water is also available there. Just around the lower end of the Breadknife, you rejoin your outward route which should be followed for the 5.2 km back to Camp Pincham car park.

MAP: Lands, 1:30,000 Warrumbungle National Park and Map 38.
WALK: One day, 12.5 km, easy grade, last reviewed August 1992, allow 4¾ hours.

39   BREADKNIFE— BLUFF MOUNTAIN

This walk in the Warrumbungle National Park features the pick of the scenic attractions of the district: the volcanic spires, domes and lava flows which are the result of volcanic activity about thirteen million years ago. The park is west of Coonabarabran, well inland.

The walk starts at Camp Pincham, next to grassy slopes and flats where kangaroos graze in large numbers. Camp Pincham lies south of the park visitor centre and in the normally dry valley of Spirey Creek.

Carry drinking water for the walk as the country is relatively arid.

Set off from the car park at Camp Pincham on a good track in wooded country, up the Spirey Creek Valley for 4 km, passing five tracks as you proceed. They fork off right at 1.2 km to West Spirey Creek, left at 1.7 km to Macha Tor, right at 2.4 km to Bress Peak, left at 2.6 km to Macha Tor and left at 3.2 km to Spirey View. The walk then involves climbing out of the valley from the Hurleys Camp turnoff.

The climb is to the lower end of the Breadknife 1 km away. There are views of nearby Belougery Spire during the steep climb. At the lower end of the Breadknife fork left uphill and pass right alongside the eastern base of the remarkable rock blade. After 400 m you should reach the upper end of the formation. However, you need to climb a little further for views. Follow the track east around the base of another blade parallel to and south-east of the Breadknife. As you climb and reach the top end walk 10 m west on to the blade for an outstanding view. Continue up some rock slopes, following paint markers which define the main track route. Within another 300 m, you should arrive at Grand High Tops for an even better view of the park.

After a break, head on westwards 600 m, at first along the tops then down to Dagda Gap. Next, walk west, climbing a little as you proceed 1.2 km to Nuada Gap, via a pleasant, forested area. Then, walk through many cypress pines. At Nuada Gap, turn left up the 1.3 km track to the summit of Bluff Mountain. At first, the track heads steeply up to the south end of the great dome which is Bluff Mountain. Then it turns back north and ascends the rock spine of the southern slopes. At the summit there is a cairn but the best views are about 150 m before you reach the summit. If you walk north-west from the cairn you will also obtain good views over the awesome cliffs.

Next, descend back to Nuada Gap and turn left. Head north past Nuada Peak and Mid Spirey View to Point Wilderness with its views to the north, then descend sharply past Ogma Rock to Ogma Gap 2.3 km away. From this saddle walk north-east towards Camp Pincham. The good track drops steeply at first, then levels out as you wander down the pleasant wooded valley of West Spirey Creek. At two points there are small caves on the right side of the track. There are many wildflowers, and parrots seem to be common. After 3 km, the track rejoins the main Spirey Creek valley track to the Breadknife. At this point you need only retrace 1.2 km of your outward route northwards back to Camp Pincham.

MAP: Lands, 1:30,000 Warrumbungle National Park and Map 39.
WALK: One day, 16.6 km, hard grade, last reviewed August 1992, allow 6 hours.

40   GUNNEEMOOROO

West of Coonabarabran is the wild Warrumbungle National Park. It features volcanic trachyte plugs and lava flows. The whole area is heavily eroded yet is dry, and few streams flow for any length of time. Undoubtedly this is one of the state's better parks and it is certainly well developed as far as tracks are concerned. There are good camping facilities at Camp Blackman and other camp areas at various points. This walk suggestion is to camp out at Gunneemooroo and to see the beautiful colourings of sunset and sunrise on the peaks. However, it is best to carry all water. What water is available is heavily used by wildlife.

The walk should start on the Spirey Creek flats at Camp Pincham car park south of the park visitor centre. Camp fires are not permitted, so carry a small stove if you wish to cook.

Set off on the excellent track up the valley of Spirey

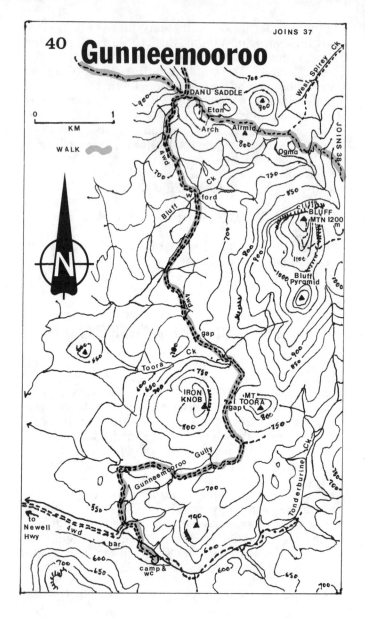

40 **Gunneemooroo**

Creek (usually dry). Walk 1.2 km to the stream's confluence with West Spirey Creek. The valley is lightly wooded. Follow the main track to keep to Spirey Creek for another 2.8 km. In doing so, avoid four side tracks which lead off up the slopes to Macha Tor, Bress Peak, Macha Tor return and Spirey View respectively. A steep climb out of the valley at the Hurleys Camp turnoff then follows for 1 km to reach the lower end of the Breadknife. As you climb there are views to nearby Belougery Spire. When at the Breadknife's lower end, fork left uphill for 400 m to pass right alongside the eastern base of the blade and to the top of the blade. Walk south-east a little to head around the base of another blade parallel to the Breadknife. When you reach its top there is an excellent view 10 m to the right.

Head further up some rocky slopes. Within 300 m you should reach the scenic Grand High Tops which would be a suitable place for a lunch break while taking in the panorama of the Breadknife and Belougery Spire.

Continue 600 m along the tops and down to Dagda Gap after lunch. Avoid the Dagda short-cut track off right and walk west, climbing slightly for 1.2 km to Nuada Gap. Pass the left-fork track to Bluff Mountain to continue past Nuada Peak, Mid Spirey View and Point Wilderness and then zig-zag down to Ogma Gap 2.3 km away. Avoid West Spirey Creek Track off right from the gap and go west near the tops for 1 km in an area of forest which is damper due to its southerly aspect. Pass Cathedral Arch Track near a saddle, then descend across Danu Scree to Danu Gap 500 m away. At this gap a jeep track is intersected, with a foot pad continuing to Mount Exmouth.

Turn south-west (left) to begin the 8.7 km jeep track descent off the range to camp at Gunneemooroo. At first the way is across the headwaters of Bluff Creek and its tributaries under the massive cliffs of Bluff Mountain. The jeep track then rises a little to pass through a gap north of Toora Creek and another gap between Iron Knob and Mount Toora. The cliffs of Iron Knob tower above this second saddle. The jeep track continues south across a plateau area from which Tonduron Spire can be seen. Then it swings west to descend Gunneemooroo Gully and turns south down through former farmland to the Tonderburine Creek valley.

Another jeep track is aligned east–west in this broad grassy valley. First, it arcs north a little from the creek where you join it. Walk up the valley via the arc, then along the south bank of the creek and reach camp within 700 m. Grassy flats attract kangaroos, and Tonduron Spire, a spectacular volcanic lava plug, is in view up the valley. Toilets are provided but there are no other facilities. The jeep track upstream provides most pleasant walking as far as the confluence of Tonderburine Creek and Tonduron Gully. While most walkers will be satisfied with the walk for the day, some may like an evening stroll up the valley a bit, in the evening when wildlife is very plentiful.

On the second day retrace the 8.7 km to Danu Saddle and drop packs for a side trip to Mount Exmouth 2.6 km west of the gap. An ideal plan would be for a lunch break on the top of Mount Exmouth which is the highest point in the National Park and where there are sub-alpine type plants. The foot track to the peak is a bit steep at times, but there are no navigation problems.

Back at Danu Saddle, after the 5.2 km side trip, go north down the jeep track for 2.3 km to Burbie Spring and on down a further 2.3 km to Burbie Creek crossing. Pass the foot track down Burbie Canyon and climb through Burbie Gap via the jeep track to reach the Belougery Split Rock track within 1 km. Double back south-east up the track towards Belougery Split Rock for 1 km to gain a saddle between the split rock and Blackmans Mountain. Take a side trip north 300 m on the main split rock track, then diverge left up

148

to the south summit a further 300 m away. This point is very rocky and steps and chains assist the ascent. After a short break to enjoy the view, retrace 600 m to the saddle.

An unofficial but fairly pronounced track descends from this gap eastwards, leading down a gully for 700 m to the main park access road. Animal pads can confuse the route a little but if you have trouble distinguishing the way, simply follow the gully closely until reaching the road. Turn right (south-east) along the road for 800 m, then turn right again on to sealed Camp Pincham Road for a final 800 m walk to the end of the two-day trip.

MAP: Lands, 1:30,000 Warrumbungle National Park (Gunneemooroo area tracks are poorly shown) and Maps 36 to 40.
WALK: Two days, 44 km (day one 20 km day two 24 km), medium grade, last reviewed August 1992, allow 7½ hours each day.

41   BARRINGTON TOPS

Barrington Tops is rather unique in northern New South Wales in that it receives snow falls and has snow grass plains, snow gums and icy conditions. Its fairly extensive plateau lies about 1500 m above sea level. It is a wild, remote part of the state where dingoes, brumbies and wild pigs can be seen and heard. The plateau is north-west of Newcastle and has lush sub-tropical forest on its slopes. Near the tops of the plateau slopes there is cool temperate rainforest with Antarctic beech trees and lyrebirds.

From the Newcastle direction motorists can drive to Lagoon Pinch, at 700 m elevation, via Dungog or Paterson, Eccleston and the Allyn River valley. Lagoon Pinch has a small picnic area. The road

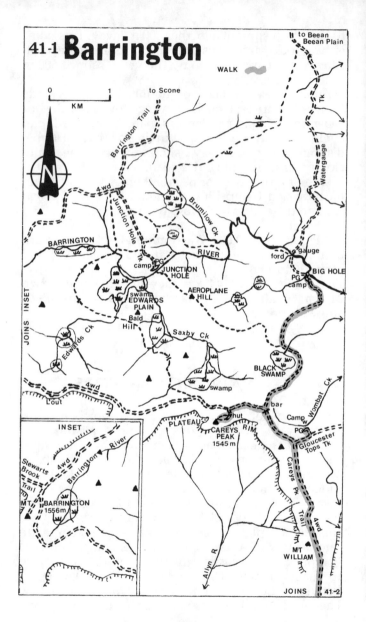

41-1 Barrington

WALK

to Beean
Beean Plain

to Scone

0   1
KM

N

Barrington Trail

Watergauge Tk

4wd

Junction Hole

Brumilow Ck

BARRINGTON

RIVER

ford   gauge

camp PG

JUNCTION
HOLE

PG
camp   BIG HOLE

swamp

AEROPLANE
HILL

EDWARDS
PLAIN

Bald
Hill

Saxby Ck

Edwards Ck

JOINS INSET

BLACK
SWAMP

swamp

Wombat Ck

4wd

L'out

bar

hut

Camp

PG

PLATEAU

CAREYS
PEAK
1545 m

RIM

Gloucester
Tops Tk

Careys Pk

INSET

4wd

Barrington River

Stewarts
Brook

Trail

MT
BARRINGTON
1556m

Allyn R

Careys Pk
Trail

4wd

MT
WILLIAM

JOINS   41-2

150

continues up the mountain from Lagoon Pinch but only as a closed jeep track. In 4 km, it climbs another 700 m to 1400 m elevation at a spot known as the Corker where the Barrington Tops National Park is entered.

Head off from Lagoon Pinch, but make sure you carry some water to drink during the steep climb ahead. North of the Corker there are still 3 km of climbing but a very gradual gradient. You should reach a junction of jeep tracks 7 km from Lagoon Pinch. To the left is Careys Peak, 2 km distant, and to the right is Wombat Creek, 400 m distant. To reach it you should follow the 20 km long Gloucester Tops Track for just 300 m then fork left for 100 m. Lunch is suggested at Wombat Creek where there are camp sites and fireplaces.

After lunch, return to the nearby junction and continue uphill north-west for 1 km towards Careys Peak to another jeep track junction. The left fork leads to Careys Peak and the right fork leads to the Big Hole. Go right (north-north-east) and walk 3 km, generally downhill, past Black Swamp to the Big Hole. It is a large deep pool on the Barrington River and is in a sub-alpine setting. It is ideal for swimming and camping. Big Hole should take some 3–4½ hours to reach from Lagoon Pinch plus the time taken for lunch. Consequently, after the hard climb an early camp should be welcome.

Next day a late start could be made too. First, retrace 3 km and then turn right for the 1 km walk west to Careys Peak. For the 1 km deviation you need go 700 m then fork left downhill to Careys Hut 100 m away. It is an old tin hut with an earth floor and no bunks or water. It is in a saddle immediately north-east of Careys Peak summit. Two foot tracks 200 m long lead from the hut to the summit where there is a sundial and panorama. The southerly aspect is especially interesting. Distinct vegetation strata can be seen on the ridge climbed the previous day. The sub-tropical vegetation joins the cool temperate forest

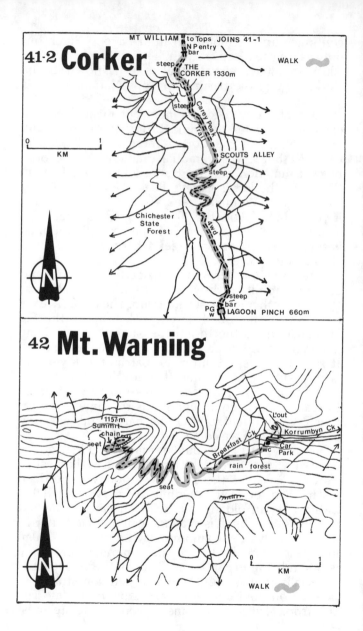

41-2 Corker

MT WILLIAM to Tops JOINS 41-1
N P entry
WALK
steep
bar
THE
CORKER 1330m

steep

Carey Peak Trail

SCOUTS ALLEY

steep

Chichester
State
Forest

4wd

steep
bar
PG
w   LAGOON PINCH 660m

0 — 1
KM

N

42 Mt. Warning

1157m
Summit
chain
seat

L'out
Korrumbyn Ck

Breakfast Ck

Car
Park
wc

seat

rain forest

0 — 1
KM

WALK

N

as a noticeable line. The Allyn River valley has eroded the southern flank of the plateau to a quite remarkable degree. Careys Peak is 1543 m high.

After the Careys Peak ascent it is suggested you retrace the tracks to Wombat Creek for lunch again. Thereafter, simply descend the jeep track back to Lagoon Pinch through the lovely forest.

MAP: Lands, 1:25,000 Barrington Tops and Map 41. WALK: Two days, 25.6 km (day one 11.8 km, day two 13.8 km), medium grade, last reviewed July 1992, allow day one 5½ hours and day two 5 hours.

42   MOUNT WARNING

A glance at the Tweed Heads National Mapping 1:250,000 sheet reveals the immensity of a vast ancient (early tertiary) volcano which we are told last erupted about 23 million years ago. It is on the border of northern New South Wales and southern Queensland. The Tweed River and other streams have eroded the central explosion crater, making it larger, but leaving an island of the more acid lava rock dome, now called Mount Warning. The old mountain once attained about 2000 m or nearly twice the present 1157 m height. The flanks of the old mountain's basaltic dome remain along the state border in the form of the McPherson and Tweed ranges, but erosion has created great low angle spurs (or Planeze) with deep gorges. Such dramatic features as the Pinnacle mark the rim of the eroded crater where the harder surface rocks have given way. The erosion caldera is about 30 km in diameter.

A most informative and enjoyable day walk to Mount Warning can be taken from the Breakfast Creek car park serving the national park which encompasses the peak. Access is via Murwillumbah and the south arm of the Tweed River valley, then up the valley of Karrumbyn Creek. Many Gold Coast visitors find the walk to be an excellent day's outing during their stay.

There are a number of name labels on trees seen beside the track as you climb.

An excellent 4.4 km long foot track leads from the car park to the summit. It is well graded except for the last short steep ascent above 1000 m elevation which has a chain handhold to assist with scaling sloping rocks. Seats along the way and distance markers also help make the walk enjoyable. Rainforest is abundant and is confined to the igneous rock areas of the main peak and associated peaks where soil depth and moisture is adequate. The upper rockfaces feature shrubby and grassy plants such as tussock grass, grass tree, blunt leaf mountain wattles, tea tree and broad leaved cassinias. Views occur only on the upper reaches and at the summit where there are spectacular views to the erosion crater walls which on average, are 15 km distant. The North Coast of New South Wales and the Queensland Gold Coast are within view as is the Tweed River and the town of Murwillumbah.

Viewing decks on the summit provide the best possible panoramas, and plaques illustrate and name the features to be seen. The top of Mount Warning, by reason of elevation and easterly aspect, is the first part of the Australian mainland to receive sun rays at dawn. The summit would be the ideal place for lunch. Water needs to be carried. There is no branch track and walkers need simply climb and descend via the same route.

MAP: Lands, 1:25,000 Burringbar and Map 42.
WALK: One day, 8.8 km, easy grade, last reviewed September 1992, allow 4 hours.
Warning: Evidently lightning frequently strikes the summit of Mount Warning during storms so avoid the top at such times.

43 BURRENDONG ARBORETUM

This special collection of Australian native plants is in the central west of the state, about 24 km south-east of Wellington, and overlooking Burrendong Reservoir. The arboretum covers 1.6 square kilometres of undulating relatively dry country but includes swampy flats and rocky hills.

A visit to the arboretum is a must for anyone wanting to learn about the native plants seen while walking in the bush. The collection is quite amazing when it is considered that the basics were established by voluntary support over some twenty years. It has only been during more recent years that some government support has been achieved. Over 5000 plants on average are added each year to the collection, and currently there are about 2000 different species. Some species are present in great numbers. There is even a fernery and rainforest section, under a vast canopy in a gully at the south-east corner of the grounds. An elaborate water reticulation system enables the arboretum to flourish in this drier climate. Presumably the water comes from Burrendong Reservoir.

Access is via Burrendong Road then south along Tara Road to where there are two entrances. The northernmost main entrance is close to the arboretum nursery and the most convenient place from which to walk. An ideal plan is to walk from the main entrance car park southwards about 700 m through the most densely planted area to the fernery canopy and to return using alternative routes. There are a few minor roads in the grounds but it is far better to walk among the plantings than to drive. One can hardly read identification labels or indeed really appreciate the plants from a car. The plantings are mostly in blocks. Seasonal variation will indicate which block is best at the time of your visit. The acacia block for example is unbelievably beautiful in early spring when a whole hillside turns yellow. There

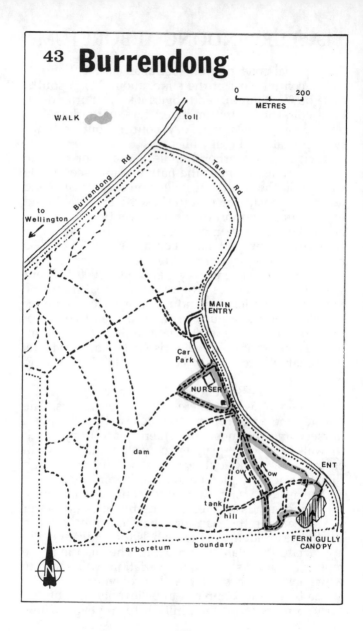

43 Burrendong

WALK

toll

0 ———————— 200
METRES

Burrendong Rd

Tara Rd

to
Wellington

MAIN
ENTRY

Car
Park

NURSERY

dam

ow   ow

ENT

tank
hill

arboretum   boundary

FERN GULLY
CANOPY

N

are large numbers of birds to be seen as they are attracted from the surrounding district to the diversity of plants and flowers. Use the map to ensure you do not miss points of interest in such a large arboretum. The western and northern margins are planted as open woodlands, while the south-east is intensively planted.

Arboretums normally contain trees and shrubs only but this collection includes smaller plants as well, especially in some mulched beds close to the nursery where water and attention are easily supplied. Under normal conditions many of them could not survive. A further distinction is that most arboretums contain plants from around the world, while Burrendong only grows Australian plants. There are even central Australian ghost gums. Mallee from Victoria, royal hakea from Western Australia and other plants that would normally prove difficult to grow away from their local region, somehow grow at Burrendong.

The arboretum is open to the public throughout the year and is somewhat informal compared with the other great place to see native plants—the National Botanic Gardens in Canberra.

MAP: Lands, 1:50,000 Burrendong and Map 43.
WALK: One day, no specific distance, easy grade, last reviewed August 1992, allow about three hours.

44   YULLUDUNIDA CRATER

East of Narrabri, some 6.6 km from the entrance to the Mount Kaputar National Park, is Green Camp car park and the start of this rewarding walk. The park has many volcanic features including lava plugs which soar skywards on the ranges. Molten rock exuded up through fissures in the earth's crust. At Yulludunida, however, the igneous rock intruded

Yulludunida

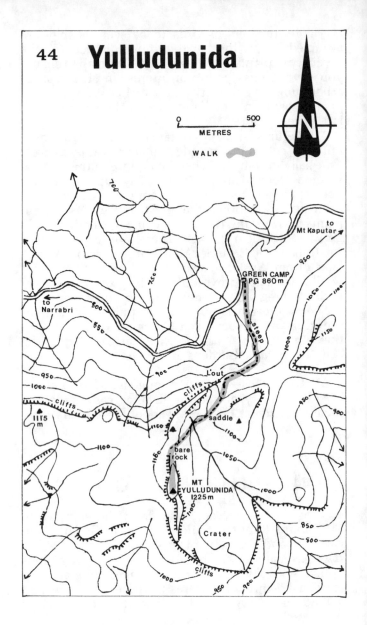

METRES

WALK

to Mt Kaputar

GREEN CAMP
PG 860 m

to Narrabri

steep

L'out

cliffs

cliffs

saddle

1115 m

bare rock

MT YULLUDUNIDA
1225 m

Crater

cliffs

across the bedding planes of surrounding rocks in thick sheets, which are now exposed. There was never a volcanic crater at Yulludunida. A basin-shaped sheet of exposed lava is the reason for the appearance of the feature today. The name of the attraction is misleading.

The walk to Yulludunida is rather steep, starting at 860 m elevation and rising to 1225 m within 2 km. The track is fairly minor and near the summit bare rock is encountered. The grading allocated is easy, by reason only of length but the terrain is very rugged and progress is slow.

From Green Camp car park (there is no camp), the pad leads south to a gully in lightly wooded country which consists mainly of white box trees and wattles. The track is then aligned near the gully as it rises steadily south-east among more white box and some black cypress pines. Hardenbergia grows in profusion as a ground cover and creates a purple splash of colour in early spring.

About 1 km from the car park the pad reaches a lookout point on a cliffline at 1020 m elevation. This cliff represents the thickness of the layer of lava present. Further climbing follows as the narrow pad leads south in scrub, to gain a saddle at 1100 m elevation. Native cherry trees and grass trees grow at the saddle and an old fence crosses. Veer right up the fence alignment and shortly the track ends at bare rock. This marks the end of the terrain which has still not eroded to the bare layer of lava. Ahead is a huge expanse of bare lava which includes the summit of Mount Yulludunida. The walk continues to this lofty bare peak. The easiest access is to contour about 100 m to the south (left) then climb a gully formation which has hand holds and foot rests. Take great care if the rock is wet. Normally the ascent is not as difficult as first feared in such wild terrain. Once on the crest, follow the ridge south to the top.

A lunch break on the top could be enjoyable although there is no drinking water available. Rock pools containing water are heavily used by wildlife. The crater-shaped layer of lava is seen to best advantage from the summit as are a number of the volcanic lava plugs at extinct volcanic vents so common in this National Park.

Retrace the same track to end the walk.

MAP: Lands, 1:25,000 Kaputar and Map 44.
WALK: One day, 4 km, easy grade (with steep terrain), last reviewed August 1992, allow 2 hours.

45   MOUNT KAPUTAR— BUNDABULLA LOOKOUT

Rising out of the north-west plains, east of Narrabri, is the Mount Kaputar National Park. It is a volcanic park centred on Dawsons Spring 53 km from Narrabri. The whole area is a heavily eroded one of trachyte plugs and massive lava flows. Dawsons Spring is the site of the ranger's office and camping facilities. It is also the starting point for this walk suggestion. It features alpine vegetation and extensive views, combined with volcanic interest. The highest peak in the park is reached on this walk, and at that height (1524 m) snow gums are very common. Wildflowers also proliferate including the vivid purple false sarsaparilla.

At the Dawsons Spring picnic ground you will notice a ford to the north-west on the creek which flows through the area (and over a small waterfall). Cross the ford, then walk a jeep track which heads uphill to the north-west to the main Narrabri road, within 400 m and at 1423 m elevation. Cross the main road and continue on a jeep track while it runs parallel to the main road. It then swings to the right and scales a spur. Within 400 m, you will meet the tourist road to Mount Kaputar itself. It is a one-way road

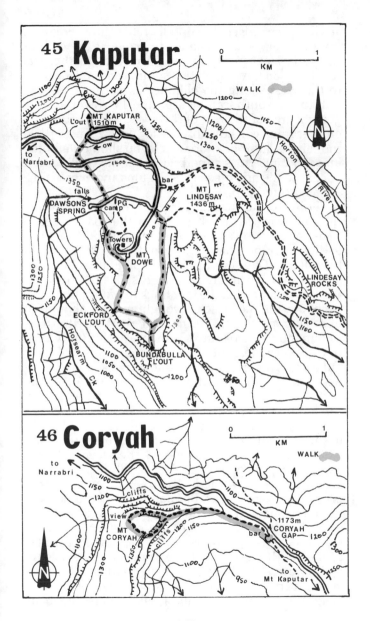

45 Kaputar

0 — 1 KM

WALK

N

MT KAPUTAR
L'out 1510 m

to Narrabri

falls

DAWSONS SPRING

IPG camp

Towers

MT DOWE

ECKFORD L'OUT

BUNDABULLA L'OUT

Horsearm CK

bar

MT LINDESAY 1436 m

LINDESAY ROCKS

Horton River

46 Coryah

0 — 1 KM

WALK

to Narrabri

cliffs

view

MT CORYAH

cliffs

1173m
CORYAH GAP

bar

to Mt Kaputar

N

at this point, used by uphill traffic only. Follow it up for a very short distance to arrive at the summit car park. Next, walk up the 20 m track to the peak top for a 360° view at the summit cairn. The view to the west, along the clifflines, is perhaps the best but, to the south, can be seen the TV tower and the general area of the rest of this walk which, from now on, becomes considerably easier. Just 25 m north of the cairn is another knob which you should definitely inspect. It provides superb views of the clifflines and valleys to the north-east. Snow gums and everlastings are all around.

Return to the summit car park and turn left down the one-way exit road. In 250 m the road becomes two-way and you should continue downhill for 400 m to the Narrabri road. Walk south for 500 m to the turnoff into Dawsons Spring camp but turn left (east) at this point. The short road east leads into a car park and the start of the foot track to Mount Lindesay.

Follow the foot track through an area abounding in trigger plants. In 200 m turn right on the track to Bundabulla Lookout, 1.5 km away. This fairly good track is very pleasant. It leads through areas of rocky outcrops and hosts of wildflowers as it gradually descends southwards. Soon, the track mounts some rocks, and views to the south-east become superb. Bundabulla Lookout is down the slopes a little from the roughly contouring track but there is a side track to the lookout. It is far better to take the detour than to short-cut and miss the views. The ascent after the lookout is quite gradual and easy. White posts in the area indicate the route as the track is often on open grass slopes and rocks. Bundabulla Lookout is 200 m from the main track and, from the lookout, views over the cliffs (150 m high) are excellent. There are many rocky ridges in view. The Kaputar Plateau lies to the south-west and Horsearm Creek Valley is the main watershed in view. Once on the main track again, turn left (west) and follow white posts across delightful grassy areas full of wildflowers: bluebells,

162

fringed lilies and pincushions. After 350 m of virtually flat walking, you will arrive at Eckfords Lookout at the top of a cliff about 150 m high and which again gives excellent views. From the lookout the pad turns back to Dawsons Spring and the track should be taken uphill towards the TV tower. Shortly before reaching the tower there is a track junction. Take the left fork. It sidles round the west side of the tower to another track junction and an Aboriginal bora ground—a ceremonial place. It is interesting that the ancient bora ground should be right at the base of one of modern man's TV pylons.

To end the walk, head west (left fork) past the bora ground, following painted markers at the edge of some cliffs. Then descend steeply through forest for about 400 m to emerge in the camp ground west of the ranger's office.

MAP: Lands, 1:25,000 Kaputar and Map 45.
WALK: One day, 6.3 km, easy grade, last (partly) reviewed August 1992, last full review April 1986. Allow 2½ hours. Park advice is that there have been no changes since.

46   CORYAH GAP— MOUNT CORYAH

Mount Kaputar National Park, east of Narrabri, is renowned as a volcanic park. There are many trachyte intrusions which have left spectacular plugs jutting skywards.

As the road climbs up the mountains towards the park centre at Dawsons Springs, it crosses Coryah Gap, 6 km short of the centre. At the gap there is an archway over the road and a car park at 1173 m elevation.

This walk suggestion enables the walker to see large sections of the national park from Mount Coryah, including Mount Yulludunida with its crater-shaped eastern rock flank. The Eulah Creek valley seems exceptionally deep from Mount Coryah and Mount Coryah itself has interesting cliffs and grass trees. The walk involves a steep climb with many steps to be negotiated. Despite the short distance, at least two hours has to be allowed for walking time. Lunch on the tops could be worthwhile but there is no water supply. Mount Coryah is 1405 m above sea level.

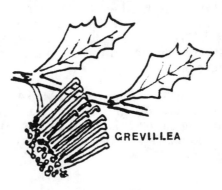

CREVILLEA

First, walk westwards uphill on the foot track from the car park. The track leads through dry open eucalypt areas of mountain gums and silver topped stringybarks. After about 1 km the track becomes much steeper and steps have been cut. The track rises up beside rocky bluffs to the base of the summit cliffs of Mount Coryah, then divides to circuit the tops.

Turn left and walk downhill along the base of the cliffs. Soon you must scale more steps up past the cliffs to the summit cairn and broad forested summit ridge. Continue over the ridge and down the foot track to arrive shortly at a lookout down the western slopes. The view is of Yulludunida Crater and the spot would be pleasant for lunch.

Next, walk to the right (north) uphill on the track. Soon it starts to sidle hard up against the base of the cliffline on the northern side of Mount Coryah. Views to the north become very good and grass trees (*Xanthorrhoea resinosa*), some of which must be hundreds of years old, abound along the cliff base. There are several rock overhangs too, and feral goats seem to like these shelters. Just before the track swings back south-east, there is a very good view of the Narrabri road about 400 m distant and virtually straight below. The track then rejoins the outward route and you should then simply retrace your outward route back to the Coryah Gap car park.

MAP: Lands, 1:25,000 Kaputar and Map 46.
WALK: One day, 4 km, easy grade, last reviewed September 1992, allow 2 hours.

47   SOUTH BALD ROCK

The highlight of this walk is South Bald Rock in Queensland. The feature is said by many to be even more interesting than the famous Bald Rock in New South Wales. Both of them are massive granite domes. The two spots are linked by jeep track and lie astride the states border. Girraween National Park in Queensland and Bald Rock National Park in New South Wales adjoin and protect the district, which is part of the huge granite belt of New England and Stanthorpe district.

Exploring the many granite formations along the border and at both Bald Rock and South Bald Rock can be an unforgettable time. Girraween means 'place of flowers' which is most appropriate as there is a very large variety of plants. The granite soils are fairly poor, trees are sparse and the strong sunlight encourages wildflowers. Rainfall is reasonably high

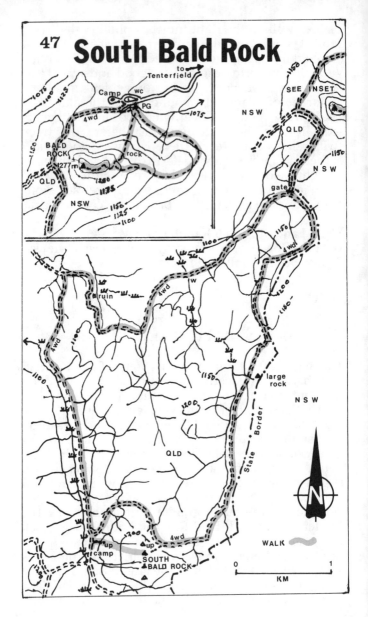

47 South Bald Rock

to Tenterfield

Camp wc
PG
4wd

BALD
ROCK
1277m   rock

QLD
NSW   1150
1125
1100

1075
1150
1125
1200
1180
1175

NSW
QLD
NSW

1150

gate

4wd

1100
1150
4wd

ruin   1200
1150

large
rock

NSW

State Border

QLD

1200

4wd

up
camp   up
SOUTH
BALD ROCK

WALK

0   1
KM

N

166

and the run-off of rain water from the vast expanses of bare granite results in quite damp localities around the edges of the rock expanses. Vegetation in these pockets therefore consists of damp-loving species, and swamps occur where granite outcrops block the streamflow. It is, however, the many granite tors, domes and precariously balanced rocks that attract walkers most.

The granite has a very coarse surface and can usually be climbed despite steep gradients and lack of hand-holds. Rubber-soled or similar non-slip footwear is essential for this walk suggestion. If the rock is wet (or icy on a cold morning) extra care is needed. Take insect repellent to combat mosquito problems at the suggested overnight camp location.

Access to the walk start is via Tenterfield, then along the Mount Lindesay Highway for 29 km. Turn west for 5.8 km to Bald Rock picnic area. Queensland National Park authorities prefer that no more than about eight walkers camp as a group at the recommended site near South Bald Rock. The aim of the walk is to complete a loop from New South Wales into Queensland for the night, then to return. Bald Rock should be seen first as a side trip without packs.

Bald Rock is an exposed dome 750 m long, 500 m wide and 200 m higher than the surrounding countryside. It is said to be the largest exposed granite rock in Australia. The rainwater run-off results in damp forest and ferns around its base. Even right near the summit, despite so much bare rock, there are plants precariously growing in crevices and depending heavily on the run-off. The suggestion is to climb the rock directly from the picnic area and to descend the longer Bungoona Track, thereby completing an anti-clockwise circuit. In so doing the steep bare rockface ascent gives easier footwear grip and anyone hesitating to walk on such exposed bare rock can re-assess the walk promptly and choose to climb and descend Bungoona Track at the far easier gradient.

Cross the footbridge at the picnic area southwards and immediately turn right on to the lesser direct pad. Walk south across flat land amid bracken for 300 m. The track ends at the base of the enormous rock. Then follow painted markers on the rock. Frequent rests will be needed because of the steepness but at each rest the views improve. Some 800 m from the walk start, the bare rock is left and an area of scrub and forest is temporarily entered. Bungoona Track links in from the left within this scrub. The way is then westwards near the tops for 400 m to the summit. Again, bare rock walking is required for this latter part. Striations of colour give the rock a distinctive appearance. On top, the vast size of the rock is well appreciated.

EUCALYPT

Retrace the 400 m and turn right down Bungoona Track. It descends gradually among massive boulders in forest and curves around in a 2.1 km arc back to the picnic ground. You can then start off towards South Bald Rock.

Between the picnic area car park and bridge there is a minor foot track off west which should be taken. Within 200 m it links to a jeep track coming out of the nearby camp area. Walk on west along the jeep track. After 1.2 km and a slight climb south-west over a saddle, you should reach the states border fence. Turn left (south) along the jeep track adjacent to the fence and pass close by the west side of Bald Rock. Downhill, the jeep track passes through a gate in the border fence after 1.3 km, then divides within Queensland. The right fork is the later return route.

Walk south-east uphill on to a ridge and keep to the jeep track which basically remains close to the fence and border. At first, there are some patches of bare rock, then later large domes and boulders lie to the left of the track. Eventually, the track swings west to approach South Bald Rock 5 km from where the border was joined. Avoid a minor foot track off left towards the rock. The track swings north-west so keep to the track as it arcs around the north side of the massive formation. Within 1.3 km, at the west side of the rock there is a junction of jeep tracks. Southwards is the suggested camping area for the night near the base of the bare rock and close to swamp.

On the second day you should start by exploring South Bald Rock as a side trip from camp. (Aim to start off for the return to Bald Rock after lunch.) There is no defined route to the summit so time must be spent choosing the best route. It is about 800 m to the top in a direct line, but to progress it may be necessary to back-track at times. Explore and enjoy this remote and complex place.

After lunch, the northbound jeep track should be followed from the junction just north of camp. It extends north 3 km to meet an east–west aligned jeep track on a grassy plain. Turn right then walk 3.8 km to the border gate, passing grasslands, swamps, creeks and granite areas. The track runs mainly south-east, then north-east.

Finally, retrace 2.5 km of the previous day's route from the border gate back to Bald Rock picnic area.

MAP: Lands, 1:25,000 Bookookoorara and Boonoo Boonoo sheets and Map 47. (The government maps lack some tracks.)
WALK: Two days, 23.4 km: day one 12.5 km, day two 10.9 km, medium grade, last reviewed September 1992, allow 6½ hours each day.

48 GIBRALTAR RANGE— DANDAHRA NEEDLES

The Dandahra Needles are the famous feature illustrated on publicity material for the Gibraltar Range National Park. The needles are granite tors balanced somewhat precariously on a steep mountain side. A visit to the attraction is the goal of most visitors to this park.

Access is from the Gwydir Highway, roughly midway between Grafton and Glen Innes. The park visitor centre is at the highway turnoff. Travel Mulligans Drive south then east for 9.4 km to Mulligans Hut picnic area beside Little Dandahra Creek. A bush camp and shelters there mark the end of the road. Mulligans Hut is beside the creek.

Cross the creek by bridge just upstream of a swimming hole and near Mulligans Hut. Then, walk north 1 km uphill slightly. Changes in the plants seen are due to variations in soil type and fertility. The granite soils support wildflowers and heaths; the richer basalt soils further up the track support rainforest-type plants.

The foot track reaches a contouring old jeep track. Next, you should turn right to walk along the jeep track. Follow it through rainforest to its end, then a foot pad on to a spur which has granite outcrops. The soils are less fertile again, so the plants are more sparse. After 1.75 km you reach Needles Lookout and a view to the Mann River Valley and beyond.

The Needles are seen to the right on the slopes and are best appreciated from this viewpoint. There is a rough pad to them from a point just back along the foot track.

Retrace the same tracks to complete the walk.

MAP: Lands, 1:25,000 Cangai (track not shown) and Map 48.
WALK: One day, 5.5 km, easy grade, last reviewed September 1992, allow 1¾ hours.

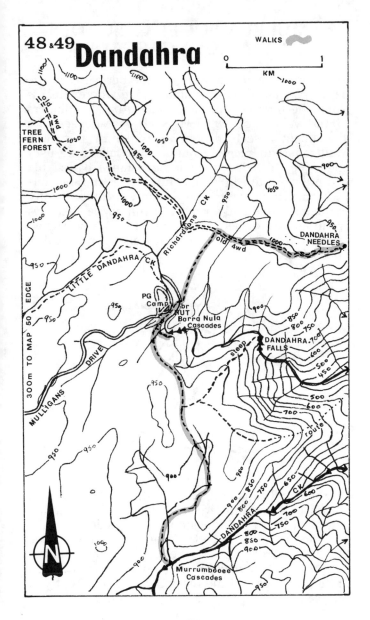

48&49 Dandahra

WALKS

0   1
KM

TREE FERN FOREST

Richardsons CK

old 4wd

DANDAHRA NEEDLES

LITTLE DANDAHRA CK

PG Camp

HUT

Borra Nula Cascades

DANDAHRA FALLS

steep

route

300m TO MAP 50 EDGE

MULLIGANS DRIVE

DANDAHRA CK

Murrumbooee Cascades

N

171

49 MURRUMBOOEE CASCADES— BARRA NULA CASCADES

There are several spots around the perimeter of the basalt plateau of the Gibraltar Range where streams leave the tops and cascade among basalt boulders to the valleys below. Two such cascades can be conveniently seen in one walk south from the Mulligans Hut picnic ground. The walk route uses an old jeep track for much of the distance. Barra Nula is quite close to Mulligans Hut. There, granitic soils predominate so that trees are mainly eucalypts, many of them stunted and sparse. Murrumbooee Cascades are in an area of better soils and in fact are reached by more than 2 km of rainforest walking in a locality of basalt soils.

EPACRIS

From Mulligans Hut, walk south 300 m, then turn left on to a pad into adjacent Barra Nula Cascades. After just 100 m, boulder-hopping is needed to reach the top of the long set of cascades where Little Dandahra Creek leaves the plateau. By boulder-hopping for about 200 m a good deal can be seen of the cascades and the recommendation is that you retrace from this point back to the main track.

Walk south 500 m on the jeep track; the eucalypt forest is then left behind in a gully. Rainforest is entered almost immediately. Go another 500 m and a track junction is reached. Keep right rather than turning off to Dandahra Falls and Junction Spur. A further 1.75 km walk in rainforest follows. The track descends over 100 m in this distance, and passes many ferns. It then reaches Murrumbooee Cascades at the junction of Dandahra Creek (South Branch) and Pigbilla Creek. A little boulder-hopping is best to gain a good vantage point and to enable you to sit on a granite boulder for lunch or a break.

Return along the same route, omitting Barra Nula on the return.

MAP: Lands, 1:25,000 Cangai and Map 49. (Note that the government map shows an incorrect alignment of most of the track route.)
WALK: One day, 6.7 km, easy grade, last reviewed September 1992, allow 2¾ hours.

50   GIBRALTAR RANGE— ANVIL ROCK

The Gibraltar Range summit includes large expanses of granite rock similar to the well known granite belt of New England—Tenterfield and Stanthorpe regions. There are huge outcrops of the rock. The granitic soils are usually poor and support dry eucalypt forest with understorey of heaths in many localities. Sedge swamps are common on the range top as the granite tends to block the peripheral stream flow, causing the swampy spots upstream of the granite. The open vegetation has brought about the good growth of wildflowers.

173

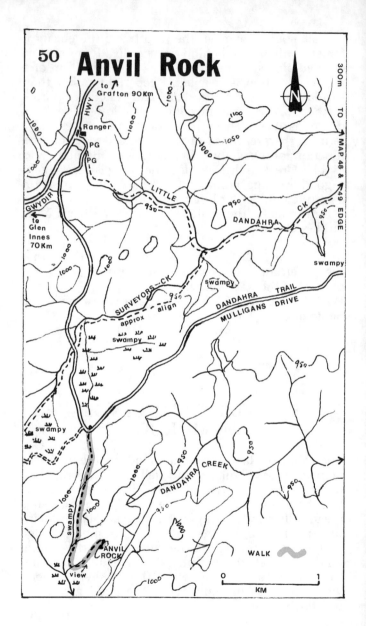

50 Anvil Rock

to Grafton 90 Km

HWY

Ranger

PG

PG

GWYDIR

to Glen Innes 70 Km

LITTLE

DANDAHRA

CK

swampy

SURVEYORS CK

swampy

approx align

swampy

DANDAHRA TRAIL

MULLIGANS DRIVE

swampy

DANDAHRA CREEK

swampy

ANVIL ROCK

view

WALK

300m

TO MAP 48 & 49 EDGE

N

1000

1100

1050

1000

950

950

950

950

950

1000

1000

450

950

1000

1000

1000

0   KM   1

One of the more interesting granite tors is Anvil Rock, which sits on a granite outcrop on the range top plateau. Anvil Rock itself cannot be climbed but walkers can explore the numerous fascinating rocks around it.

Access to the walk start is from the Gwydir Highway, slightly west of the halfway point between Grafton and Glen Innes. Mulligans Drive leaves the south side of the highway adjacent to a National Park visitor centre. Travel this gravelled road south 3.5 km to gain the track head. The walk involves very little climbing or descent. But after persistent rain the middle section could be wet underfoot where the track leads along the margin of a sedge and tea tree swamp. In some places the scenery reminds one of the button grass plains of south-west Tasmania.

Head off south into dry eucalypt forest with acacias, banksias, tea tree and heathland shrubs to be seen at first. After about 800 m, and immediately to the west of some granite rocks, the sedge swamp begins. The track threads a way between rock and swamp. Some 1.5 km south of the walk start, the track turns north-east and there is a view ahead of Anvil Rock, silhouetted against the sky. Then follows a minor climb for 500 m to the feature.

Retrace the same track, after exploring the rocks.

MAP: Lands, 1:25,000 Cangai (track alignment incorrectly shown) and Map 50.
WALK: One day, 4 km, easy grade family suitability, last reviewed September 1992, allow 1½ hours.

Never Never

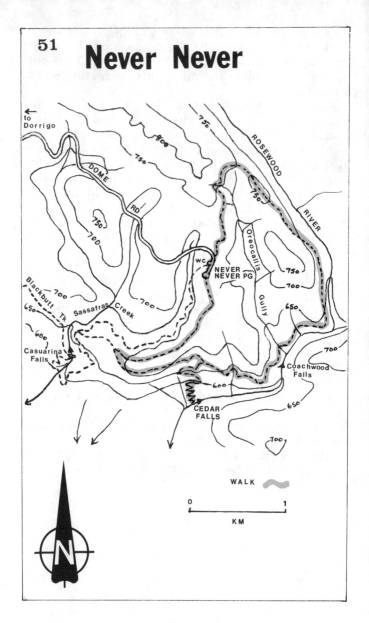

51   NEVER NEVER—
ROSEWOOD RIVER

The Dorrigo Plateau is a remnant of an old volcano centred on Ebor about eighteen million years ago. Today the plateau supports rich farmland and the town of Dorrigo. Especially on the eastern edge of the plateau, humid coastal air masses result in high rainfall, which has eroded an escarpment and given rise to rainforest on the escarpment and spurs. There are rich basalt soils and poorer yellow clay soils in the area. Sub-tropical rainforests exist on the better soils and warm temperate rainforests where clays occur, such as those at Never Never picnic ground east of Dorrigo.

Never Never has coachwood trees, hoop pines, brush box, blackbutt, tallow-wood and many ferns as the main forest types. Never Never also has a walking track circuit known as the Rosewood Track. The track grade is gradual. Coachwood Falls which are passed on the walk are pleasant but relatively small. Later, a side track leads off down zig-zags to the more impressive Cedar Falls. The falls and the rainforest ensure an enjoyable walk.

Just south-east of Dorrigo township is the National Park rainforest centre, a large and elaborate park visitor centre where, if you wish, you can first call to gain some impression of rainforest environments. The (partly sealed) road to Never Never (Dome Road) passes the centre. The picnic spot in the lush dense forest is some 9.5 km from the centre.

Start the walk from the upper (southern) end of the grassy clearing in the forest to walk the circuit anti-clockwise. For 1 km follow an old logging track down a spur crest. There are many eucalypts along this ridge and it is obvious that the ridge has been heavily logged in the past, thus removing the old-growth rainforest. There are many cut logs by the track and even the type of regrowth trees indicates that man has changed this part of the forest perhaps for centuries.

A track junction is reached next. Double back on the left fork to contour in damp forest for 700 m to the Cedar Falls track. Take this side trip down the zig-zag track for 1.4 km. About 180 m elevation is lost and will have to be regained in the return but the effort is well rewarded. It is this return climb which causes the day's walk to have a medium grading rather than easy.

Once back on the contouring track, walk east in more damp forest for 1 km and Coachwood Falls are seen. A pause by them or a lunch break might be appreciated. Thereafter, the way ahead for some 2.7 km is up the Rosewood River valley and over a ridge back into the Never Never picnic ground. During this section of the walk the rainforest is seen at its best. It is on steep, east-facing slopes near the river and is damp, mossy and ferny.

MAP: Lands, 1:25,000 Brooklana and Map 51.
WALK: One day, 8.2 km, medium grade, last reviewed September 1992, allow 3½ hours.

52 TRIAL BAY—GAP BEACH

Smoky Cape Range rises abruptly from the ocean near South-West Rocks and several beautiful beaches nestle in the coves formed by the spurs of the range. Gap Beach is the most difficult of access and also perhaps the most attractive. It is backed by some littoral rainforest and flanked at each end by rocky bluffs. During dry weather four-wheel-drive vehicles can get to within 200 m of the beach, but normally the cove is reserved for walkers.

Historic Trial Bay Gaol at Laggers Point is another attraction near South-West Rocks. It dates from 1876

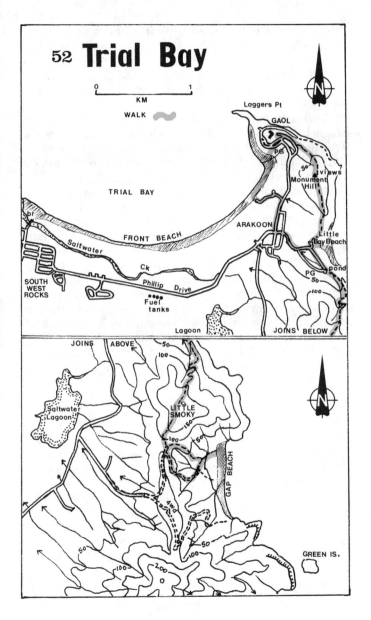

52 Trial Bay

0 _____ 1
KM

WALK 〜

Laggers Pt

GAOL

PG

Views

Monument Hill

TRIAL BAY

ARAKOON

Little Bay Beach

FRONT BEACH

pond

Saltwater

PG

Ck

Phillip   Drive

SOUTH WEST ROCKS

Fuel tanks

Lagoon

JOINS BELOW

N

JOINS   ABOVE

50

100

Saltwater Lagoon

LITTLE SMOKY

100

150

50

GAP BEACH

4WD

50

50

100

100

200

GREEN IS.

N

and its use has included the internment of German people (mostly from German Pacific colonies) during the First World War. Today it draws tourists and is surrounded by lawns, kiosk, camp and picnic facilities. Coastal scenery, beaches and walking tracks add interest.

A walk from the gaol locality to Gap Beach includes these historic attractions, three lovely beaches, views, wildflowers and forest. Access to the gaol entrance and car park is to South-West Rocks from Kempsey then east via Phillip Drive. For a small fee you can tour the gaol before setting off on the walk. Any season is suitable but beach weather would be ideal. In spring too, there tend to be carpets of boronia and hakea flowers near Little Bay and Monument Hill.

Start off on a foot track which leads east up the crest of a spur from the gaol car park. Within 500 m you should reach the top of 76 m high Monument Hill. As you climb, the castle-like gaol is seen on the point behind, with a broad seascape of Trial Bay and the Pacific. Trial Bay was named after the brig *Trial*, which was seized by convicts in Sydney in 1816 and wrecked here on her passage north. There is a memorial on Monument Hill in memory of Germans who died in the gaol during internment.

Continue along the track which descends the crest of a ridge. Heathland plants and wildflowers are usually good in the locality and there is a broad panorama of coastal scenery. Little Bay then comes into view ahead. Descend the track to this lovely ocean beach from a car park and picnic area 900 m from Monument Hill. A short break would be worthwhile before next climbing a hill.

A one-way-traffic circuit leads south-east 300 m from the main Little Bay Beach access car park. Take this road for the 300 m to another picnic area and car park adjacent to an old reservoir which is now a home for varieties of ducks. Presumably the reservoir once serviced the gaol. A fence surrounds the storage and a foot track leads off beside the fence nearest the ocean.

Follow the track to climb almost to the summit of Little Smoky (200 m elevation). This 1.25 km climb is on lightly wooded slopes and includes some zig-zags. The top of the peak is just to the left of the track and has no view. The banksias there seem to attract a lot of birds. Continue over the ridge and descend about 100 m elevation over 500 m distance in damper forest to an old jeep track on a saddle of the range crest. Walk the jeep track south 200 m, then diverge left to descend off the range via the jeep track into a basin which backs Gap Beach. After

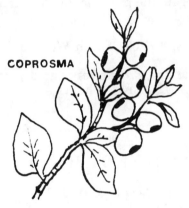

COPROSMA

500 m a rough car parking place is reached. Two pads lead off the jeep track towards the beach. Take the left fork north-east pad to the north end of Gap Beach 300 m away via a littoral rainforest revegetation area. Fencing guides you to the beach. Note the track linking in from the left as you near the beach. This track is the later return route.

Spend time on the 1 km long beach, perhaps enjoying lunch on the small dune tops or rocks at the southern end. There will probably be surfers to watch if the jeep track is trafficable. On a warm day a swim might appeal.

After the break, leave the beach from the north end and diverge right, on to the foot track almost immediately. Climb this track for 500 m, rising 100 m, to pass through cool forest and gain the jeep track on the range crest again. Turn right and retrace the foot track over Little Smoky to Little Bay car park 2.05 km away. Instead of retracing further, turn left down sealed Little Bay Road for 400 m as it curves to meet the gaol access road. Turn right (north) and go another 400 m towards the gaol but then join a gravel road off left to car parking areas and the front beach of Trial Bay. This gravel road section is also 400 m long. Finally, turn right along the beach for 500 m to regain the prominent gaol entrance area on the headland.

MAP: Lands, 1:25,000 South-West Rocks and Map 52.
WALK: One day, 8.7 km, easy grade, last reviewed September 1992, allow 3½ hours.

53   NORTH BROTHER MOUNTAIN

Between Port Macquarie and Taree is delightful Camden Haven, an area of river, lakes and ocean. North Brother Mountain (490 m high) dominates everything as it rises sharply from sea level amid the lakes and inlet that virtually encircle it. A glance at a topographical map helps one to better appreciate how the mountain rises from the encircling waters rather like a volcanic cone in a lake-filled crater. Middle Brother and South Brother Mountains are nearby and were named by Captain Cook when he discovered and sailed the coast.

Following a bicentennial grant there is now a sealed road to a lookout on top of North Brother and the ascent of the mountain is a tourist attraction. For

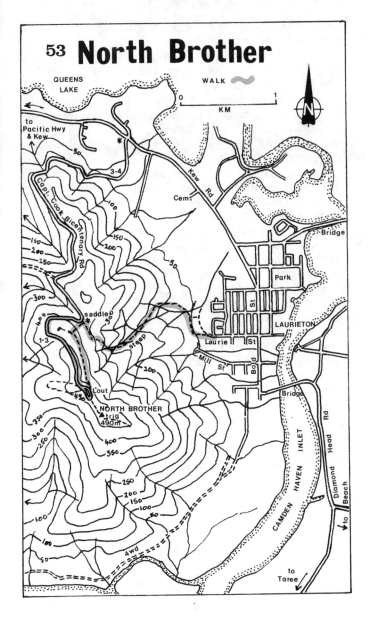

53 North Brother

QUEENS LAKE

WALK

0   1

KM

N

to Pacific Hwy & Kew

3·4

Capt. Cook Bicentenary Rd

Kew Rd

Cem.

Bridge

50

100

150

200

250

300

400

saddle

1·3

steep

50

Park

St

LAURIETON

Laurie   St

Bo

Mill St

L'out

450

NORTH BROTHER
trig
490m

200

300
350
250
400
350

Bridge

250
200
150
100
50

100

50

4wd

CAMDEN HAVEN INLET

Diamond Head Rd

to Beach

to Taree

183

many years walkers have made their way to the top by several routes but today only the road and one steep track remain. The walking track is directly from Laurieton and involves strenuous climbing, with the need to carry drinking water. The track could prove slippery when wet. The walking track starts at the top end (west end) of Laurie Street which intersects the main street in the centre of town. The reward for the effort is one of the better views along the New South Wales coast.

For the first 1.5 km of the walk beyond Laurie Street you need to climb more and more steeply from 40 m elevation to 390 m, where you join the mountain road (Captain Cook Bicentennial Road) at a saddle and road bend. The climb is within forest.

Leave the road again virtually where it was joined to continue on the foot pad. You need to climb another 100 m over a distance of 700 m to the summit lookout. Most of this last section is across steep slopes, but rising only gradually after an initial steep pinch. On top there are good views from two separate lookout points while the forest blocks north-west and south-east views. (There is a very short forest loop walk on the mountain top to satisfy the tourists who arrive by road.) As an alternative, return by first walking down the sealed road for 1.3 km to the saddle and road bend then join in the foot track to retrace the pad 1.5 km steeply down to Laurie Street.

MAP: Lands, 1:25,000 Laurieton and Map 53.
WALK: One day, 5 km, medium grade (despite the short distance), last reviewed September 1992, allow 3 hours.

54   DIAMOND HEAD

This headland fronting the Pacific between Port Macquarie and Taree is reached by road south from Laurieton. The headland achieves 114 m height at Diamond trig point to give excellent coastal views and a view to nearby North Brother Mountain. The best base for a walk to Diamond Head is Diamond Head picnic area at the south end of long and beautiful Dunbogan Beach. There is a circuit track system with easy grades amid a variety of coastal type plants. Two beaches are included in the circuit. The track starts at the entrance of the picnic area.

Head off to climb south-east on open heathland slopes where wildflowers are good. Within 500 m the circuit track is reached. Turn left (east) to continue the gradual climb for 800 m to the trig point. Colourful boronia, banksia and flannel flower displays are to be seen in spring as the trig is approached. The way is then south near rugged and scenic clifflines for 1.3 km to the north end of Kylies Beach. The cliffs include a blowhole and clay-coloured rocks. It is a good idea to walk the 400 m return distance on a pad to the blowhole area as a side trip. Just before reaching Kylies Beach the track divides. The right fork leads to Indian Head picnic area. Take the left fork at the saddle and descend to the beach then follow the beach south for 500 m.

The mouth of a small creek is then reached, adjacent to a four-wheel-drive beach access point. The track to follow leaves the jeep track to cross the creek near its mouth, then heads inland for 400 m to Kylies Hut. This routing bypasses nearby picnic and camping areas. Kylies Hut is in a grassy clearing frequented by kangaroos. Kylie Tennant, the author, lived in the hut and wrote a novel about Diamond Head.

Continue from the hut north just 300 m to Indian Head picnic area. Again, kangaroos are often seen feeding on the grass. To the east side of the clearing take the left-fork track to walk through coastal scrub

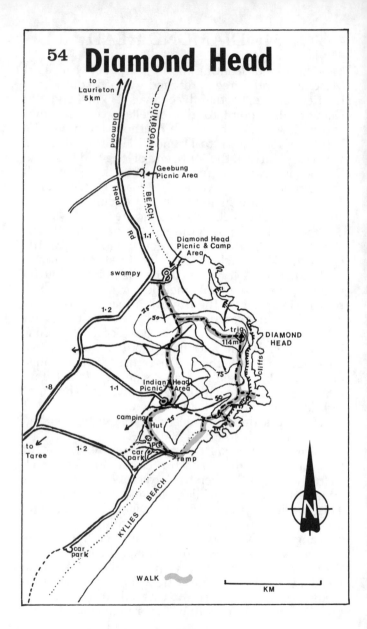

54 Diamond Head

to Laurieton 5 km

Diamond Head Rd

DUNBOGAN BEACH

Geebung Picnic Area

1.1

Diamond Head Picnic & Camp Area

swampy

1.2

25
50

trig 114 m

DIAMOND HEAD

75

cliffs

Indian Head Picnic Area

.8

1.1

50

camping

Hut 25

25

to Taree

1.2

PG

car park

ramp

KYLIES BEACH

car park

WALK

KM

N

and forest for 1.1 km. Tree ferns and coral ferns grow in a gully you cross in the forested part. Finally, turn left and retrace 500 m north-west down to Diamond Head picnic area.

MAP: Lands, 1:25,000 Laurieton and Map 54.
WALK: One day, 5.5 km, easy grade, last reviewed September 1992, allow 2 hours.

55   DARK POINT

The Myall Lakes National Park is some 300 km north-east of Sydney and features magnificent white sand beaches with dunes which are backed by the Myall River and associated lakes. Dark Point (or Little Gibber) is of volcanic origin and extends seaward from the surf beaches. Offshore are further volcanic outcrops forming the Broughton Island group, while there is an extension of volcanic ridges further inland. These volcanic features are aligned at right angles to the coastline. Once the sea extended much further inland so that there were many more islands.

This walk recommendation is to undertake a circuit which includes the surf beaches, Dark Point and the backing sand dunes. In the 1960s and 1970s sand mining took place in the dunes and disused mining access tracks can now be walked together with foot tracks to complete the interesting circuit. Spring is clearly a good time to enjoy the tea tree, banksia and heathland of the dunes and summer is of course ideal for the beach. The walk has year-round appeal and walkers have the Lions Club of Tea Gardens to thank for installing and maintaining the foot tracks.

Access to the walk start is best from Tea Gardens and Hawks Nest, north along Mungo Brush Road for about 9 km to a spot known as Robinsons Crossing. There, the former sand mining old Mungo Trail temporarily abuts the west side of Mungo Brush Road. For ease of navigation the circuit is best walked anti-clockwise.

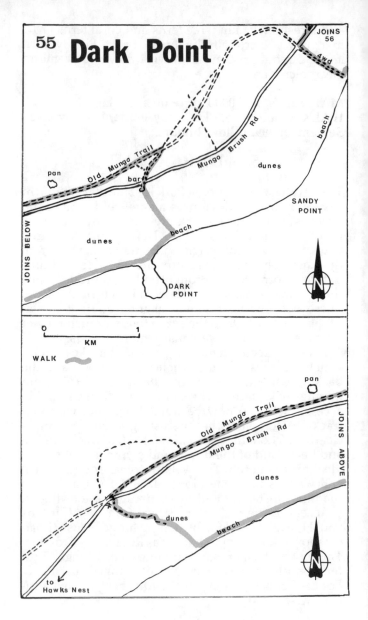

55 **Dark Point**

JOINS
56

4wd

Old Mungo Trail

Mungo Brush Rd

pan

bar

dunes

SANDY
POINT

JOINS BELOW

dunes

beach

beach

DARK
POINT

N

0   1
KM

WALK

Old Mungo Trail

pan

Mungo Brush Rd

JOINS ABOVE

dunes

dunes

beach

to
Hawks Nest

N

188

First, the walk is through bottlebrush scrub then over massive sand dunes to the ocean beach. Signposts mark the start of the foot track through the scrub. This pad links on to an old jeep track within 150 m, and then leads east to shifting sand dunes just 700 m from the walk start. The dunes encroach on the scrub and track so that there is a sudden change of surroundings to a complete lack of vegetation and views of the Pacific Ocean.

Cross the dunes for 400 m to the shore, then wander along the beach for 2.5 km north-eastwards (left turn). This brings you to an isthmus linking the beach to Dark Point, an ideal spot for a break and perhaps a swim if the day and the surf are suitable.

The plan is next to head inland again to gain Mungo Brush Road. This is best achieved by continuing further along the beach for 400 m then climbing on to the dunes and walking 700 m roughly north-west in an area of heavy wind scouring of the dunes. The route is well used, so normally many footprints should be evident on the dunes. As you reach the road, there are signs and a car park as a guide.

Cross Mungo Brush Road on to an old sand mining track which leads north-east 400 m to a T intersection with Old Mungo Trail. The junction is well within heathland. Turn left (west) at the junction to continue. There is in fact a short-cut pad near the intersection but it is quite difficult to discern so best remain on the main track. Ahead the heathlands and the birds that they attract are a major attraction in spring. For 3.3 km the Old Mungo Trail can be followed in virtually a straight line back to the walk end at Robinsons Crossing. Old Dune Trail forks off right into the scrub during this last segment of the day's walk.

MAP: Lands, 1:25,000 The Branch and Bombah Point sheets and Map 55.
WALK: One day, 8.4 km, easy grade, last reviewed July 1992, allow 3 hours.

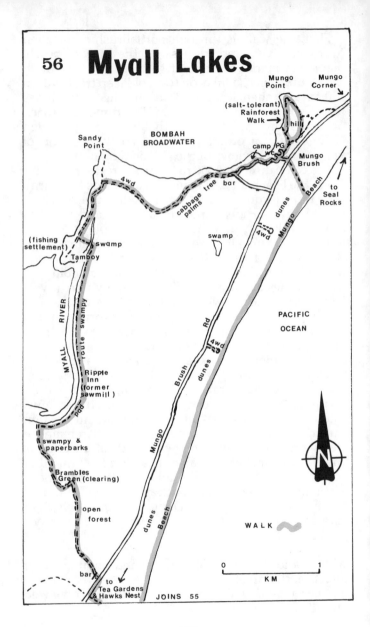

56 **Myall Lakes**

Mungo Point

Mungo Corner →

(salt-tolerant) Rainforest Walk →

hill

BOMBAH BROADWATER

Sandy Point

4wd

camp PG
wc

Mungo Brush

bar

cabbage tree palms

Mungo Beach

to Seal Rocks

dunes

(fishing settlement)

swamp

Tamboy

swamp

4wd

Mungo

PACIFIC OCEAN

MYALL RIVER

route swampy

pad

Brush

Rd

dunes

4wd

Ripple Inn (former sawmill)

swampy & paperbarks

Brambles Green (clearing)

Mungo

open forest

Brush

dunes

Beach

N

WALK

0   1
K M

bar

to Tea Gardens & Hawks Nest

JOINS 55

56   MYALL LAKES

The Myall Lakes National Park is some 100 km north-east of Newcastle and features a diversity of water environments and a network of walking tracks to aid enjoyment of the locality. Magnificent white sand beaches have long been a great attraction for summertime campers in the Mungo Brush area on the shores of Bombah Broadwater. Myall Lakes however has much more to offer. There are lakes, the Myall River, rainforest, swamplands, shifting sand dunes, heathland wildflowers and cabbage palm groves. Much of the district is sandy but volcanic ridges are aligned at right angles to the coast and extend into the sea at Dark Point and form the Broughton Island group. In the 1960s and 1970s there was sand mining among the dunes. In the 1920s a sawmill operated at Ripple Inn. Today there is little evidence of these industries, only some old tracks and a rusting sawmill boiler. The tracks are now useful access for walkers.

A most interesting circuit is suggested from the Mungo Brush camping complex and picnic area. A long surf beach walk is included near the end of the circuit. Spring is an ideal time for the walk because the heathland flowers are in bloom and the swampy paperbark forests are beginning to dry out. September to November have the least rainfall. Walkers need to wear old footwear and socks and should expect to wade in ankle-deep water for short distances, especially during autumn and winter. In summer, the beach is the principal attraction.

Access to the walk start is best from Tea Gardens and Hawks Nest along Mungo Brush Road for about 19 km. Here, on the shore of Bombah Broadwater, is a large fully equipped picnic and camp area with boat ramp access to the lakes and a shelter among Illawarra flame trees. Immediately north is Mungo Point and a 28 m high volcanic hill covered with rainforest. The forest is distinctive, and adapted to survive the harsh coastal conditions and salt-laden winds. The recommendation is that a 1.2 km long track circuit be walked through the rainforest. Then set off on the main walk circuit to see other types of vegetation as a contrast. The rainforest loop circuits the hill and passes an old Southern Cross windmill. During this initial loop ignore two pads off east to Mungo Corner and keep close to the base of the hill. Collect water next for use during the main walk loop.

Set off from the picnic and camp area to follow an old jeep track through cabbage palm groves westwards near the lake shore. Some 2 km away, turn left in the vicinity of Sandy Point. Remain on the main track for 600 m south towards a tiny fishing settlement called Tamboy. The locality is littered with old cars and rubbish but is soon bypassed. As Tamboy is approached look for a track marking system off east from the jeep track. These markers guide walkers for 1.3 km through an area of swampland adjacent to the Myall River. There is no track. Persevere with wet feet if the paperbark forest is flooded so as to see an environment so remarkably different. You need simply to carefully follow the many markers on the trees. In July 1992 a pack of cards were being used as some of the markers and the last card seen was the joker! Ripple Inn, the old sawmill site on the banks of the Myall River should then be reached and a defined track then begins again. The sawmill boiler lies between the track and the river. Cabbage palms and swamp mahogany trees then become noticeable among the continuing paperbarks and casuarinas. Some 800 m along the riverbank track is a clearing and the end of a jeep track.

Follow the jeep track south through open forest which then includes red gums, past a former farm site at Brambles Green and on through banksia stands to regain Mungo Brush Road within 1.8 km. The typical sandy tracts and coastal vegetation are pronounced. Walk 200 m south on the road (right turn), to turn on to a jeep track. Walk it south-east

Govetts Leap, Grose Valley, Blue Mountains

Blackheath, Blue Mountains

Kanangra Walls, Blue Mountains

Mount Gower from Lagoon Road, Lord Howe Island

for 500 m in dune country to the beach.

The beachcombing phase of the walk then follows. For 4.6 km you need simply to wander north-east along the beach. It is a truly magnificent white sand beach, the likes of which are renowned overseas as the Australian beach image.

The rainforest-covered hill at Mungo Point can be seen rising slightly above the dunes as the 4.6 km stretch is nearing completion. The position of the hill top is a rough guide as to where to look for a sign on the dunes marking a good foot track north-west 500 m through coastal scrub directly to Mungo Brush Road and picnic area. At two points during the long beach walk there are four-wheel-drive vehicle access points to the beach. The northernmost of these is some 500 m south of the foot track beach exit spot leading to the end of the walk.

MAP: Lands, 1:25,000 Bombah Point and Maps 55 and 56.
WALK: One day, 13.5 km, medium grade, walk last reviewed July 1992, allow 5 hours.
Note: Ankle deep water is a possibility for short distances at certain times of the year, and suitable old footwear is essential.

57   HAWKS NEST—YACAABA

New South Wales is undoubtedly endowed with some spectacular coastal scenery and the image overseas residents have of Australian beaches seems to be an image of New South Wales beaches rather than of other states. Such places as Port Stephens must surely rank as world class, especially because of the fine, white sand beaches, beautiful lakeland and dominating peaks and headlands around the margin of the lake. It certainly is one of the best areas in New South Wales.

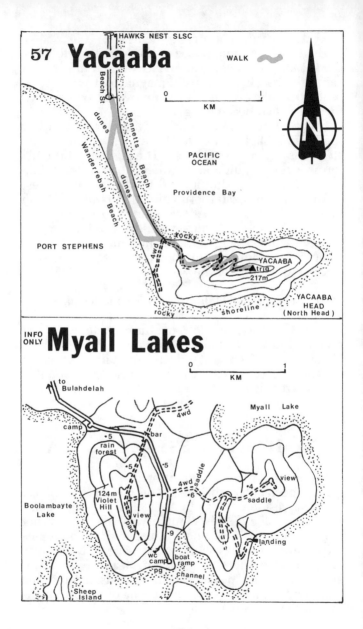

57

Yacaaba

HAWKS NEST SLSC

WALK

Beach St

Bennetts Beach

Wanderrebah Beach

dunes

dunes

0 _____ 1
KM

N

PACIFIC OCEAN

Providence Bay

rocky

PORT STEPHENS

4wd

YACAABA
▲ trig
217m

YACAABA HEAD
(North Head)

rocky   shoreline

INFO ONLY **Myall Lakes**

0 _____ 1
KM

to Bulahdelah

Myall Lake

4wd

camp

bar

•5
rain forest

•5   •5

4wd   saddle

•4   view

124m
Violet Hill

view
pad

•6   saddle

Boolambayte Lake

•9

landing

wc
camp
pg

boat ramp

Channel

Sheep Island

This walk suggestion commences at Hawks Nest and includes a climb to Yacaaba (North Head).

The head is 217 m high and dominates the northern side of the entrance to Port Stephens lakeland. It is connected to Hawks Nest by a 2 km long sand spit so that both Pacific Ocean and Port Stephens beaches are on the walk route.

Access to Hawks Nest is along the Pacific Highway past Karuah then to Tea Gardens and over the big bridge across the Myall River, then east along Kingfisher Street, south along Mungo Brush Road and east along Booner Street to the ocean foreshore and surf club. Start the walk at a car park in the sand dunes 1 km south of the surf club along Beach Street. At the car park the spit is only about 300 m wide.

Walk on to the ocean beach then turn south and walk about 200 m to then veer on to some bare sand dunes for a good general view. Keep going south over the dunes and then diverge westwards across the spit to Wanderrebah Beach on the inlet. There are good views to the west across Port Stephens and to Nelson Bay. Walk south-south-east for 1.4 km along Wanderrebah Beach. The relatively calm waters will probably be dotted with yachts and fishing craft.

As you reach the foot of Yacaaba (North Head), cross the spit to the ocean beach. You should see both a jeep track and a foot track next to each other, leading off the end of the beach. Enter bushland by going up the left fork foot track. It tends to be overhung by a South African plant, boneseed, which is considered a noxious weed in Australia. The plant is clearly becoming a major problem on the nearby dunes and in Yacaaba itself. Follow the foot track uphill amid very large banksias for 800 m to where the slopes steepen. The track then begins to zig-zag steeply up in more forest to the ridge crest within 450 m. Take note of the spot where the ridge is gained for ease of descent later. A small pad, somewhat rocky underfoot, then leads east for just 150 m to a trig point on the summit. The climb to it has a minor rise.

Vegetation is tending to obscure the broad views that were once a feature of the peak but by moving about a little you can look to South Head, Nelson Bay and out to several rocky islands in the ocean. There is no water supply on the top, but lunch could be eaten while you have a break after the climb.

EPACRIS

To return, use the same track routing to the ocean beach. Once on the beach a swim might be welcome and then you should merely follow the ocean beach north-north-west back to the car park. If you are lucky you might see a dingo in the dunes area. It seems they are present and fairly unconcerned about the presence of people.

MAP: Lands, 1:25,000 Port Stephens and Map 57.
WALK: One day, 6 km, easy grade, last reviewed July 1992, allow 2½ hours.

58 BARREN GROUNDS— COOKS NOSE

This walk to two quite spectacular lookout points overlooking Brogers Creek and Kangaroo Valley 400 m below, is at Barren Grounds. This reserve is on a typical hanging swamp plateau, almost completely encircled by sheer cliffs. The plateau is mostly at about 600 m elevation. It has extremely thin top soil with many bare sandstone expanses. Therefore, vegetation is mostly sedge and heathland, with vast numbers of wildflowers and only a few trees.

The plateau was originally reserved in 1956 to protect the habitat of the rare ground parrot and the rare eastern bristlebird. Today the twenty square kilometre plateau remains remote and aloof with the chief aim being the preservation of the landscape and 160 species of birds. There is a picnic area and a bird observers field studies centre. Otherwise, facilities are low key and cater only for walkers. Access is from the Robertson to Jamberoo road 800 m south on to the plateau to a picnic area and shelter.

Set off south from the picnic area, past a barrier and the field studies centre for 1.1 km. Then turn right (west) to continue on the former jeep track, rather than take a left fork foot pad. The first 1 km is across quite open, almost bleak, sedge plateau. Then ahead is a 450 m stretch of sheltered track. Along the southern edge there is a line of banksias, acacias and other thriving shrubs together with coral ferns. These appear to have grown as a result of a man-made culvert on the high side of the track which traps and re-directs water. At the west end of the shelter belt, double back south-east at a T junction so as to take the Cooks Nose Trail uphill. It swings south, and after 750 m divides into two very minor former jeep tracks which effectively are now foot tracks. Both forks lead

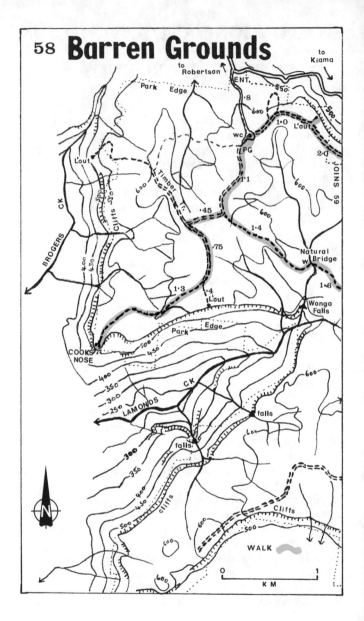

to Kiama

to Robertson

Park Edge

ENT.

.8

550

600

500

wc

LPG

L'out

1.0

2.0

JOINS 59

L'out

Timber Tr.

600

1.1

.45

600

.75

1.4

Natural w Bridge

1.3

.4

L'out

1.6

Wonga Falls

Park Edge

500

COOKS NOSE

600

400
350
300
250

LAMONDS

CK

600

falls

falls

300
350
400
450
500

cliffs

Cliffs

600

500

WALK

N

O   1

K M

198

to vantage points on the plateau rim. The left fork is 400 m long and the right fork 1.3 km. Take the 400 m track first. The last 30 m on to the rocks is a bit scrubby but offers no real problems. There is a superb view which will compel a break, but there is better to come. Next, take the 1.3 km pad which leads to Cooks Nose through an area thick with shrubs and a few trees. Banksias and hakeas are the main shrubs lining the track until it ends among eucalypts on Cooks Nose. Sandstone outcrops line the escarpment rim and are a good spot for a lunch break while taking in the view. The headland will be hard to leave because of its beauty but when you do you need to retrace 3.6 km back to the picnic area.

MAP: Lands, 1:25,000 Kangaroo Valley and Map 58. WALK: One day, 8 km, easy grade, last reviewed November 1992, allow 3 hours.

59 SADDLEBACK—NATURAL STONE BRIDGE

Barren Grounds is a 600 m high plateau covering about twenty square kilometres and almost totally surrounded by sheer cliffs. The plateau soils are extremely shallow and overlie sandstone, so plants are mostly sedge and heathland with very few trees or even substantial shrubs. Wildflowers thrive in the direct and strong sunlight and generous water supply. Much of the plateau lacks good drainage and swamp conditions are widespread.

This walk is a circuit on the plateau but visits two viewing points on the escarpment rim. It also visits a natural sandstone bridge over the principal stream; Lamonds Creek. Birds are a great attraction and the plateau is the home of the rare ground parrot and the rare eastern bristlebird. A bird observers field studies centre and a picnic area are the only intrusions into this wilderness area. Access is from the Robertson

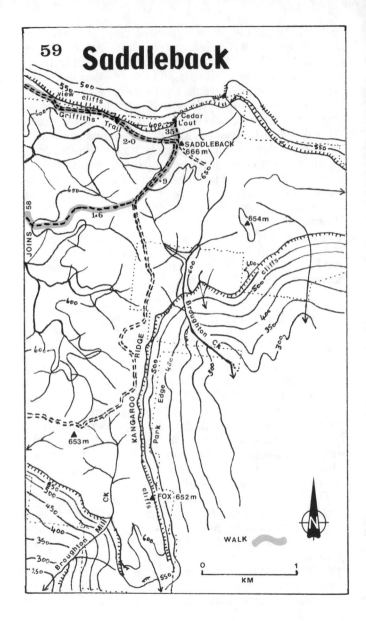

59 Saddleback

JOINS 58

Griffiths Trail

view cliffs
550   500
600
2.0   400   35

Cedar L'out

▲ SADDLEBACK
666 m

550

650
9
600   1.6

654 m

500 cliffs
600   500
400   350   300

Broughton Ck

600

KANGAROO—RIDGE

Park Edge

500   450   600   300

▲ 653 m

▲ FOX 652 m

cliffs

550   500   450   400   350   300   250

Broughton Mill CK

600

550

WALK

0   1
KM

N

to Jamberoo road then south 800 m to the picnic spot.

The walk starts off eastwards on an old jeep track which leads near the northern plateau rim for 3 km to Saddleback trig. Just near the walk start is a short nature trail which could be bypassed. Better to walk the suggested route, which is one long fine nature walk. Just 1 km from the walk start, however, you should take a side trip off left 150 m each way to see the view from Illawarra Lookout. The lookout is next to a powerline support pole and the view is of the Jamberoo district and beyond. Further on, towards Saddleback trig, the margins of rainforest that drape the slopes around the plateau are seen. Overall, though, the vegetation remains sedge and heathland.

At the trig there is a crossroads of old jeep tracks. Take the north fork 350 m downhill to see the impressive view towards Port Kembla from Cedar Lookout. The rocks on the cliff rim could be used for a break or lunch spot before you retrace the 350 m to the trig.

Continue south-west across the plateau for 900 m, then diverge right on to a well trodden foot track to the Natural Stone Bridge 1.6 km distant. During the gradual descent towards Lamonds Creek there are broad views towards Kangaroo Valley. At the creek there is a good water supply suitable for drinking and could be an alternative lunch spot. The creek flows underground temporarily to form the bridge and immediately upstream there is a large deep pool.

Across the bridge, climb gradually for 1.4 km north-westwards to meet the old jeep track system again. Turn right and walk 1 km across more sedge and heathland in a fairly bleak location to regain the picnic ground.

MAP: Lands, 1:25,000 Kangaroo Valley and Map 59.
WALK: One day, 9 km, easy grade, last reviewed November 1992, allow 3¾ hours.

60 Minnamurra Rainforest

to falls

seats

MINNAMURRA RIVER

br

br

br

fig

gully

CAR PARK

to Jamberoo

VISITOR CENTRE

wc

toll

Kiosk

br

br

0   200
METRES

WALK

N

60 MINNAMURRA RAINFOREST

That the rainforest preservation lobby has in recent years clearly succeeded in gaining political attention is evidenced by lavish spending of Commonwealth National Rainforest Funding on rainforest centres, especially at Dorrigo and to a lesser extent at Minnamurra. Millions of dollars have been spent creating elevated walkways, viewing platforms, educational centres, kiosks and souvenir shops amid rainforests. To many true bushwalkers, what has been created is quite uninviting, having absolutely no sense of wilderness, solitude or adventure. The centres appear politically motivated and no doubt expect to be self-supporting as tourist attractions.

Clearly, though, for bushwalkers the educational aspect of the centres is good, with reference reading and display material, videos and plant labelling available. At Minnamurra there is even a perfumed garden to bring scented native plants to visitors' attention. School groups would no doubt also appreciate the educational aspect, provided the students are at least into their teen years.

Minnamurra centre is located about 40 km south of Wollongong in a valley below Minnamurra Falls. Access is via Albion Park or Kiama and Jamberoo. The centre is open to the public daily 9 a.m. to 5 p.m. with an entry fee payable. The 600 m high Illawarra Range and its escarpments lie west of the valley, protecting it from cold south-west weather, and so rainforest grows well in a microclimate created by warm moisture-laden sea breezes that enter the horseshoe-shaped valley from the east. As well, the soil is the rich volcanic type resulting from an ancient lava flow. The rainforest is significant in that it is among the farthest south in Australia of its subtropical type.

This walk is included to satisfy those people who wish to learn more about the plants they see as they walk other rainforest areas. Lyrebirds are present as are many other birds and there are also reportedly platypus in the Minnamurra River.

The Big Fig Rainforest Walk and a shorter Lyrebird Walk are linked to create a figure eight circuit, virtually all of which is on elaborate elevated walkways including suspension bridges and five river crossings.

Minnamurra Falls consist of two levels: the lower level is 50 m high and the upper 25 m. They are about 600 m upstream of the westernmost end of the elevated walkway. In November 1992 work had started on a walkway to these falls from the present walkway, so that in the future these lovely waterfalls will add interest to the present forest walk. Access to the falls has been closed for over two years, pending construction of the elevated walkway and falls viewing platform. The recommendation is that once accessible, the falls be visited in addition to completion of the Big Fig and Lyrebird circuits. The outing should prove educational to most visitors and if you can cast aside your yearning for wilderness then you will probably quite enjoy your visit.

MAP: Lands, 1:25,000 Kangaroo Valley (track detail not shown) and Map 60.
WALK: One day, 1.2 km, easy grade, last reviewed November 1992, no specific time.

61   DRAWING ROOM ROCKS

Drawing Room rocks are sandstone rocks that resemble actual-sized tables and chairs. They are on the rim of an escarpment. While seated on the 'chairs' you have one of the better coastal views in New South Wales. From an altitude of 600 m the panorama is of Nowra, Berry, Gerroa, the Shoalhaven River and the Pacific Coast.

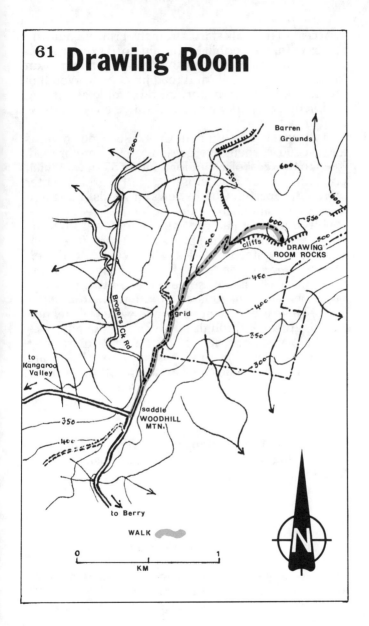

Barren Grounds

600

600

550

500

550

600

500

DRAWING ROOM ROCKS

cliffs

450

400

350

300

grid

Brogers Ck Rd

300

to Kangaroo Valley

350

400

saddle
WOODHILL MTN.

to Berry

WALK

0   1
KM

N

Access to the walk start is from the Princes Highway at Berry. Take Woodhill Mountain Road from the east end of the town of Berry northwards, about 6 km to a 350 m high saddle and road junction at Woodhill Mountain. Leave transport on the saddle as turning is difficult and parking space is scarce on the narrow road ahead.

Start walking on Brogers Creek Road northwards for just 200 m, then diverge right on to a minor road. Keep to the crest of a spur for another 550 m, at which point the minor road crosses a cattle grid to enter private property. Good views towards Kangaroo Valley are gained from this section of roadway. A well trodden foot pad can then be followed from the grid up the crest of the spur within forest. The track is not overly steep but rises significantly to Barren Grounds and the sandstone tops. As it climbs it leads along the west side of some bluffs a little, to a zig-zag which easily negotiates a route to the top of the bluffs. Thereafter, you need to follow the well defined but rough track through scrub as it gradually rises on to a plateau and swings to the right to arrive at the main escarpment rim. Drawing Room Rocks are seen to best advantage as you approach them. They are 1.5 km from where you left the road.

After a break at the cliff rim, return down the same routing.

MAP: Lands, 1:25,000 Kangaroo Valley and Map 61.
WALK: One day, 4.5 km, easy grade, last reviewed November 1992, allow 2¼ hours.

62   TALLOWA DAM

This virtually flat walk is to an escarpment rim high above the Shoalhaven River. The rim view includes the river gorge and upstream to Tallowa Dam at the

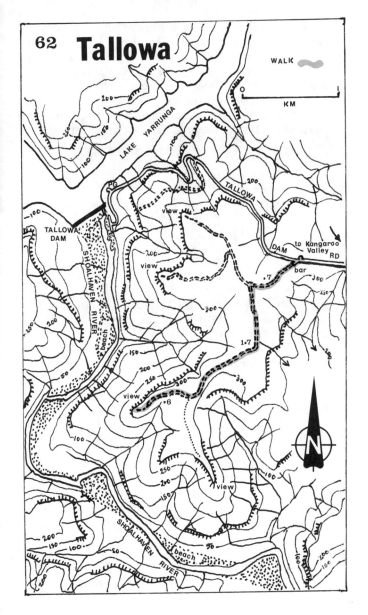

WALK

KM

LAKE YARRUNGA

200

150

100

PG

TALLOWA

view

200

TALLOWA DAM

view

200

to Kangaroo Valley RD

DAM

.7

bar

200

250

100

300

1.7

200

SHOALHAVEN RIVER

beach

150

200

250

300

200

view

.6

N

100

250

200

view

150

100

200

150

100

50

SHOALHAVEN RIVER

beach

50

200

150

100

50

200

100

180

confluence of the Shoalhaven and Kangaroo Rivers. Access is from Kangaroo Valley along Tallowa Dam Road westwards to 80 km speed limit signs which are 19.7 km from the Mossvale Road turn-off in Kangaroo Valley. Immediately west of the speed limit signs is a small road cutting and fire access road turn-off on the left of the cutting. Park above the cutting, opposite the start of the fire trail and its road barrier.

EUCALYPT

Set off south along the fire trail on part of the Brooks Plateau, amid fairly uninteresting scrub. After 700 m take the left fork south and simply follow it for 2.3 km to its end. As you progress, the plants and scenery become more interesting. The track gradually swings west to terminate on a sandstone bluff, and the last 500 m are quite attractive, with wildflowers and patches of bare sandstone. Boronia is one of the main plants present. From the end of the jeep track there is a foot pad off right and it gives almost immediate access to the escarpment rim, rocks and views.

A short scramble along the rocks on the rim westwards is scrubby but worthwhile. You gain better views of the river below, but the view to the dam is excellent without any scrub bashing. Lunch is recommended at the vantage point before retracing the route.

MAP: Lands, 1:25,000 Burrier and Map 62.
WALK: One day, 6 km, easy grade, last reviewed November 1992, allow 2¼ hours.

63 BOMADERRY CREEK

Adjacent to the Princes Highway bridges over the Shoalhaven River at Nowra is Bomaderry Creek. The creek has a catchment area of only about 22 square kilometres, yet just near its confluence with the Shoalhaven it has carved its way through a sandstone gorge with cliffs up to about 20 m high. The creek's volume of water, mainly from the Cambewarra Range, seems greater than might be expected for such a small catchment. Within the gorge there are a number of rock overhangs and ferny glens and along the rim there are several lookouts. A walking track system leads to all the main features and there is a principal track head and picnic area just 400 m from the Princes Highway. The towns of Nowra and Bomaderry are very close, but the gorge seems totally remote, with many lyrebirds and water dragons to be seen. Pleasingly, there is a remarkably low incidence of introduced weeds, unlike so many other bushland sites near towns.

Access to the walk start at the Weir Track head is via Narang Road, Bomaderry which leads west off the highway just north of the Nowra tourist information centre and 2 km north of the Shoalhaven River bridges.

Revegetation with such native plants as bottlebrush (Callistemon) has altered a former quarry site into a pleasant picnic spot and car park. Adjacent is a weir which dams the Bomaderry Creek waters. To best appreciate this walk an anti-clockwise circuit is suggested.

Cross the creek on stepping stones below the weir and walk the track downstream for 2.75 km via the western bank. About 1 km from the weir crossing you pass a bridge at Rock Crossing. At the lower end of the circuit there are two tiny bridges at She Oak Crossing. Toward the end of the 2.75 km stretch, as you near She Oak Crossing there are two short ladders which ease the climbing of some rock across the track.

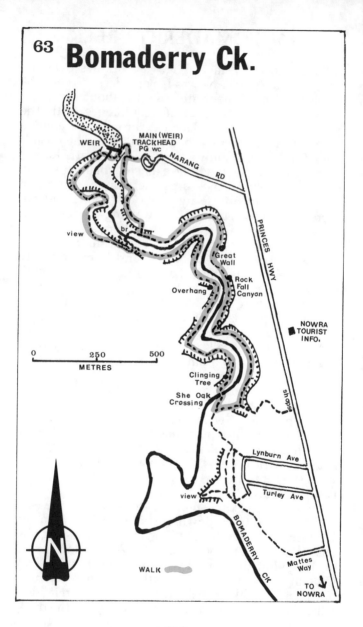

63 Bomaderry Ck.

WEIR

MAIN (WEIR)
TRACKHEAD
PG wc

NARANG RD

PRINCES HWY

view

br

Great
Wall

Rock
Fall
Canyon

Overhang

NOWRA
TOURIST
INFO.

0   250   500
METRES

Clinging
Tree

She Oak
Crossing

sh ape

Lynburn Ave

Turley Ave

view

BOMADERRY CK

N

WALK

Mattes
Way

TO
NOWRA

210

Watch for the remarkable Clinging Tree south of these ladders; a large spotted gum (*Eucalyptus maculata*) has grown on to a cliff face in a most unusual manner.

Cross the creek at She Oak Crossing to return upstream on the east bank. Rock Fall Canyon and the Great Wall are just two of the sandstone features that make this walk so appealing. It is 2.75 km back to the picnic area. As you progress, you pass two tracks off right, both of which lead up to the Princes Highway. You of course also need to bypass the left-fork Rock Crossing bridge during the upstream walk. Throughout the whole of the circuit the track routing varies and is aligned to be above the cliffs at times and to be within the gorge at others.

MAP: Lands, 1:25,000 Berry and Map 63.
WALK: One day, 5.5 km, easy grade family suitability, last reviewed November 1992, allow 2¼ hours.

64   JERVIS BAY BOTANIC GARDEN ANNEXE

Australia is a vast country. Its native flora is widely dispersed and it is important that a collection be assembled for research, identification, education and enjoyment. The Australian National Botanic Garden is principally in Canberra, but there is an annexe at Jervis Bay. Visitors to both gardens see the largest collection of Australian native plants in the world. There are more than 5500 species and a vast number of cultivars. The collection represents about one-third of all known Australian flowering plants, conifers and ferns. Certain parts of Australia are particularly rich in plant life; the Sydney sandstone basin has among the most diverse flora in the world. It nowhere near matches areas such as South Africa's Flynbos near Cape Town, but we can take great pride in our flora.

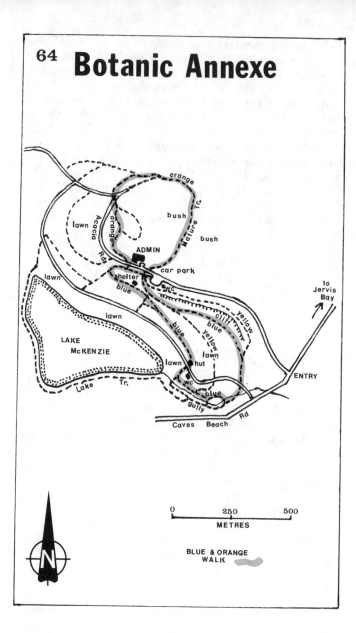

64 Botanic Annexe

orange

bush

Nature Tr.

lawn

Acacia Rd.

orange

bush

ADMIN

car park

lawn

shelter

blue

wc

lawn

cliff

yellow

to Jervis Bay

LAKE McKENZIE

lawn

blue

yellow

lawn

hut

lawn

ENTRY

Lake Tr.

wc

blue

gully

Caves Beach Rd.

0 250 500
METRES

N

BLUE & ORANGE WALK

212

The Jervis Bay annexe was established to allow the cultivation of frost-sensitive native flora in coastal conditions, more favourable than those of Canberra. The grounds cover nearly a square kilometre and include Lake McKenzie as a natural feature which also supplies the needed water. Most of the soils are sand dunes or sandstone outcrops. There are three colour-coded walking routes through the garden plus a Lake Trail which skirts the southern and western shore. The usual lawns and picnic sites are provided, but unlike Canberra with its background traffic noise, there is solitude and the sound of birds attracted to the nectar of so many plant species. Plant labelling in the beds is relatively good.

Access is from the Princes Highway south of Nowra, along Jervis Bay Road then south 2.1 km on Caves Beach Road to the entrance, some 43 km from Nowra. Entry is free and leaflets are available at the car park.

It is an excellent plan that undertakes at least the blue-coded and orange-coded circuits to complete a figure eight through the grounds. You should recognise many of the native plants seen elsewhere in the bush. The blue route is about 1 km long and the orange about 800 m.

A yellow-coded route is about 800 m long and the Lake Trail, including access, is about 2 km. The grounds are closed on Saturdays, Christmas Day and Good Friday only. A visit to the garden is both educational and enjoyable and you should gain a better appreciation of the flora seen during other walks.

MAP: Lands, 1:25,000 Sussex Inlet (limited use only) and Map 64.
WALK: One day, 1.8 km, easy grade, last reviewed November 1992, no specific time.

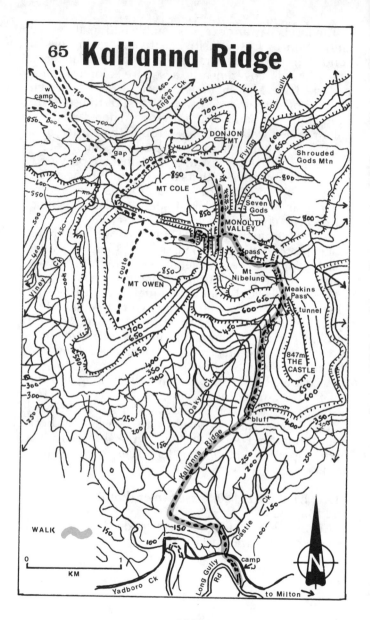

65 Kalianna Ridge

WALK

0   1
KM

N

214

65 KALIANNA RIDGE— MONOLITH VALLEY

The Monolith Valley section of the Budawangs is one of the best walking areas of New South Wales, but it is isolated and generally requires an overnight walk. Kalianna Ridge, however, provides access for agile people wanting to make a day trip. Access to Kalianna Ridge is from the Milton to Brooman and Nelligen road west up the Clyde Ridge Road 7.8 km to fork right for 4.4 km to the Pigeon House turnoff. Keep left at this fork and continue 9.5 km on Yadboro Road to cross the fork right off Long Gully Road on to Clyde River. Go on up around ridges 4.6 km then a dirt road on the Yadboro River flats. These flats are popular bush camping places and a suitable place to leave transport.

An old jeep track leads north-west along the south bank for 500 m to a ford across Yadboro River.

At the outset there is sometimes an obstacle in that the river can get quite deep and fast-flowing. If in doubt, do not take risks, but do carry bathers with a view to making a good attempt to see the wild places beyond. Usually, the water is no more than knee deep but it can be quite cold.

Head across this ford on to a foot track which at first leads along Castle Creek 300 m then rises up west on to Kalianna Ridge. The foot track is actually an overgrown jeep track and it then continues up the ridge crest. Some 3 km from Yadboro River the old jeep track ends below a bluff and some 320 m higher elevation than Yadboro River.

The bluff must then be scaled. There are three options. If proficient on bare rock, simply climb up the spur crest. An alternative is to chimney up a steep rocky ravine just left. The third option is to walk about 100 m to the left to locate a steep bypass around the main bluff. All three routes are difficult and great care is needed, especially if the rock is wet. Once past the bluff the rest of the ascent has no major obstacles.

Once on top, diverge left to contour north for 1 km along the base of massive cliffs. Boulders, ferns and a camp cave are passed as you pass under the towering Castle cliffs. You then enter Oaky Creek's upper valley and ascend steeply up slopes north-easterly. At cross foot tracks turn left to climb directly into forested Meakins Pass. (The alternatives at the cross tracks could interest anyone wishing to see a tunnel. One could climb straight up the slopes from the cross tracks to some cliffs, then walk east (right) 200 m to see the tunnel. From there one could double back, contour west, then descend a little into Meakins Pass.)

The pass marks the start of incredibly wild terrain and is 5 km from Yadboro Creek. A track leads off east to the Castle nearby, but another route, off north-west, leads to the beautiful Monolith Valley. The Castle climb is extremely rocky and exposed, requiring some degree of care. If time permits and the inclination exists, on the return walk you could try ascending the Castle, but it is better to see the wonderful Monolith Valley first, and this will be very time consuming.

From Meakins Pass, climb any of the several pads north-west. They soon join and lead up along the east side of more cliffs. The route continues under impressive cliff overhangs to a big ravine through the cliffs 400 m from the pass. There are a stream and cascade in the ravine and the track divides below the ravine. Climb the left-fork pad up through the ravine into wild, rocky terrain. A few steep sections must be negotiated before Nibelung Pass is reached about 1 km from Meakins Pass. Then the route gets easier and Monolith Valley can be explored. It will take at least three hours to climb the 6 km from Yadboro River to Nibelung Pass and about two hours to descend the route later.

Spend as much time in Monolith Valley as possible.

There are several tracks to enable exploration of huge chasms, cliffs and dome-shaped sandstone outcrops. Places such as the Seven Gods should not be missed. When time has passed, simply descend back to Yadboro River.

Walkers who are hesitant on rock should take about 10 m of rope to assist them over difficult parts of the route, such as any climbing of the Castle and perhaps for the bluff scaling and descending of the main Kalianna Ridge pad.

About 3 km of walking in Monolith Valley is perhaps ideal to see it well.

MAP: Lands, 1:25,000 Corang and Map 65.
WALK: One day, 15 km, hard grade, last reviewed November 1992, allow 8 hours.

66 AGGIE GAP—MOUNT AGGIE

The Brindabella Range along the western boundary of the A.C.T. is relatively close to Canberra. At Mount Aggie amid alpine surroundings it attains 1496 m altitude. In winter the area becomes snowbound but once the snow melts the plants grow rapidly and blossom in summer to make a carpet of colour. It is therefore best to time this walk for summer.

Access from Canberra is via Cotter Road and Brindabella Road to the A.C.T.–New South Wales border, then south along Mount Franklin Road on the range crest basically, for 17.6 km to Aggie Gap. An old jeep track along the border alignment links Aggie Gap and Mount Aggie direct, but the jeep track has been closed for much of its length for regeneration and to control erosion.

A walking track circuit has been installed to give access to Mount Aggie and this circuit has particular interest in that it leads through a stand of alpine ash trees as well as the more common snow gums.

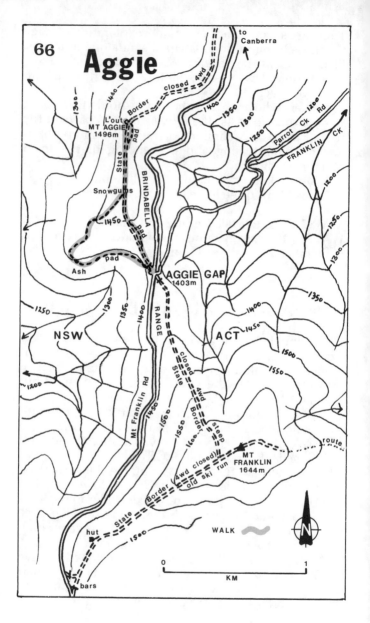

Head off west from Aggie Gap on the foot track. Soon the track descends into the alpine ash (*Eucalyptus delegatensis*) forest. The forest floor here is remarkable for its lack of plant understorey. Continue on the track and you pass out of the ash stand and ascend a spur among snow gums (*Eucalyptus pauciflora*). The spur climb is basically north-eastwards. When 1.6 km from the walk start, the old border jeep track is reached. Turn left uphill on the jeep track and, as the rocky top of Mount Aggie is neared, watch for the continuation of the foot track on the right. The foot track avoids a closed steep section of the jeep track by leading among gums close to the jeep track alignment. It reaches the top of Mount Aggie 550 m from where the jeep track was joined. The rocky summit permits good views westwards; masses of trigger plants and alpine everlastings can be seen there in season.

After a break on the hilltop retrace the 550 m down the foot and jeep tracks, then continue down the jeep track towards Aggie Gap. Again, watch for the foot track alignment off left to avoid the closed section of steeper jeep track ahead. Wander down the foot track to gain Aggie Gap within another 550 m. The last few metres are on the old jeep track and all of the 1.1 km descent route off Mount Aggie to Aggie Gap is within snow gums.

MAP: Lands, 1:25,000 Tidbinbilla and Map 66.
WALK: One day, 3.25 km, easy grade family suitability, last reviewed February 1992, allow 1½ hours.
Note: The district is snowbound in winter.

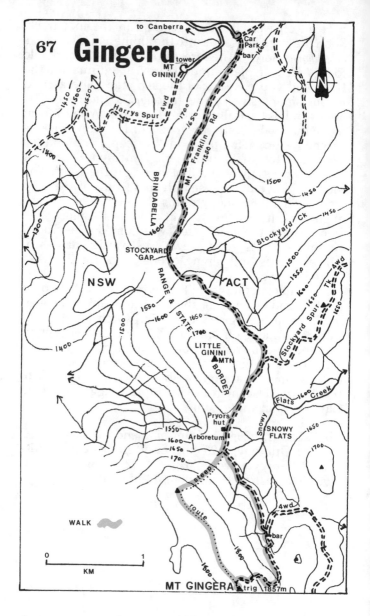

67 **Gingera**

to Canberra

Car Park
bar

MT GININI
tower

Harrys Spur

4wd

Mt Franklin Rd

BRINDABELLA

STOCKYARD GAP

NSW

RANGE & STATE

ACT

Stockyard Ck

Stockyard Spur Tk 4wd

LITTLE GININI MTN

BORDER

Pryors hut

Arboretum

Flats

Creek

Snowy

SNOWY FLATS

steep

route

WALK

0   1
KM

MT GINGERA trig 1857m

N

220

67 MOUNT GINGERA

The Brindabella Range west of Canberra has some lovely places to walk. The range rises to 1857 m above sea level at Mount Gingera and, as such, is quite alpine in its vegetation and receives regular snow falls in winter. The Mount Franklin Road provides access except, of course, when blocked by snow.

From Canberra you need to travel via the Cotter Road and Brindabella Road to the range top, then south past Bulls Run, and Aggie Gap to Mount Ginini, 21.5 km south of Piccadilly Circus. There is a radio link station on the summit of Mount Ginini. Some 600 m before the installation a lesser road forks off left to a car park and gate within 300 m.

This walk is within the Namadgi National Park in the A.C.T.

The first 2.9 km of the walk route are along the eastern slopes of 1763 m high Mount Ginini to Stockyard Gap. There are old, gnarled snow gums and a few wildflowers beside the road to hold your interest. Stockyard Gap has a small clearing on the west side of the road with a small dam in the clearing. You should next walk a further 1.4 km up around the north-eastern slopes of Little Ginini to a lovely grassy alpine saddle on the east side of the road. Minor Stockyard Spur jeep track leads off left at the saddle. Continue for another 700 m on the road to a saddle at the northern end of Mount Gingera. Pryors Hut (open) and some Scots pines are on the west side of the road. About 200 m past the hut, leave the jeep track and climb south-west, straight up through lovely grassy and flowering slopes to the north-western end of the elongated summit of the peak. The climb is over a distance of only about 600 m and the altitude difference is some 200 m. (The best spot to leave the jeep track is just east of a tiny creek so as to avoid scrub.)

Once on the top, there is easy walking for the rest of the day among alpine vegetation and the views are certainly unrivalled anywhere else near Canberra. Large areas are open and wild horses and feral pigs are sometimes seen grazing on the lush grasses. From the tops you can look down on Snowy Flats, an alpine plain immediately to the north of the peak and to the distant Cooleman Plains away to the south-west. Numerous far-off peaks can be seen, including much of the northern Kosciusko National Park. It is suggested you wander south-east along the summit and pick a spot for lunch. There is no water supply. The tops extend for about 1.2 km and culminate at a trig point at the south-east end where there are more views.

From the trig point, retrace 100 m to where you should locate a minor jeep track which services the trig area. The track should then be followed down, roughly east then north-west 1 km on to the Mount Franklin Road. The descent is most pleasant and through fine snow-gum slopes. Turn left at the Mount Franklin Road and walk north-west for 1.2 km so as to complete a circuit back to Pryors Hut and arboretum.

From here on, the route is simply a retrace of the outward route.

To really enjoy this walk it is essential to linger, to take particular notice of the alpine flowers and shrubs, the old gnarled snow gums, twisted by severe winters, and to admire the views. It is essentially a summer walk which needs fine weather. In mist or fog the trip would not be very enjoyable.

MAP: Lands, 1:25,000 Corin Dam and Map 67.
WALK: One day, 14 km, easy grade, last reviewed February 1992, allow 5½ hours.
Note: The area becomes snowbound in winter.

68   TINDERRY TWIN PEAK

The Tinderry Range south of Queanbeyan provides some quite hard walking, mostly over trackless and very rocky terrain. Tinderry Peak itself could only be regarded as a hard grade overnight trip without tracks. However, Tinderry Twin Peak (North Tinderry) can be reached on a day walk, provided essential map and compass experience is used. It is still a hard walk though. The summit is wild and boulder covered and reaches 1570 m. The walk should not be undertaken in fog or in bad weather when navigation could become a problem. Water should be carried, especially in hot weather.

Access is best from the Monaro Highway at Michelago then north-east along the minor Michelago to Queanbeyan road for about 8 km to Mount Allen fire trail start. Much of the distance to the peak can be covered using this and the West Tinderry fire trail for 4.75 km.

Start the walk at 810 m elevation at a locked gate. Then begin the long climb south-east for 3 km, rising to 1200 m at the junction of West Tinderry fire trail. The climb has several very steep sections and could be unpleasant in hot weather because of the sparse tree cover and exposure to the sun.

Next, turn left for 500 m of fairly level walking eastwards, followed by a resumption of climbing for 1.25 km, rising to 1350 m. This brings you to the crest of the jeep track. Another 1.75 km distance must be covered to the mountain top which can be seen from the track. Note the map position carefully and use a compass for the rest of the climb. Ensure that the fire trail is left at its very summit then scrub-bash in light scrub eastwards along the ridge crest. Keep to the highest ground for 500 m. Then, begin to climb around the south-west side of a hill which lies immediately north of Tinderry Twin Peak. The aim is to gain the saddle between the two peaks. Some bare rock assists passage but the pace will be slowed

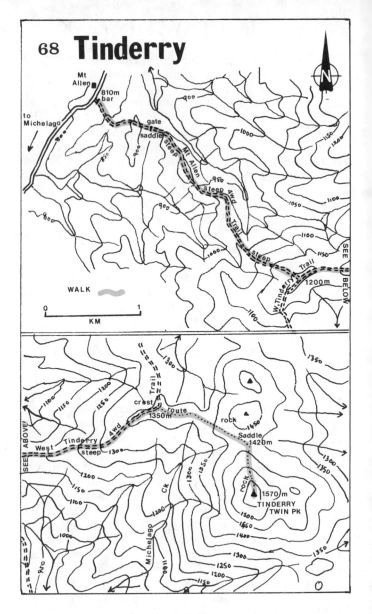

68 Tinderry

Mt Allen

810m
bar

to
Michelago

gate
saddle

steep

Mt Allen

steep

4wd

Trail

steep

W.Tinderry Trail

1200m

WALK

0   1
KM

SEE BELOW

crest Trail

1300

4wd

route

1350m

rock

West Tinderry

steep

Saddle
1420m

SEE ABOVE!

Michelago   Ck

rock

1570 m
TINDERRY
TWIN PK

224

Neds Beach, Lord Howe Island

Lagoon and Mount Eliza from Lovers Bay, Lord Howe Island

Lord Howe Island, View of North End Island from Summit of Gower

Wollomombi Gorge

by scrub and fallen timber. Feral pigs and goats frequent the saddle area which is 1 km from the fire trail and only 70 m higher, at 1420 m elevation. Alpine vegetation covers the whole of the tops and some of the snow gums have especially beautiful trunks.

Finally, turn south to ascend the final 150 m over 750 m to the rocky summit. The way is not easy. It involves some scrambling around and over boulders, and scaling bare, sloping rock. There is no trig point at the top. The best views are gained by climbing onto boulders. Some 2 km south Tinderry Peak looks most impressive with its huge rock faces.

To return, take particular care as you descend north to the saddle so as not to head off into scrub-choked valleys. Likewise, maintain the correct route as you sidle down to the fire trail. Once on the trail, retrace the upward route.

MAP: Lands, 1:25,000 Michelago and Tinderry sheets and Map 68.
WALK: One day, 13 km, hard grade, last reviewed February 1992, allow 5½ hours.

69   BADGERYS LOOKOUT— SHOALHAVEN RIVER

The Shoalhaven River near Marulan assumes grand proportions and has eroded a gorge about 500 m deep. The valley is quite steep-sided and winding, but the river bed is relatively broad with lovely, sandy beaches and delightful camping spots. It provides endless possibilities for swimming, fishing, sun-baking, climbing, photography and even floating about on airbeds. The catch is that to return from the river you must ascend 500 m. Most people are deterred by the climb so you could have a paradise virtually to yourselves.

Shoalhaven

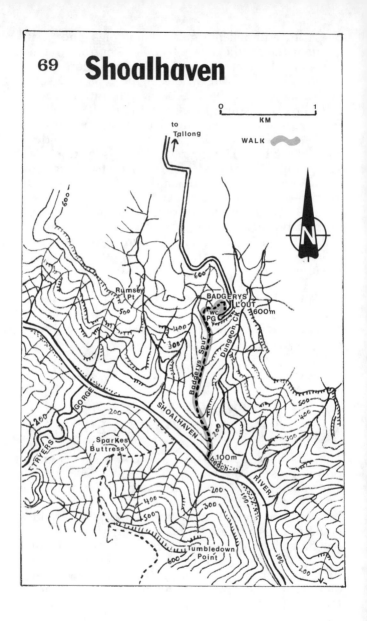

to Tallong

WALK

0   1
KM

N

Rumsey Pt

BADGERYS L'OUT
WC
PG
600m

Badgerys Spur

Dungeon Ck

ST RIVERS GORGE

SHOALHAVEN

600

500

400

300

200

100m

Sparkes Buttress

beach

RIVER

200

300

400

500

600

Tumbledown Point

100

200

Some 7 km south of Tallong railway station, a small town on the main southern railway, is Badgerys Lookout. It is a little-visited lookout on the gorge rim. There are several other places where one could descend to the river by foot track but this route is the shortest and hence the steepest. It is only 2.5 km from the lookout to the riverside.

Rock climbers frequent the cliffs just west of the lookout and its picnic facilities. A pad leads west to these cliffs. Take care to start the walk on a lesser track which leads north from midway between the toilets and the picnic table at the west end of the car park. The correct track starts by leading north down into a gully, then turns west to follow that gully and swings south right around the western end of the knob on which the lookout is situated. It then sidles on to Badgerys Spur and descends generally southwards to the river. Despite the short distance involved, you should allow well over an hour for the steep, slow climb out later.

MAP: Lands, 1:25,000 Caoura and Map 69.
WALK: One day, 5 km, medium grade, last reviewed October 1992, allow 2½ hours.

70   LONG POINT—SHOALHAVEN RIVER—BUNGONIA GORGE

The Shoalhaven River has eroded a gorge 500 m deep near Marulan. At a number of places sidestreams, such as Ettrema and Bungonia creeks, have carved impressive ravines on their way to the mighty Shoalhaven. This walk suggestion, like other overnight recommendations in this book, must surely be one of New South Wales' best walks. The Shoalhaven has lovely, white, sandy beaches and camping places and Bungonia Gorge would probably rank as one of the

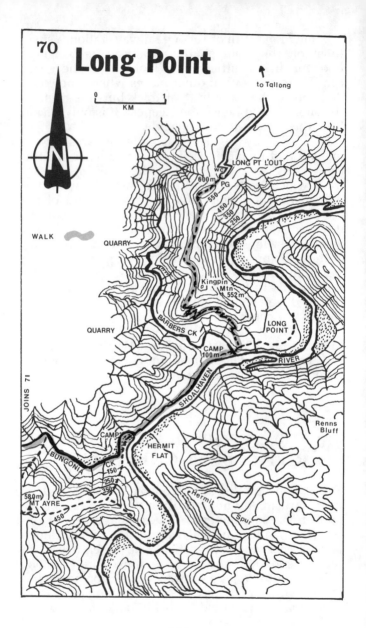

70 **Long Point**

to Tallong

0   1
KM

N

WALK

QUARRY

LONG PT L'OUT
WC
600m
PG
550
450
350
250

Kingpin
Mtn
552m

QUARRY

BARBERS CK

LONG
POINT

CAMP
100m

RIVER

SHOALHAVEN

JOINS 71

CAMP

BUNGONIA

CK
150
250
350

HERMIT
FLAT

Renns
Bluff

580m
MT AYRE

450

Hermit

Spur

most rugged anywhere in Australia. Take your bathers, a lightweight airbed for floating about on the river and a bath towel (rather than a huge beach towel).

Long Point Lookout, 5.7 km south of the small town of Tallong on the main southern railway, is perhaps the easiest place from which to descend to the Shoalhaven as the track is well graded. The track leads off south-west from the lookout car park which has picnic facilities and tank water. At first the pad is on a sharply defined spur and then leads down south into a saddle nearby.

Kingpin Mountain, which is really just part of the Long Point Spur, is then skirted via its western and southern slopes. There are a couple of minor uphill grades to cross gullies and there are a number of zig-zags before the track emerges at the confluence of Barbers Creek and the Shoalhaven River, some 4 km from the car park. Most of the way is well graded.

While the area near the bottom of the track is very pleasant, it is suggested that you follow the river's north bank upstream for 2 km to the mouth of Bungonia Creek. Along the way there are magnificent sandy beaches and perfect swimming places, so it is suggested that you linger and enjoy it.

On those rare occasions when the river is high it may be necessary to walk amid light scrub and keep above the river level in one locality. At the mouth of Bungonia Creek there are sand and swimming places as well as a lovely grass camping place. It is suggested that you establish camp there and, after lunch, set off without packs and, preferably, in just bathers and sandshoes (providing it is warm enough) up Bungonia Creek. At first it is easy walking, simply following the stream bed, beaches and minor south bank pad. But, in 2 km, you reach the start of the canyon area at Troy Walls. On the way, there are signs warning of quarry blasting nearby at certain times. Naturally, you should heed those warnings.

From Troy Walls upstream, the scenery is breath-

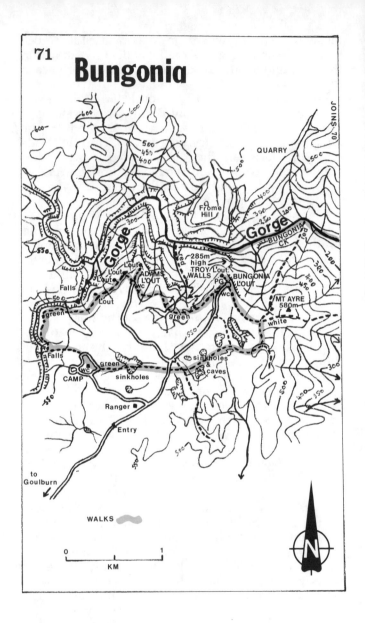

71

Bungonia

QUARRY

Frome
Hill

Gorge

Gorge

BUNGONIA
CK

600

500
450
600

500

550

300

285m
high
TROY
WALLS

L'out

ADAMS
L'OUT
wc

L'out

L'out

Falls

L'out

L'out

L'out

BUNGONIA
L'OUT

PG
wc

MT AYRE
580m

300

200

300

250

200

green

red

300

200

300

450

550

green

white

500

Falls

green

wc

300

sinkholes

sinkholes
&
caves

CAMP

Ranger

Entry

500

450

350

350

400

550

500

500

to
Goulburn

WALKS

0   1

KM

JOINS 70

N

taking and the walking becomes far more difficult. Huge boulders slow progress. Aim to get right into the canyon, to obtain a good appreciation of this incredible place before returning to camp in the idyllic gorge.

Next day you should return to the base of Long Point Spur by about mid-afternoon. Lunch can be somewhere by the river, and plenty of time can be spent swimming and floating about on that airbed. If the weather is cooler, you could take a stroll upstream along the Shoalhaven beyond Bungonia Creek or wander along the lovely grassy flats downstream from the base of the Long Spur. When you must leave this paradise, allow plenty of time for the climb back out to Long Spur Lookout. Wet that towel and use it to wipe your face and keep you cool as you ascend.

MAP: Lands, 1:25,000 Caoura and Map 70.
WALK: Two days, 18 km (day one 12 km and day two 6 km), medium grade, last reviewed October 1992, allow day one 6 hours and day two 2¾ hours.

71   BUNGONIA TOPS

South-east of Goulburn is Bungonia Caves at a belt of limestone rock close to the Shoalhaven River. There are a number of limestone caves, although none is tourist orientated.

The Shoalhaven River has eroded a truly massive valley and its tributary Bungonia Creek which descends through the limestone belt, has one of Australia's most spectacular gorges, with sheer cliffs up to 285 m high. This gorge though is 500 m deep and this walk is a circuit which visits all the main features without actually descending into the gorge.

Access from Goulburn is south-east to the tiny

settlement of Bungonia, then some 9 km further, north-east. Good camping and picnic facilities are provided and there is a network of walking tracks linking the camp ground with the caves and lookouts. Some of the tracks are colour coded for ease of navigation. The green-coded circuit is the recommended route of this walk. For convenience, the walk is based on the camp area which is just to the north once the park is entered. A small fee is payable for entry to the park.

From the north-western edge of the camp area, take the green-coded track westwards down among fairly sparse eucalypt forest for 600 m to Bungonia Creek. This starts a clockwise circuit. In the creek vicinity the track turns north from near a cascade to begin following close to the rim of the gorge through which the creek tumbles. There are views across the still shallow gorge to a rock formation called the Devils Pulpit. After another 1.4 km, at Jerrara Lookout, the view from the track begins to become awe-inspiring as the creek cuts deeper and deeper. Jerrara Falls can be seen across the gorge but Bungonia Falls are out of sight far below. Some 200 m onwards you should reach a picnic area and shelter at the end of a road. Take the 400 m return side trip north to Adams Lookout from the road end to see the amazing view of Bungonia Canyon downstream. The panorama is eastwards, over some of the most rugged terrain imaginable.

Back at the road end, continue along the green-coded track another 1.25 km, passing Mass Cave Track off left midway and joining the red-coded track from the canyon a little later. Bungonia Lookdown is then reached. It is perhaps the most magnificent of the views and includes the Shoalhaven River. Again, there is a picnic area and shelter at a road end.

Head south-east on the combined green, red and white codes track for 500 m, then at a saddle and cross foot tracks, turn south (right) to retain the green code only. The other routes lead to the gorges. After

350 m turn west (right) to begin the westward walk via several sinkholes and caves back to the camp 1.9 km away. You pass near Hogans, Drum and Grill Caves. Then, after 1.1 km you cross a road.

For most of the distance sparse eucalypt forest predominates but as you near the camp the track passes through a pleasant grassy basin of another sinkhole area.

MAP: Lands, 1:25,000 Caoura and Bungonia sheets (foot tracks not shown) and Map 71.
WALK: One day, 6.7 km, easy grade, last reviewed October 1992, allow 3 hours.

BANKSIA

72 GIBBERGUNYAH

This delightful bushland tract, complete with lyrebirds and ferny ravine, seem surprisingly little known, yet is close to the towns of Mittagong and Bowral. What is known as Glen Link Track is especially attractive and peaceful. There is a colour-coded network of jeep tracks and foot tracks through

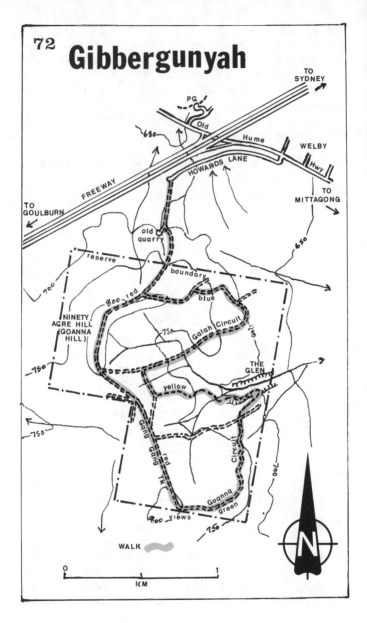

72

Gibbergunyah

TO SYDNEY

PG

Old

650

Hume

WELBY

Hwy

FREEWAY

HOWARDS LANE

TO MITTAGONG

TO GOULBURN

old quarry

reserve

boundary

650

700

800 red

blue

NINETY ACRE HILL (GOANNA HILL)

750

Galah Circuit

760

THE GLEN

750

yellow

750

Gang Gang Tk

red

Circuit

760

Goanna

Green

800 views

750

WALK

N

0   1

KM

the bushland, and this suggestion follows the best of them. The area is on the Mittagong Range and within the headwaters of Gibbergunyah Creek. During the walk there are views of nearby Mount Gibraltar (the Gib) and Bowral.

To reach the walk start you need to take Howards Lane, Welby. This road parallels the Hume Freeway westwards from where the freeway crosses over the old Hume Highway west of Welby. Leave transport 800 m along Howards Lane where it turns south to leave the freeway. To travel further is very rough and turning is awkward. Regrettably though, the start of the walk then becomes a short road bash uphill and with a sometimes hot north aspect. However, the bushland is not far away.

Walk up the rough lane to pass an old quarry and to steeply ascend past a sign on a spur. A display map there of the track system is somewhat inaccurate and of the yellow-coded track system is quite wrong.

About 1 km from the walk start the crest of the range is gained, the freeway noise is left behind and the sounds of birds predominate. A clockwise circuit is suggested once the hill has been climbed. First, turn hard left on to the blue-coded jeep track. The aim is to use the blue Galah Track to gain access to the yellow Glen Link Track. This involves descending eastwards then turning back south-west over a ridge and across a damp forested creek gully and up to a junction of jeep tracks 1.6 km away. From there, walk south 300 m (left turn), then turn east (left again) down the yellow coded Glen Link foot track. For 1 km you then wander down forested slopes with many wildflowers and birds to hold your attention. Lyrebirds seem quite common. The Glen is the highlight of the walk. It has sandstone cliffs and many ferns, plus a seat upon which to sit and listen to the myriad birds. Take a break or have lunch in the Glen.

From the ravine the track turns sharply up a spur crest in an area that is excellent for wildflowers. Then, within 300 m, it reaches the green-coded Goanna Circuit jeep track and a seat. To continue, walk the green-coded route clockwise south then west, up to the ridge top 1.2 km away via more forest and to where there are views to Bowral and the Bowral Country Club. Some houses abut the bushland at the spot.

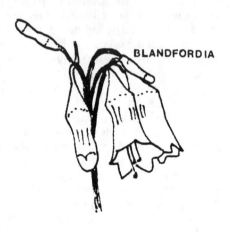

BLANDFORDIA

The red-coded Gang Gang Track should then be followed north-west along the range top for 1.6 km through sparse forest and good wildflower country. During this 1.6 km stretch avoid tracks off right and left to maintain the tops. The circuit is then completed and you need to descend north 1 km to Howards Lane, retracing the earlier route.

MAP: Lands, 1:25,000 Mittagong (Howards Lane and some tracks not shown) and Map 72.
WALK: One day, 8 km, easy grade, last reviewed November 1992, allow 3¼ hours.

INLAND REGION (SOUTHERN)

73   WEDDIN MOUNTAIN RANGE

Near the mid-west town of Grenfell are the Weddin Mountains, a largely undeveloped forested range amid vast agricultural lands. Near the north-west end of the range there are two walking tracks. One track leads to bushranger Ben Hall's cave, and the other, a longer track, ascends to the top of the range from the western end of Holy Camp Road. Peregrine Lookout is passed during the ascent to a trig point known as Eualdrie trig. (National Park literature and signs include an extra 'R' in the name Euraldrie, seemingly incorrectly.) The Weddin Range rises about 350 m above the surrounding farmlands so that views are a feature of the suggested walk.

From Grenfell, turn west off the Barmedman Road 1 km out of town, then travel west via Holy Camp Road for 14 km to a picnic area at the road end. Toilets and fireplaces are provided. Most of the distance is on sealed road. The walking track ahead is rocky underfoot and sturdy footwear is necessary. A disused eroded logging track is followed west from the picnic area at the start.

Head off uphill through sparse forest of native cypress (Callitris) and ironbark to an isolated sandstone block known as Ben Halls Rock. The track then leads into a gully where the vegetation changes to include ferns. This is the head of Carabagel Creek where boulders need to be skirted and where rocky terrain ensures more difficult walking. Soon, the track rises to the left out of the gully and leads on to a spur crest. A 50 m long side track forks off left on the spur to Peregrine Lookout, an outcrop of rock from which there are good views to the farmlands below. Already, about 180 m elevation has been gained from the car park over a distance of 1.5 km. Peregrine falcons can sometimes be seen in the lookout vicinity.

73

Weddin Mtns.

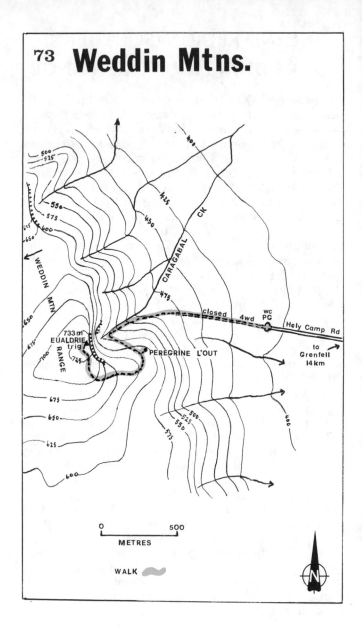

WALK

238

From the viewing point, the track gradually rises through stringybark forest and through an area prolific with wildflowers in spring. It is a more gentle slope than that below Peregrine Lookout and avoids the steep terrain and cliffs east of Eualdrie trig by curving in a semi-circle to approach the trig cairn from the south. It is 750 m between the two lookouts and a further 133 m elevation is gained to reach 733 m. A rocky outcrop at the trig provides a view similar in aspect to Peregrine Lookout but is more commanding due to added height. Vegetation includes many wattles (acacias), but prevents any significant views westwards. Return using the same track system.

MAP: Lands, 1:50,000 Marsden (no track shown) and Map 73.
WALK: One day, 4.5 km, easy grade, last reviewed July 1992, allow 2½ hours.

74 WOOLSHED FALLS AND BLUFF

The Cocoparra Range north of Griffith is a good district for adventurous walkers who enjoy exploration of wild places in rugged terrain and with virtually no foot tracks. Use of map and compass results in the locating of many interesting and scenic features in a dry inland situation where the vegetation is sufficiently sparse to enable fairly easy penetration. One gets a real feeling of outback Australia, reinforced by the presence of the old Whitton Stock Route immediately adjacent to the western edge of the range. The range consists of very ancient tilted and uplifted sedimentary rock with subsequent erosion creating gorges and cliffs. Creeks in the range rarely flow, so walkers need to carry water. Given the distance from most settled areas in New South Wales,

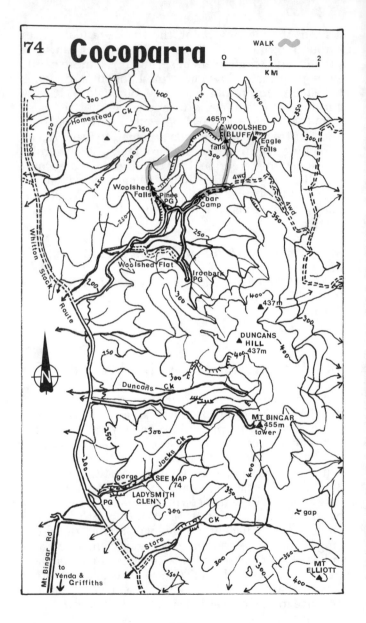

74

Cocoparra

WALK ～

0 1 2
KM

465m
WOOLSHED BLUFF
Eagle Falls
falls

Homestead Ck

Whitton Stock Route

Woolshed Falls
Pines PG
4wd
bar Camp
4wd

Woolshed Flat
Ironbark PG

437m

N

DUNCANS HILL
437m

Duncans Ck

MT BINGAR
455m
tower

Jacks Ck

gorge   SEE MAP 74
LADYSMITH GLEN

PG

Ck

Store

MT ELLIOTT

gap

Mt Bingar Rd

to Yenda & Griffiths

a good option is to camp in an area provided at Woolshed Flat. Toilets and fireplaces are provided.

Access is best from the Murrumbidgee Irrigation Area town of Yenda northwards some 22 km via Myall Park Road, Mount Bingar Road and the Whitton Stock Route. Woolshed Flat has a camp ground plus two picnic areas at The Pines and at Ironbark picnic area. Each is serviced by short roads from the stock route.

While there are many possible routes for walks the most interesting seems to be a circuit from The Pines picnic area. It is the first picnic spot after leaving the stock route and is only 250 m from (usually dry) Woolshed Falls.

The main feature in this dry rocky locality is a cliffline from Woolshed Falls to Woolshed Bluff. The cliffs are up to 50 m high and extend right across the northern side of Woolshed Flat. The sparse trees are mainly native cypress, yellow box and red gum. Kangaroos are common and there is an abundance of bird life, especially parrots.

Set off with map and compass on the foot track for 250 m to Woolshed Falls via the creek gully area. There are three sets of falls. From the first, climb up among rocks to the right of the falls then follow the creek gully up to the two upper falls. At each set of falls a little easy scrambling is needed to get above rock. The cliffs adjacent to the falls are low but become higher and higher as you walk north-eastwards.

Follow the creek gully among sparse scrub and native cypress. In spring, you will see wildflowers and orchids. About 600 m from the walk start, proceed due east some 300 m to the cliff rim area. Acacias will be seen during the climb. The cliff tops can then be used as a navigation guide and followed among rocks and scrub north-east 1.4 km, then south-east 500 m, until Woolshed Bluff is attained. There are good views over most of the distance.

Next, it is best to walk north-east about 300 m so that a steep descent down through cliffs can be made off Woolshed Bluff. Once below the cliffs an adjacent gully can be followed 1.4 km downstream. In following the gully another dry waterfall is seen. Then eventually the gully has a confluence with a main valley creek bed. There is a jeep track adjacent to the south side of this main creek. Turn right and walk the jeep track 500 m to a road barrier. Then continue on the road as it passes through the Woolshed Flat camp area and within 1 km returns you to The Pines picnic area. Just 400 m before the walk end, the road to Ironbark picnic area will be seen leading off to the left.

MAP: Lands, 1:50,000 Lake Wyangan and Map 74.
WALK: One day, 6 km, easy grade (but with good navigation skills needed). Walk last reviewed May 1992, allow 2½ hours.
Note: At the height of summer this walk is probably best avoided because of heat.

75   JACKS CREEK

The Cocoparra National Park north of Griffith contains some delightful walking areas that are quite distinctive. One gains the feeling of the great Australian outback, of distance, space and vivid colours. Cocoparra is a dry region, largely covered with native cypress trees. The terrain is rocky, being influenced geologically by fault lines and the subsequent erosion over millennia of tilted and uplifted sedimentary rocks. Where it descends off the western side of the Cocoparra Range on to the adjacent plains Jacks Creek has eroded a gorge known as Ladysmith Glen. It is interesting that Jacks Creek rarely flows yet has eroded a gorge with cliffs up to 44 m high.

Best access is from the Murrumbidgee Irrigation Area town of Yenda northwards 15 km via Myall Park

75

Jacks Creek

LADYSMITH GLEN

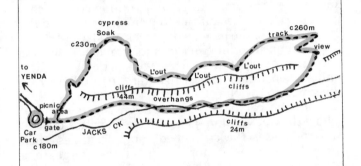

cypress
Soak

c230m

track c260m

view

L'out

to
YENDA

L'out

L'out

cliffs

cliffs
44m

overhangs

picnic
area

gate

Car
Park
c180m

JACKS CK

cliffs
24m

SEE MAP 74
FOR SURROUNDING
RANGES

0   500

METRES

WALK

Cocoparra Range

243

Road and Mount Bingar Road. The Jacks Creek watershed drains the western slopes of Mount Bingar. A 300 m long roadway leads into a picnic area and car park from the Whitton Stock Route to service the lower end of Ladysmith Glen. From it there is a 2.5 km circuit foot track in the gorge and along the dry tops north of the gorge. The track is well defined and informative signs and seats have been placed along the route. Yellow box, red gum, white cypress and kurrajong trees are the main species, and kangaroos are common. There are three constructed lookouts along the cliff rim to provide views into the gorge. Despite the usually dry creek and lack of pools, frogs live in the cliff crevices and manage to survive between creek flows. The walk circuit is best undertaken anti-clockwise to minimise the climb from the gorge to the cliff rim.

From the car park, pass through a gateway and follow the track east up Jacks Creek. The track crosses and re-crosses the creek bed some six times, then ascends out of the north side of the gorge to a viewpoint. Thereafter the track zig-zags, then begins the return westwards along the tops. The three constructed lookouts are serviced by the track and are passed before the pad diverges from the cliff tops to cross to a nearby spot known as the Soak. Clearly there must be more underground water in this locality than elsewhere, as the adjacent trees grow far more vigorously. There is a seat at the soak. Finally, the track descends south-west through the picnic area fireplaces to the gateway and car park.

MAP: Lands, 1:50,000 Lake Wyangan and maps 74 and 75.
WALK: One day, 2.5 km, easy grade family suitability, last reviewed May 1992, allow one hour.

The red gum forests along the Murrumbidgee and Murray Rivers provide a distinctive type of walking sometimes overlooked by walkers. At Barooga, the Murray River is broad and mature with white sand beaches. Bullanginya Lagoon (Barooga Creek) forms an anabranch of the main river system. The resulting forested island has billabongs and reed beds and attracts a lot of waterbirds. The forest is pre-dominantly magnificent red gums (*Eucalyptus camaldulensis*). Kangaroos and emus are plentiful. A minor forestry road stretches 9 km across the length of the island and has three short lateral roads leading to beaches. The ideal time for a walk is in summer when the beaches hold special appeal. The rest of the year is good, too.

Access to the island is from the Barooga to Cobram (Victoria) river crossing. There are two gateways off the causeway about midway between the two towns. The westernmost entry has a better road surface and starts just 300 m on the New South Wales side of the Murray River. Take this road north for 400 m to where the other entry road links, then drive a further 700 m to another road junction. Parking is easy. The roads may be impassable after a lot of rain, especially further into the forest.

The suggestion is that the left fork road be walked south-west 300 m to the banks of the Murray River, then that the road be followed basically west another 500 m to a small beach at a river bend. Across the river you see the popular beach and tourist spots in Cobram. Next, the river bank should be walked. There are cattle pads in places and tracks elsewhere but be prepared to cross grass and dodge trees in the sparse forest. After 2 km a second, better beach is reached. On again another 1.5 km is a third even nicer beach. This could be a good spot for a break if desired.

The river bank should next be followed another

Barooga Forest

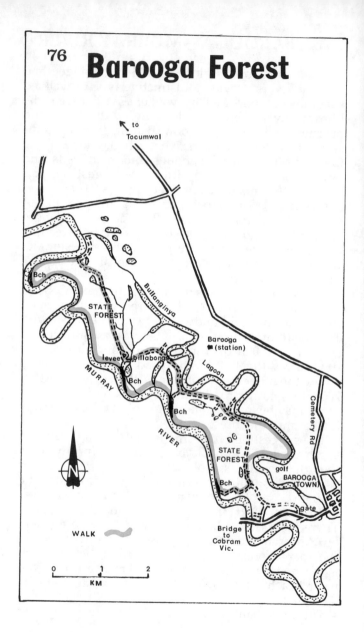

to
Tocumwal

Bullanginya

STATE
FOREST

Barooga
(station)

Lagoon

levee billabongs

MURRAY

Bch

Bch

RIVER

STATE
FOREST

golf

Bch

BAROOGA
TOWN

Cemetery Rd

gate

Bridge
to
Cobram
Vic.

WALK

0   1   2
KM

4.5 km, passing remote beaches to then gain the island forestry road near the north end of the island. This is a good camp location if you wish to convert this day walk to an overnight outing. It is advisable to carry mosquito repellent if camping though.

To begin the return route it is best to follow the road back through the forest for 5.8 km so as to see bird life at several billabongs. At two points the road abuts Bullanginya Lagoon, and at the 5.8 km stage the lagoon is again alongside. Next, leave the road to follow the lagoon edge 2.2 km south-eastwards then back west till you reach a sharp bend in the lagoon. Head 200 m west into the forest away from the lagoon to regain the forestry road, then turn left and go south 500 m on the road, to the end of the walk circuit.

MAP: Lands, 1:50,000 Tocumwaal and Map 76.
WALK: One day, 17.5 km, medium grade, last reviewed May 1992, allow 6 hours. Walk can be converted to an easy overnight trip if desired.
Note: The entire route is on river flood plain and on rare occasions the walk therefore may need to be abandoned due to flooding.

77 CAMPBELLS ISLAND

Near the small Riverina town of Barham there is a bridge over the Little Murray River to Campbells Island. The Little Murray is an anabranch of the broad Murray River. The resulting Campbells Island is within a large red gum forest on the river flood plains. From the bridge, Campbells Island Road services the island forests and is useful for walkers. The bridge is 8.7 km north-west of Barham via North Barham Road for 4 km then west on Cappiellos Lane 1.5 km to enter the forest. Little Murray Road should then

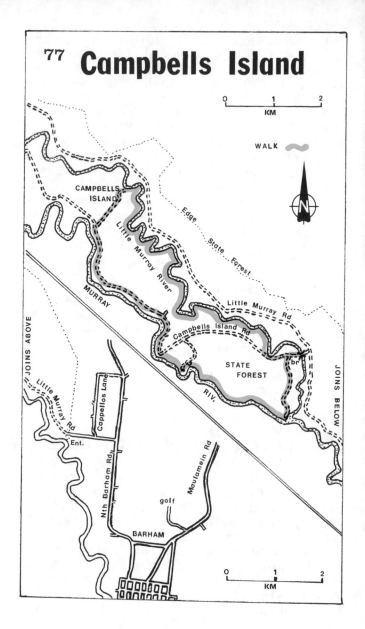

77 # Campbells Island

WALK

CAMPBELLS ISLAND

Edge State Forest

Little Murray River

MURRAY

Little Murray Rd

JOINS ABOVE

Little Murray Rd

Coppellos Lane

Campbells Island Rd

STATE FOREST

br

JOINS BELOW

RIV.

Ent.

Nth Barham Rd

Maulamein Rd

golf

BARHAM

0   1   2
KM

0   1   2
KM

be followed 3.2 km north-west and north to suitable car parking spots.

The recommendation is to take a circuit walk from the bridge via the banks of the Murray River, returning along the banks of the Little Murray River. A 1.2 km stretch of road can be used to cross the flood plain between the two rivers near the farthest point. Over half the circuit is without tracks or roads but grassy places and lack of significant forest understorey improve progress. Beaches along the Murray are an added attraction, especially in summer when swimming may appeal. By walking clockwise, navigation is easier and the walk duration time can be better judged as you proceed.

Head off over the bridge and for 300 m west, then turn south to walk a side road for 1.5 km to the junction of the Murray and the Little Murray. This confluence is a pleasant place featuring river vistas. Next, follow the banks of the broader Murray River north-west for 2.3 km to gain a second side road. There are no tracks to follow for this section but animals have created pads in spots. Turn left along the road till it ends 300 m later at a bend in the river. This bend is a recognised camp locality.

Continue north-west along the river bank for 700 m. The main Campbells Island Road should then be reached where it abuts the Murray for the first time after crossing the island from the walk starting point. The road then closely follows the Murray for 4 km north and north-west. The road, the river bank, or a combination of the two can then be walked for 3.7 km to reach the walk turn-around point. Several camp spots are passed along the way. The walk could be converted to an overnight trip if you desire. Any of these camp places could be used. Mosquito repellent should be carried if staying overnight.

Cross the island on the 1.2 km long side road which leads off north-east so as to reach the banks of the Little Murray 10 km from the walk start. Kangaroos seem more common at this end of the island.

Turn right to follow the banks of the Little Murray. Again there is no foot track but animal pads assist passage. Fallen tree branches typical of red gum country hinder progress a little but overall walking is easy. Waterbirds seem to be in greater numbers on the Little Murray than the Murray. To walk close to the river for the whole of the distance back to the bridge and end of circuit is 8.5 km, given the meandering nature of the river. The last 600 m is probably best undertaken using Campbells Island Road which is close to the banks. Much of the meandering is within the first 4 km so if you want to shorten the journey then this 4 km section offers the best opportunities. The magnificent old trees, animals and waterbirds will, however, probably induce most walkers to complete the full distance and not short-cut river bends.

MAP: Lands, 1:50,000 Barham and Map 77.
WALK: One day, 18.5 km, medium grade, last reviewed May 1992, allow 6½ hours.
Note: The entire walk region is on river flood plain and on rare occasions flooding may require the walk to be abandoned.

78   HUME AND HOVELL TRACK—
BURRA CREEK

As part of Australia's 1988 Bicentennial celebrations the long-distance Hume and Hovell Walking Track was established to commemorate the journey of explorers Hamilton Hume and William Hovell. Their party travelled from Sydney overland in the summer of 1824–25 to the present-day site of Geelong, Victoria. The commemorative track roughly follows the route of the explorers and near Tumbarumba leads down-stream along Burra Creek to Tumbarumba Creek. At

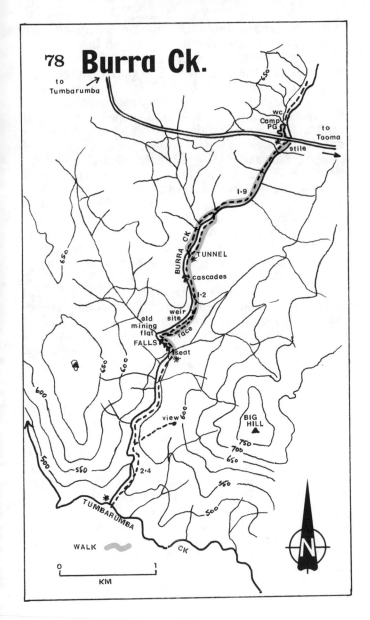

78 **Burra Ck.**

to Tumbarumba

to Tooma

wc
Camp
PG

stile

1·9

BURRA CK.

TUNNEL

cascades

1·2

weir site

race

old mining flat

FALLS

seat

view

BIG HILL

750
700
650

650
600

600
550

500

2·4

TUMBARUMBA

WALK

CK

0   KM   1

N

the time of the expedition, Hume, an Australian-born man, was aged just twenty-seven and English-born Hovell was thirty-eight. Six convicts travelled with and assisted the explorers. The party climbed the slopes of nearby Big Hill and saw the snow-capped main range of the Snowy Mountains. First settlement by squatters running sheep and cattle came straight after the explorers, so that for some years thereafter the district was a pastoral region.

The Tumbarumba goldfield was, however, proclaimed in 1866 and this extended to Burra Creek by 1872. The Tumbarumba to Tooma road now passes across the Burra Creek goldfield and the road is surrounded by former alluvial workings. The creek has been altered by dams, water races and a tunnel and the field was still worked as late as the 1930s. Considerable alluvial tin was won during the gold-rush period.

Where the Tumbarumba to Tooma road crosses Burra Creek 8.5 km south-east of Tumbarumba, Henry Angel Flat picnic and camp area has been established on the north side of the road. Henry Angel was one of the six convicts in the Hume and Hovell party. Downstream along Burra Creek, south of the road, land has been reserved and the long distance track leads 5.5 km in the reserve to the confluence with Tumbarumba Creek. The reserve is unfenced so stock graze on the reserve and adjacent farmland.

It is suggested that a walk be taken from the picnic and camp spot for 3.1 km to the base of a set of three waterfalls which were described in Hovell's journal. Burra Creek loses 100 m altitude from the base of the third waterfall to Tumbarumba Creek so the falls base is a convenient turn-around point.

Cross a stile on to pasture from the south side of the road opposite the picnic and camp area, then follow the track down the west bank. Willows and some prunus trees line Burra Creek in former swamp lands. When 1.2 km south of the road, look for rocks placed by gold miners to shore up the stream banks.

Just downstream, a channel was blasted through granite to drain the upstream swamp and facilitate alluvial gold mining. The rock shoring was needed to stop erosion as the swamp drained. The channel can be seen where the walking track divides and leads along both banks temporarily. There is a 70 m long man-made tunnel 1.9 km south of the road. Tunnel entry and exit viewing platforms have been constructed for walkers. These platforms are on either side of the creek and the tracks rejoin above the tunnel and continue on down the east bank. The tunnel, like the upstream channel, was built to lower the creek bed and drain the swamp.

Continuing downstream, the creek begins to descend more rapidly and cascades are passed within 400 m. A small weir is seen next. It was built to divert creek water into a flood raceline to supply water for gold panning downstream. The track divides again at the weir so that one route is beside the creek while the other follows the old raceline a few metres higher up the slopes. The creek makes a sharp turn from south-west to south-east next, and at the bend there are a lot of tailings where rock was dumped after treatment. There was an old mining flat across the creek at the bend and the tracks converge at the bend too. The track then descends past three lovely waterfalls to a seat on grassy banks below the third falls. The spot is ideal for a rest before returning upstream.

MAP: Lands, 1:25,000 Tumbarumba and Map 78.
WALK: One day, 6.2 km, easy grade, last reviewed January 1992, allow 2¼ hours.

Warogong

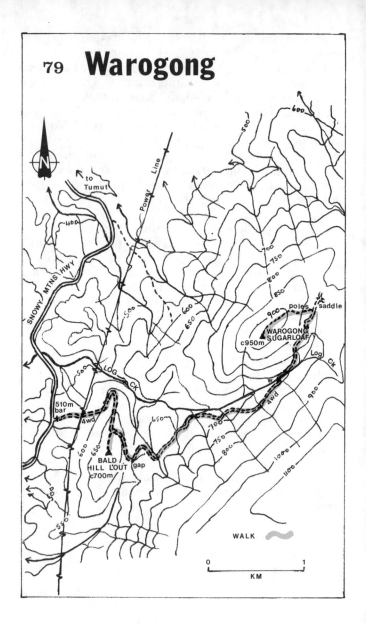

79 WAROGONG SUGARLOAF

Where the beautiful Tumut river valley emerges from the Alps and the Kosciusko National Park on to the undulating country around Tumut township, there is a 950 m high peak known as Warogong Sugarloaf. It stands slightly separated from the high country to the south and the east and affords expansive views of Tumut and the river valley. The ascent is significant in that the available walking track starts at the Snowy Mountains Highway at 510 m elevation and a more than 440 m climb is involved. The walk holds a great deal of attraction because of the large mobs of kangaroos seen on the grassy open spurs and the common sighting of lyrebirds and wombats in the fine forests of the upper reaches of Log Creek. Apart from the fact that the peak is normally below the winter snowline, enabling winter walking, there is an added attraction in the splendid view of the Tumut Valley and Blowering Reservoir from the summit of 700 m high Bald Hill near the beginning of the walk.

To reach the track start, travel south from Tumut along the Snowy Mountains Highway for about 16 km. The northern edge of the Kosciusko National Park is in the vicinity. Orange marker posts indicate the route to follow eastwards up the slopes from a jeep track barrier. The jeep track is mainly used to service pylons of a high voltage electricity transmission line nearby, and once past the line it is less intrusive. National Park authorities recommend seven hours to set aside for the walk but five hours would seem adequate under normal conditions.

Head off east up the jeep track under the powerlines and climb steeply to gain a northern spur of Bald Hill. Briar roses are prolific on the grassy slopes and kangaroos seem to be ever present. Head on up the spur of Bald Hill as the jeep track turns south and 1.5 km from the walk start, continue south 250 m up a gentle rise on to the summit of Bald Hill. A rest to enjoy the panorama will then no doubt be appreciated as already 190 m elevation will have been gained. Warogong Sugarloaf lies less than 2 km (as the crow flies) north-east and, misleadingly, appears heavily timbered when seen from Bald Hill.

Retrace 250 m and turn east (right) down the continuation of the old jeep track still on open grassy slopes. The jeep track then leads across saddles and intermediate gullies until at 2.5 km from the walk start it enters forest near the south bank of Log Creek. For the next 1.2 km there is a considerable climb in fairly damp forest on the southern slopes of the creek valley. Lyrebirds seem quite common in this locality. Next, the creek is crossed at a ford and drinking water is usually available at the spot. More climbing for another 1 km follows to a spot 200 m south of a prominent saddle. (The jeep track all but ceases at the saddle.) Marker posts indicate the route to follow westwards up a fairly sparsely timbered slope on to Warogong Sugarloaf where there is a cairn 500 m from the jeep track. Make sure you walk an additional 50 m south into thick scrub from the cairn so as to scale rocks and attain a fine view to the south and of Blowering Reservoir. In the vicinity of the cairn views are best towards Tumut and out over the undulating country to the north-west.

Return using the same track system.

MAP: Lands, 1:25,000 Blowering and Map 79.
WALK: One day, 11 km, medium grade, last reviewed July 1992, allow 5 hours.

HAKEA

Mount Warning

South West Rocks, Trial Bay

Laurieton from North Brother

Myall Lakes

Yarrangobilly Caves are located just off the Snowy Mountains Highway, about 75 km south of Tumut. The limestone formations are in a belt some 12 km long running north–south, and 1.5 km wide. The Yarrangobilly River flows along the west side of the limestone belt with great bluffs of limestone up to 200 m high flanking the river. There are sinkholes feeding the limestone area with water and these occur even as far north of the main tourist spot as the tiny locality of Yarrangobilly.

In former times Yarrangobilly Caves was a popular holiday destination serviced by Caves House guest house. A warm spring was used to fill a thermal pool and tennis, horseriding, picnics, walking and of course cave tours were all attractions. Today, the region is within the Kosciusko National Park; Caves House is closed and the area is relatively quiet. Activities are confined to picnics, thermal pool swimming, walking and limited caves inspections. Glory Hole Cave, however, is now set up as a self-guiding facility and inspection of it is easily incorporated into walk itineraries. It is therefore suggested that Glory Hole Cave be included in a figure-eight circuit walk which takes in all the best features of the locality.

Glory Hole Cave is quite cool and the path within is 470 m long, so take warm clothing. The walk passes the thermal pool and the Yarrangobilly River so include swimming gear if a swim is desired. There are dressing sheds near the pool. The thermal water is only just warm (27°) so may not appeal in cooler weather.

Two narrow, winding, gravel roads lead down to link the Snowy Mountains Highway with Yarrangobilly Caves visitor centre (ranger station) and 300 m down from it is the Glory Hole car park where the walk should commence. Pay the entrance fee to Glory Hole Cave at the visitor centre before setting off on the walk.

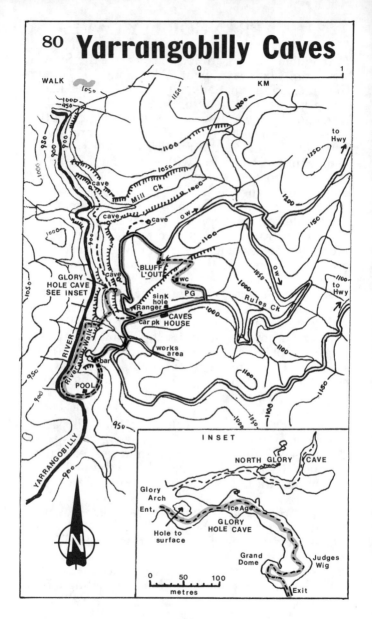

80 Yarrangobilly Caves

WALK

KM

to Hwy

Mill Ck

cave
cave
cave o w

cave

BLUFF
L'OUT

GLORY
HOLE CAVE
SEE INSET

wc

sink
hole
Ranger

PG

o w

Rules Ck

to Hwy

CAVES
HOUSE

car pk

RIVER

works
area

River Walk

bar

POOL

YARRANGOBILLY

N

INSET

NORTH GLORY CAVE

Glory
Arch
Ent.

Hole to
surface

Ice Age

GLORY
HOLE CAVE

Grand
Dome

Judges
Wig

Exit

0   50   100
metres

The walk involves following the road from the car park first for 500 m to turn left into a large picnic area uphill from the visitor centre. Head across the picnic area to locate the start of the Bluff Lookout Walking Track north-westwards beyond a toilet block and near a cliff base. Next, climb to the Bluff Lookout 90 m higher and 600 m distant to view Caves House and its vicinity. Continue about 200 m on the track northwards to meet a one-way (uphill) traffic road. Turn left and descend the road. Unlike vehicles, walkers are permitted to descend the road which leads via the rim of the limestone bluffs overlooking the Yarrangobilly River and via a zig-zag to Glory Hole car park 1 km away. What is known as the Lookout Walk Circuit (2.6 km long) is then completed. A second and more interesting circuit of identical length lies ahead.

Walk the roadway 500 m around to the thermal pool access car park, avoiding the road off left up to the Snowy Mountains Highway. The car park is high on a bluff overlooking the river. Descend the steep roadway south from the road barrier for 400 m to the thermal pool. The river is virtually adjacent to the pool. A break here might be appropriate for a swim. A riverside track can then be taken upstream for 700 m. Then the track needs to be ascended steeply eastwards via a small limestone ravine for 250 m. About 60 m is gained in altitude by the time Glory Hole Cave access path is reached as it sidles down 250 m, past bluffs from the nearby car park to the cave entrance at Glory Arch. The cave should then be entered for your self-guided tour. The cave is said to be less than 100 000 years old, so is quite young in geological terms. It is illuminated and there are many beautiful limestone formations to discover at your leisure before exiting at the rear of the cave back to the car park.

MAP: Lands, 1:25,000 Yarrangobilly and Map 80.
WALK: One day, 5.2 km, easy grade, last reviewed January 1992, allow 2¼ hours.

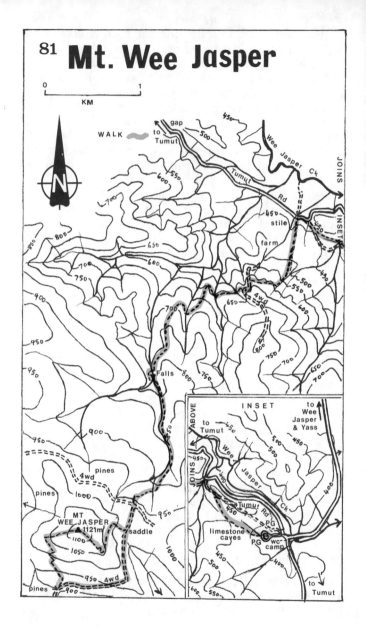

81 Mt. Wee Jasper

0   1
KM

WALK
to Tumut

gap

Wee Jasper Ck

Tumut Rd

JOINS INSET

stile

farm

4wd

Falls

pines

4wd

pines

MT WEE JASPER
▲ 1121m

saddle

pines

4wd

INSET

to Wee Jasper & Yass

JOINS ABOVE

to Tumut

Wee Jasper Ck

Tumut Rd

PG

limestone caves

PG

wc-camp

to Tumut

81   WEE JASPER

Wee Jasper is a tiny settlement beside the Goodrabidgee River arm of Lake Burrenjuck, some 80 km north-west of Canberra. The surrounding country is steep with forested slopes and tops. The valleys are farmed.

Hume and Hovell originally explored the district and today the long distance Hume and Hovell Walking Track passes through Wee Jasper and over nearby Mount Wee Jasper. The track system to the mountain is mostly within eucalypt forest and every now and then there are splendid views. The track is designed for long distance through-walks, but a day walk can be taken to Mount Wee Jasper from Fitzpatrick Track head 4 km south of Wee Jasper. (James Fitzpatrick was one of the six men assigned to accompany Hume and Hovell.) At the track head there are full facilities for picnics and camping. To the west there are interesting limestone outcrops and caves. A short track links the track head to the alignment of the main long distance route. The walk is suitable for any time of the year except very hot summer days as some of the walk is on steep spurs which have a northerly aspect and they receive strong sunlight.

A climb of some 720 m elevation is necessary to gain the summit. Midway through the climb there is a pleasant 8 m waterfall in a rocky gully. But, carry water for drinking as the waterfall area is the only reliable source of water and it too may dry up in summer. The falls are 5 km out from the walk start.

From Fitzpatrick Track head start the climb west at the rear of the camp and picnic area. The foot pad to follow climbs among limestone outcrops and limestone caves. Kurrajong trees are passed, then the track descends across a broad gully to cross an old jeep track and to abut the Wee Jasper to Tumut road. It then climbs a little again between the old jeep track and the road to meet the road 1.3 km out from the walk start. The main Hume and Hovell Track crosses the road at this point where it is surrounded by farmland.

Turn left to climb a stile to follow the main walking track 700 m south up a spur through a paddock. The track remains fairly close to a fence until it enters eucalypt forest near a second stile. Views of the Wee Jasper Creek valley are quite good before the forest. For 3 km the track then sidles and climbs across steep spurs and gullies until the waterfall is gained at 780 m elevation. During the climb the old Hayshed fire trail is temporarily the route to follow. Kangaroos, wallabies, wombats and echidnas seem common on the slopes. The benched foot track is generally good, but has several quite steep pinches. Take a break at the falls.

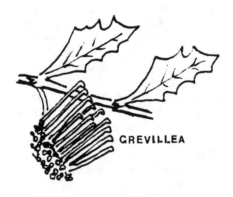

GREVILLEA

Beyond the waterfall the forest is more stately and damp. Ferns, reeds and lyrebirds are to be seen. The track leads south up the creek valley for 1.5 km to gain a contouring logging road. There are extensive pine plantations in the area, especially west of Mount Wee Jasper but only a little of it is seen during the walk. However, the track leads beside pines for the next 500 m of climbing beyond a gate at the logging road. From the gate walk south up a jeep track for

300 m to a saddle, then turn west and go another 200 m on a track between pines.

More climbing among eucalypts follows for the final 800 m to the rounded top of Mount Wee Jasper. The track climbs south-west for 400 m to a spur, then ascends north-west up the rocky spur crest to the summit trig at 1121 m elevation. Blackwood trees grow on the top, as do tall eucalypts. Views are limited to a few spots. Lunch and a well-earned rest are recommended here if the waterfall area was not used earlier.

To return, the long distance track should first be followed 400 m west down another spur crest on an old jeep track. This section is a bit rocky and is set amid fine eucalypts. Next, the track descends south as a foot pad via zig-zags to another jeep track in a gully 800 m away. Turn left on to the jeep track to then leave the long distance walking track system. Head east to walk to and climb a spur south-east of Mount Wee Jasper. Continue on the jeep track as it leads north until a saddle is gained at the head-waters of Racecourse Creek. At this point you should have completed a walk circuit. The latter jeep track section totals 1.2 km and is through damp forest.

Thereafter, retrace the long distance walking track route for the 300 m north down the jeep track, through the gate and by foot pad back down to Fitzpatricks Track head.

MAP: Lands, 1:25,000 Couragago and Map 81.
WALK: One day, 17 km, hard grade, last reviewed August 1992, allow 6½ hours.

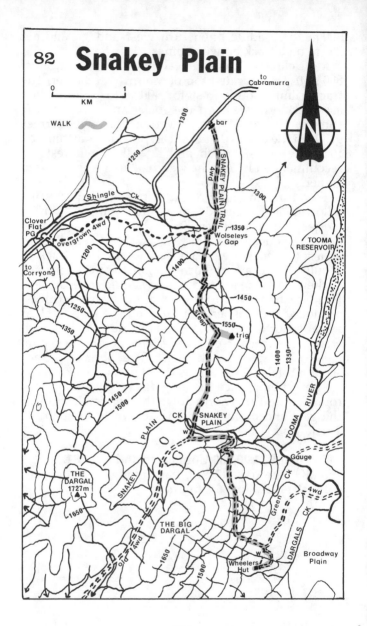

WALK

to
Cabramurra

0   1
KM

N

1300

bar

1250

SNAKEY PLAIN TRAIL
4wd

1300

Shingle   Ck

1350
Wolseleys
Gap

Clover
Flat
PG

overgrown 4wd

TOOMA
RESERVOIR

to
Corryong

1200

1400

1450

1250

1350

steep

1550

trig

1400

1350

1450

1500

CK

SNAKEY
PLAIN

TOOMA   RIVER

w

Gauge

SNAKEY   PLAIN

THE
DARGAL
1727m

Green   Ck

4wd

DARGALS   CK

1650

old   4wd

THE BIG
DARGAL

1650

1500

w

Wheelers
Hut

Broadway
Plain

SNOWY MOUNTAINS AND FAR SOUTH COAST REGION

82 SNAKEY PLAIN— WHEELERS HUT

To most people, Snowy Mountains walking seems to involve a trip to the Kosciusko summit area. It is quite obvious that very few people walk to many of the other beautiful places further north in the National Park such as the area right next to the Kiandra–Khancoban main road. No doubt many people travel through Cabramurra and see some of the alpine plains, flowers and snow gums but do not make the effort to walk. If only they knew how lovely such places as Far Bald Mountain, Round Mountain and Snakey Plain are.

Snakey Plain does not appear to have snakes, but maybe the name keeps people away. It is right alongside Big Dargal Mountain. It gives a really good view of massive Mount Jagungal to the south-east and has a crystal clear stream flowing through it, with grassy banks providing a perfect lunch spot.

Further along the track is rustic Wheelers Hut in another delightful alpine plain setting and an excellent overnight stopping place.

To reach the area, travel the Tooma Road to a south side turnoff 2.5 km west of Tooma Dam. The spot is on a rise and marks the start of Snakey Plain fire trail. At this point you are about 1300 m above sea level. Snakey Plain is at 1500 m, so a little climbing is involved. Note that the 1:50,000 scale map Khancoban incorrectly shows Snakey Plain fire trail too far east as far as Wolseleys Gap.

The trail should be followed south at first, through open forest without views. About 1.5 km from the Tooma Road, after mostly fairly level walking, you should descend slightly to Wolseleys Gap, where there is an overgrown east–west road. At the former junction, cross the saddle then continue south up grassy Snakey Plain fire trail. Once away from the lushness of the small saddle, the track becomes more pronounced and climbs steadily on to open grassy slopes above the treeline, on the northern side of the Jagumba Range. Views to the north-west become quite good and alpine flowers proliferate. Tooma Reservoir also comes into view as you ascend. The track reaches some tops just 100 m west of a trig point, on a small summit, which is worth visiting as a minor side trip. The trig is 3 km from the Tooma Road and is dilapidated.

It is a further 1.5 km from the range top to Snakey Plain and the trail traverses some truly delightful alpine 'garden' settings. About December–January especially, the area ranks as one of the best displays of flora in the Snowy Mountains. The trail is well defined and gradually descends to Snakey Plain which is very green and dominated by Big Dargal Mountain. The stream, flowers, views and snow gums all contribute to make it a paradise for walkers. Mount Jagungal can be seen from the middle of the plain where Wheelers Hut fire trail leads south-east down off the plain.

Follow the jeep track down gradually off Snakey Plain to enter extensive stands of alpine ash, then descend steeply across a gully. Thereafter, sidle down the eastern slopes of Big Dargal Mountain. The way is basically southwards until 2.5 km from Snakey Plain. At this point the track emerges from forest on to the alpine grass plains along Dargal Creek and turns north-east to rise on to a low ridge. Wheelers Hut is 300 m south-west of this bend and low point on the track, but the hut is across a creek and difficult to see from the track. However, a quite minor 500 m long jeep track forks off south, crosses the small creek then turns west and approaches the hut up the grassy slopes. There are no track markers and in fog or snow the hut could be difficult to locate without accurate map reading.

Wheelers Hut is an historic two-roomed cattlemen's hut with bunk space for six persons. It has an east-facing verandah with a pleasant view and has a rear (woodshed) verandah as well. The hut is of slab timber, lined with tar paper and has a huge fireplace. It gets very cosy with a fire. Water is available from the small creek about 100 m north, and a toilet is provided outside. Replace any wood used and ensure the hut is left tidy. The plains adjacent to the hut are the site of the old Toolong diggings and a short wander about the area can be a most pleasant addition to the day's walk.

On the second day, use the same tracks to retrace the route back north.

MAP: Lands, 1:50,000 Khancoban and Map 82.
WALK: Two days, 15 km, spread over two days of 7.5 km, easy grade, last reviewed January 1992, allow 4 hours for each day.
Note that the whole district becomes snowbound in winter.

83   ROUND MOUNTAIN—
MOUNT JAGUNGAL

The Snowy Mountains country has a wide variety of walking venues, but perhaps the two best spots are the main range and the Mount Jagungal area. The former features exposed tops and views and the latter, rambling alpine country including alpine plains, lovely snow gums and a few majestic peaks, exposed like the main range, and giving excellent views. Mount Jagungal dominates everything else for a huge area and rises up to 2061 m, about 500 m higher than the surroundings. There are good camping possibilities in many places, but it is suggested that you try a two day walk, camping at the foot of mighty

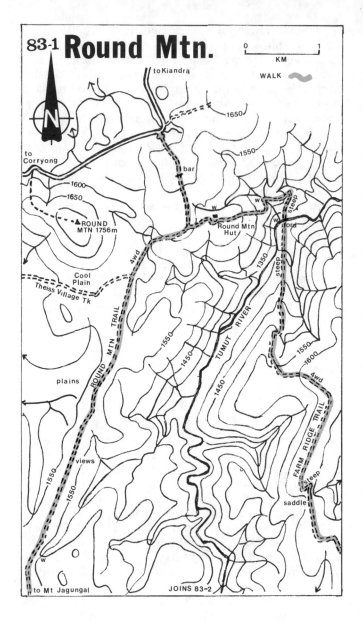

83-1 **Round Mtn.**

0 KM 1

WALK

N

to Kiandra

to Corryong

1650

1550

1600

1650

bar

w w steep

ROUND MTN 1756m

Round Mtn Hut

w ford

steep

Cool Plain

Theiss Village Tk

4wd

1350

TUMUT RIVER

steep

plains

1550

1450

1450

1550

1600

4wd

FARM RIDGE TRAIL

views

1550

1550

steep

saddle

w

to Mt Jagungal

JOINS 83-2

Jagungal—or Big Bogong as it is also known. The camp spot is in the extreme headwaters of the Tumut River.

To reach the walk area, travel along the Tooma Road between Kiandra and Khancoban. Some 19 km west of Cabramurra is the start of Round Mountain Trail. It leads off from the south side of the road as a jeep track, but there is a barrier about 750 m south and the track is open to walkers only beyond that point. Round Mountain itself is just next to the turnoff.

Start off south along the trail and past the vehicular barrier. After 1.5 km Farm Ridge Trail leads off east to Round Mountain Hut and Thiess Village track leads west after the first 2.5 km. You should generally walk south-south-west across delightful alpine plains, abounding with flowers, gradually rising up the Toolong Range.

One broad swathe of the area has been burned in recent years, but regrowth is progressing well and the added sunlight seems to encourage the growth of more flowers.

About 10.5 km from the walk start, the track forks to the south-east off Hellhole Creek Trail. An old hut (Derschkos Hut) is passed 2 km later.

Near the base of Jagungal, another 2 km on, Grey Mare Trail is met. Its eastern extension leads to O'Keefes Hut, Farm Ridge and on to the Far Bald Mountain area. Turn east and follow this track for about 350 m to where you cross the small stream which is the extreme upper headwaters of the Tumut River. There are several camp spots near the stream. (One large spot is 400 m uphill beyond the ford, beside the track.)

To finish the day, a side trip to the summit of Jagungal is a must. The top is 2.5 km away and scrub is dense on the lower slopes. An ascent track leads up the east side of the bank of the Tumut from the ford, then mounts a spur south-eastwards. An alpine meadow-covered, main spur can then be followed to the summit. Take care to note the surroundings at the spot where the main spur is attained to facilitate

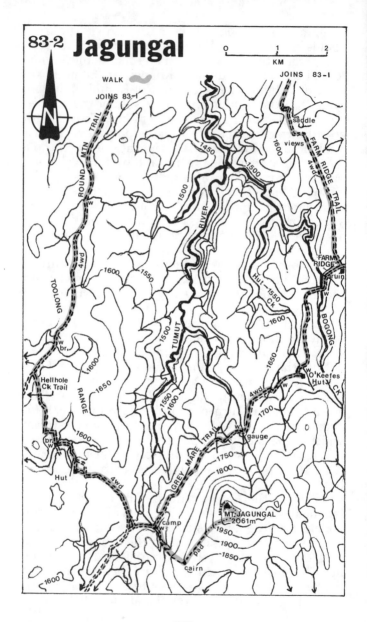

83-2 **Jagungal**

your later return, especially if fog is a possibility. The top is a mass of granite boulders and is quite impressive. Due to the rocky terrain, the final few hundred metres approach is better made from the east. Views from the top are surely some of the best in the state.

On the second day, follow the Grey Mare Trail in a north-easterly direction through snow gum country. After 2.6 km, you pass a gauging station near a creek which has a reliable water supply and camp spots. A further 1.8 km along the trail is O'Keefe's Hut. It lies to the right of the track in a large natural clearing, is in good condition and has a creek water supply close to the doorway.

The jeep track should then be followed northwards along a ridge for 1.3 km, and down across Bogong Creek and up steeply to Farm Ridge, a further 1.4 km away.

Farm Ridge is the site of an old alpine grazing property, and abandoned stockyards and ruined buildings can still be seen. Farm Ridge Trail forks off left from Grey Mare Trail at this spot. It should be followed north-west uphill. The ridge becomes quite lightly timbered and there are many very pleasant alpine clearings along the way. About 3 km from Grey Mare Trail the headwaters of a south-flowing stream could provide water for a meal break at an idyllic lunch spot on an alpine meadow with a superb view of Mount Jagungal.

After lunch, continue north-west 1 km, then north 1.4 km. The trail then leaves the ridge and turns west. It descends gradually for about 1 km, then again turns north to descend steeply down a well defined spur for 1.5 km to the treeless Tumut River flats. A normally easily negotiated ford should be reached after 500 m of walking northwards across the flats. The spot is not very good for lunch or camping. A steep climb north follows, to attain a spur crest within 400 m. At this point the trail doubles back south-west and climbs for 1.3 km to Round Mountain Hut. Midway between these points is a creek with a reliable water supply. Round Mountain Hut is in good condition, with camp areas around it. Water lies 100 m north in a creek. There is bunk space for seven people.

To rejoin the Round Mountain Trail, continue uphill for a further 400 m amid snow gums. Turn north and retrace the previous day's walk route for 1.5 km to the Tooma Road and the end of the walk.

MAP: Lands, 1:50,000 Khancoban and Maps 83–1 and 83–2.
WALK: Two days, 39.1 km (day 1 20 km and day 2 19.1 km), medium grade, last reviewed February 1992, allow 8 hours for each day.
Note: The district is snowbound in winter.

84   MOUNT DROMEDARY

Over 220 years ago, in 1770, Captain Cook named Mount Dromedary because the peaks appeared like a dromedary camel when viewed from off the coast. The summit is 797 m high and is an isolated volcanic cone formation. It resembles Mount Warning near the Queensland border in some respects because of its geology, aspect and vegetation. Captain Cook also named Mount Warning as he continued north up Australia's east coast.

Mount Dromedary was once heavily covered with cool temperate rainforest, but the discovery of alluvial gold in the streams on the mountain slopes in the 1850s caused much clearing. The timber was used by the miners for fuel for steam-powered mining machinery and for construction. Today, a small amount of rainforest remains and the old mining tracks now provide excellent walking routes to the summit. Much of the peak is now covered by relatively small timber with many tree ferns and much

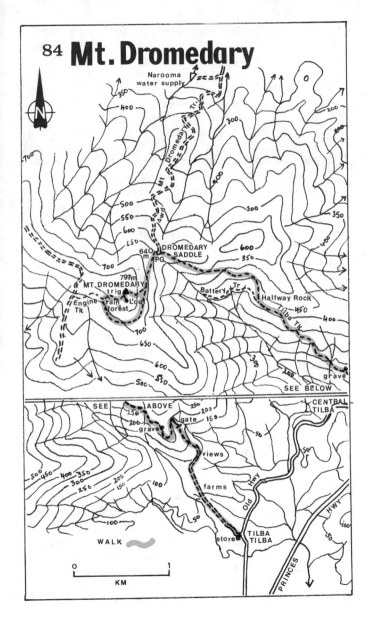

84 Mt. Dromedary

Narooma
water supply

N

Mt Dromedary

4wd

DROMEDARY
SADDLE

640
m
PG

797m
MT. DROMEDARY
trig
L'out
rain forest

Engine
Tk

Battery Tr

Halfway Rock
Tilba Tk

grave

SEE BELOW

SEE ABOVE

CENTRAL
TILBA

gate
grave

views

farms

Old Hwy

TILBA
TILBA
store

WALK

PRINCES HWY

0   1
KM

low scrub. The rainforest depends for its existence on frequent mists and heavy rainfall on the higher slopes as well as protection from drying winds. While there are many peaks near the coast of New South Wales which are clothed in rainforest, Mount Dromedary is one of the better ones to climb because of ease of access and because of views from the summit. The climb is moderately hard in that 800 m elevation needs to be gained over the 5.5 km distance. The walk starts virtually at sea level. A flora reserve surrounds and includes the mountain.

There are two approaches to the mountain top. One is from the Narooma water supply area via a jeep track to Dromedary Saddle where it is joined by the alternative route up the south-east slopes. This latter route is by far the most enjoyable and most of its climb is in the shade of the south aspect rather than the warmer northern spur. This is therefore the recommended walk. About 4½ hours is best set aside for the walk although fit young walkers could halve the time.

The recommended route has access from Tilba Tilba, now just off the re-aligned Princes Highway south-west of Narooma. The track leaves the old highway along the north side of Pams general store. Car parking is available in front of the house next door. Drinks and lunches are on sale at the store, including cut lunches. Initially, the track is a minor roadway through dairy farm country for 1 km along the route of the old miners' pack horse trail. Respect the adjacent private property and leave gates you pass as you found them.

Set off for the 1 km across the farmland to where the road rises into forest and enters the flora reserve 1.5 km from the walk start at an altitude of about 180 m. From here on the track is reserved for walkers although it is wide enough for maintenance vehicles all the way up to Dromedary Saddle. The climb rises past Chinamans Grave and through forest up to Half Way Rock, at a track junction 2.75 km from the walk start. The left fork is Battery Trail along which miners lived and worked in the early days. Little remains to be seen on this 800 m long side track so best to keep to the right fork major route. Continue north-west up the slopes until you reach Dromedary Saddle.

Dromedary Saddle lies at 640 m elevation. It is the junction of the two access routes, has tank water, toilet, fireplaces, tables and a visitors' book. It is 4.8 km from the walk start and is a good lunch spot. By the shortest route it is only 700 m short of the summit. The best plan is to take this shortest route called the Summit Track then to return to the saddle via the Rainforest Trail. Watch for lyrebirds and wallabies in this locality as you head off up southwards to the summit trig point. Within 400 m, fork right to climb steeply to the top. Views improve as the top is neared and at the top you can see Montague Island, Narooma and much of the coast. Bermagui can be seen by walking a few metres south of the trig point. There is a seat on the peak top.

To return, take the Rainforest Trail south-west down into fine stands of pinkwood (*Eucryphia mooreii*), sassafras (*Doryphora sassafras*) and both soft and rough tree ferns (*Dicksonia antarctica* and *Cyathea*). The forest floor has a light covering of ground ferns and mosses.

The track descends to join with Engine Track some 300 m from the summit trig point. Turn left to continue on up the Rainforest Trail, over a spur crest and around the slopes to rejoin the Summit Trail 700 m from the trig. Then retrace the 400 m down to Dromedary Saddle. Thereafter, retrace the 4.8 km down to Pams store.

MAP: Lands, 1:25,000 Central Tilba and Map 84.
WALK: One day, 11 km, medium grade, last reviewed February 1992, allow 4½ hours.

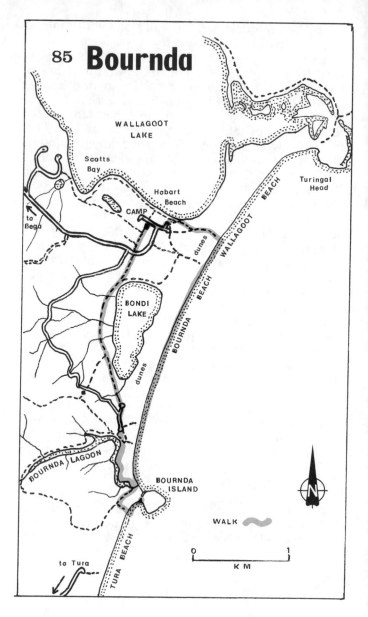

85 **Bournda**

WALLAGOOT LAKE

Scotts Bay

Hobart Beach

CAMP

to Bega

BONDI LAKE

dunes

dunes

BOURNDA BEACH

WALLAGOOT BEACH

Turingal Head

BOURNDA LAGOON

BOURNDA ISLAND

WALK

TURA BEACH

to Tura

N

0   1
K M

85 BONDI LAKE— BOURNDA ISLAND

On the South Coast, south of Tathra and just 3.4 km off the Tathra to Merimbula road is the start of a network of walking tracks among salt and freshwater lakes, a lagoon, and along a superb surf beach.

Wallagoot Lake is central to the area. It is suggested that a circuit walk be taken from the Hobart Beach camp ground on the southern shore of Wallagoot Lake. The camp has full facilities if needed and includes a large picnic shelter where the walk should start. The diversity of water environments is one of the main features of the walk and there are large numbers of kangaroos to be seen. The beach could be used for a swim if the weather is warm enough.

Head off south from behind the picnic shelter into tea tree for 300 m. Cross the camp access roadway after avoiding two tracks off right, both of which lead to Scotts Bay. Straight across the access road the track continues south to Bondi Lake via a former jeep track. A foot track links in from the left. This junction is adjacent to the north-west shore of Bondi Lake and there are good views south across the lake, especially just east of the track junction. The old jeep track continues, and lies close by Bondi Lake's western shore. But the lake is mostly out of view. Head south, and across grassy flats where kangaroos seem plentiful. After wet weather the old jeep track gets swamped a little. Walking across the grass at times may be preferable to getting wet feet. When 2.5 km from the walk start you reach the Bournda Lagoon picnic and car park areas. (Avoid a minor track off right to a schools field studies unit.) A very short track loop links the car park with the lagoon. Use the loop to gain access to the eastern shore of this serene spot. Walk the shore for 500 m to where the lagoon enters the sea, then ford the mouth or cross rocks to its south bank.

This spot is at the southern end of 4.5 km long Bournda Beach. Adjacent is Bournda Island which should next be investigated. The foot track to be followed leads up on to a headland and divides. Take the left fork down on to Tura Beach which is just south of the headland. Then walk out across an isthmus to Bournda Island. The rocks, views and crashing waves all make this locality ideal for a lunch break.

To return, retrace the outward route the short distance to the mouth of Bournda Lagoon then walk the surf beach for 3 km northwards. Two tracks lead off the beach back to the Hobart Beach camp ground but the southern one can get inundated so use the northern one. The wooden steps of each track start can be seen leading up the sand dunes which back the beach. The two tracks are only 300 m apart. Keep to the constructed track and steps as you cross the dunes to abide by erosion control measures. The dune separates the beach from the inland lakes system. Immediately west of the dune-crossing keep right as the track divides. Within 200 m this right fork gives access to the shore of Wallagoot Lake. From the lake shore, tracks lead into adjacent car parks and the Hobart Beach camp ground.

MAP: Lands, 1:25,000 Wolumla and Map 85.
WALK: One day, 7 km, easy grade, last reviewed February 1992, allow 2½ hours.

86   MOUNT IMLAY

In the far south, beyond Eden, and close to the Victorian border is very prominent 886 m high Mount Imlay. It is far higher than any of the surrounding country. The top is rocky and has cliffs in several places. Views from the summit make the fairly steep climb most rewarding.

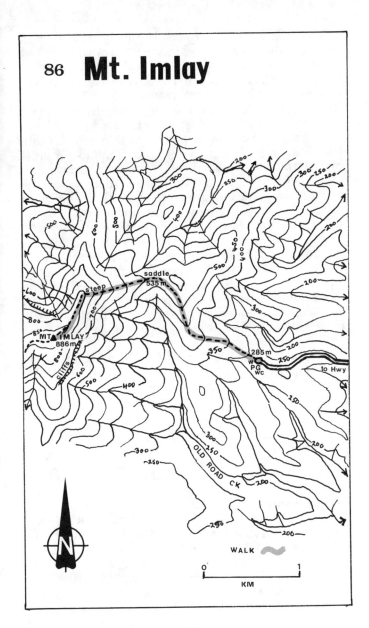

saddle
535 m.

steep

MT. IMLAY
886 m.

CLIFFS

350

285 m
W
PG
WC

to Hwy

OLD ROAD CK

N

WALK

0   1

KM

Access is from the Princes Highway, 14 km south of Eden, then 9.6 km west along Burrawong Forest Road to Burrawong picnic ground. Here, there are tables, fireplaces and tap water. The walk involves climbing from 290 m to 886 m over a distance of 3.5 km. In several spots it is quite rocky underfoot. About 3½ hours should be set aside for the walk.

The track to follow is mostly within forest. From the picnic area, it leads west at first, up a spur crest on a former jeep track. The track then turns north and keeps scaling the spur crest then sidles the western slope of the spur into a saddle 1.5 km from the walk start. Thereafter, the track keeps to the highest ground on the spur crest westwards into progressively more rocky and broken ground. Finally, it leads along tops south-west to a trig point among low tea tree. The view includes Towamba River valley, Twofold Bay and lighthouse, Womboyn Lake and The Cobberas westwards in Victoria. On a clear day you can see Mallacoota Inlet in Victoria. The return route is back down the same spurs.

MAP: Lands, 1:25,000 Mount Imlay and Kiah sheets and Map 86.
WALK: One day, 7 km, medium grade, last reviewed February 1992, allow 3½ hours.

87 RENNEX GAP—GIANTS CASTLE

About 8 km up the main Kosciusko (Summit) Road beyond the Kosciusko National Park visitor centre and at the very head of Sawpit Creek is Rennex Gap. The spot is 1600 m above sea level and the gap was named after the engineer in charge of road construction between 1906 and 1909. (Some literature lists the name as Rennix.) The road has in fact been realigned as it approaches the gap from the east and

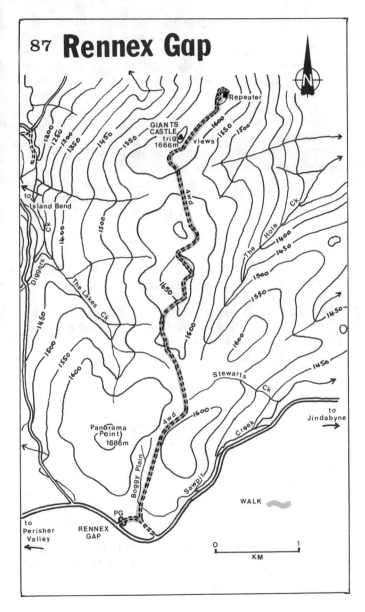

87 **Rennex Gap**

N

Repeater

GIANTS
CASTLE
trig
1666m   views

to
Island Bend

1200
1250
1300
1350
1450
1550

1600
1550
1500

4wd

The Hole Ck

1500

1650

1600

1400
1450

Diggers Ck

The Lakes Ck

1450

1500
1550
1600

1500

1550

1600

1600

1450

Stewarts Ck

1450

to
Jindabyne

4wd   1600

Panorama
Point
1686m

Boggy Plain

Sawpit

Creek

WALK

PG

to
Perisher
Valley

RENNEX
GAP

0   1
KM

281

the old route (about 500 m long) on Boggy Plain marks the start of this walk suggestion. A jeep track forks off the old road and leads north, gradually ascending on the small plain. The suggested walk passes through alpine vegetation and forested areas and the route leads along the tops out to a radio repeater tower on granite tors.

At the walk start there are a couple of snow poles to indicate the alignment of the minor jeep track. Thereafter, the track is more defined. Walking is fairly straightforward and the way is roughly northwards.

Midway along the walk there are good views westwards to the main range. Further on there is a trig point on a boulder-strewn top 1666 m high, known as Giants Castle. The rocks can only be climbed by true rock climbers. Another 750 m along the track is the turn-around point where the radio repeater stands and where there are views of Lake Jindabyne and the Snowy River.

MAP: Lands, 1:50,000 Berridale and Map 87.
WALK: One day, 12 km, medium grade, last reviewed January 1992, allow 4¾ hours.
Note: The district is snowbound in winter.

88   PERISHER VALLEY—
THE PORCUPINE

From Perisher Valley ski village in the Snowy Mountains, there is an alpine walk which has traditionally been promoted by Kosciusko National Park authorities. It leads on to the Ramshead Range in the Porcupine Rocks area.

Perisher Village lies at 1725 m and the Porcupine attains 1960 m elevation. The walking track is amid alpine snow gums (*Eucalyptus pauciflora*) and herb-lands, with the gums being sufficiently sparse to

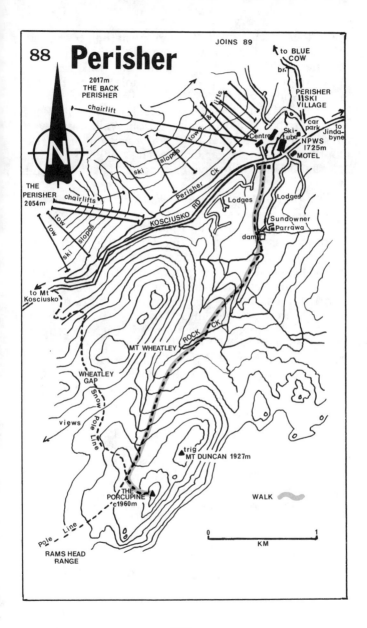

88 **Perisher**

to BLUE COW

br.

PERISHER SKI VILLAGE

2017m THE BACK PERISHER

chairlift

car park

to Jinda-byne

Centre

Ski Tube

ski slopes

tows & lifts

NPWS 1725m

MOTEL

THE PERISHER 2054m

chairlifts

Perisher Ck

Lodges

Lodges

tow ski slopes

KOSCIUSKO RD

Sundowner

Parrawa

dam

to Mt Kosciusko

MT WHEATLEY

ROCK CK

WHEATLEY GAP

Snow Pole Line

views

trig MT DUNCAN 1927m

THE PORCUPINE c1960m

WALK

Pole Line

RAMS HEAD RANGE

0   1

KM

permit good views. Wildflowers are at their best about December and January. Snow poles define the route of the walk, but if fog is about the walk is better not undertaken. In winter the whole region is completely snowbound.

Start the walk on the Kosciusko (Summit) Road near Perisher Valley Skitube station. Walk south-west across nearby Rock Creek and turn left on to the foot track before Eiger Chalet. The track system was re-aligned in 1992 to give better access from the main road.

Follow the track close to Rock Creek to a small reservoir about 600 m from the Skitube station. The old track alignment used to start near this reservoir. It now passes the lower (western) side of the dam and leads south-west away from the village area. Snow poles indicate the general direction of the track, but they do veer away from the track a little at times. On the tops, and some 2.3 km from the dam there is a junction of pole lines. Take the track from the junction 200 m south-east up to reach Porcupine Rocks on the very crest of the Ramshead Range. The rocks are south-west of nearby Mount Duncan which has a conspicuous trig point on its top. There is a superb view from the rocks of Bullocks Flat far below in the Thredbo River valley. The Skitube terminal can be seen on the flat.

After a break, retrace the route to Perisher Valley.

MAP: Lands, 1:50,000 Mount Kosciusko and Map 88. WALK: One day, 6.2 km, easy grade, last reviewed January 1992, allow 2½ hours.
Note: The district is snowbound in winter.

89 BLUE COW MOUNTAIN

The Skitube in the Snowy Mountains provides excellent year-round underground railway access to the top of the Perisher Range at Blue Calf Mountain and is ideal for transporting walkers. Blue Calf Mountain is north-west of Perisher Valley ski village and reaches 1900 m above sea level. The Swiss-style rack railway extends for 8 km and is best joined at Bullocks Flat outside Jindabyne. It can also be joined at Perisher Valley station. Outside the top station at Blue Calf Mountain is a lookout which provides a panorama of the main range, including Mount Kosciusko. Mount Twynam dominates the view and much of the upper Snowy River valley is seen. Just 1.4 km northwards is the summit of Blue Cow Mountain, 1981 m high.

HOVEA

The name Blue Cow commemorates a small piece of local history. In the very early days of pastoral leases in the high country, about the mid 1800s, a man named Spencer ran cattle in the locality. It is said that one of his cattle kept avoiding the annual autumn roundup and was usually found later blue with cold on the peak. Many of the place names in the district were named by Spencer and usually related to his cattle.

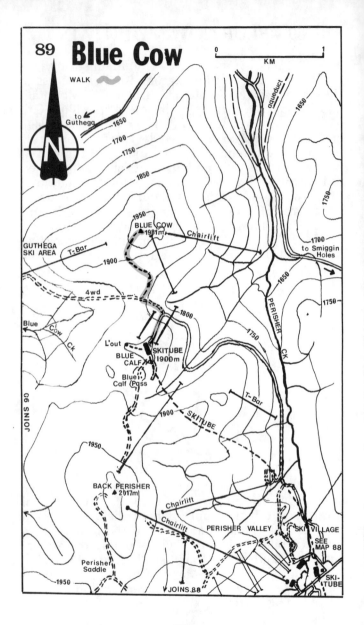

89 Blue Cow

WALK ~

to Guthega

0 ———————— 1
KM

BLUE COW
▲1981m

Chairlift

GUTHEGA
SKI AREA

T-Bar

4wd

to Smiggin
Holes

PERISHER CK.

Blue Cow Ck

JOINS 90

L'out

BLUE CALF

SKITUBE
1900m

Blue
Calf Pass

SKITUBE

T-Bar

BACK PERISHER
▲2017m

Chairlift

Chairlift

PERISHER VALLEY

SKI VILLAGE

SEE
MAP 88

SKI-
TUBE

Perisher
Saddle

JOINS 88

A short walk to the summit of Blue Cow Mountain is recommended and is most rewarding for views. Unless fog is about the whole route of the suggested walk can be seen from just about any point along the way and navigation, normally, would not be a problem. If there is fog, the walk would be better abandoned. Extreme care would be necessary as the route 'to the summit is across alpine grass and herbland and the route is not well defined. Keep to the crest of the Perisher Range on a road, down slightly across a saddle then northwards steeply up to the summit on a minor track. Use the same short route for return.

MAP: Lands, 1:50,000 Mount Kosciusko and Map 89. WALK: One day, 2.8 km, easy grade family suitability, last reviewed January 1992, allow 1½ hours.
Note: The district is snowbound in winter.

90   SKITUBE—BLUE COW MOUNTAIN—MOUNT TWYNAM

At the northern end of the Perisher Range in the Kosciusko National Park are Blue Calf Mountain and Blue Cow Mountain. These two high points at 1900 m and 1981 m have suddenly been accessed by the Skitube rack rail trains via an 8 km line, mostly underground, from Bullocks Flat near Jindabyne. The highest station on Blue Calf Mountain opens up many walk possibilities to Guthega, Mount Twynam, Mount Tate, Whites River, Schlink Pass and of course Blue Cow Mountain. If several days walking is intended, it is now often less expensive to use free car parking at Bullocks Flat, travel by Skitube and avoid the (expensive) daily car park fees within the Kosciusko National Park. Alternatively, private transport can be left at Perisher Valley ski village and the Skitube

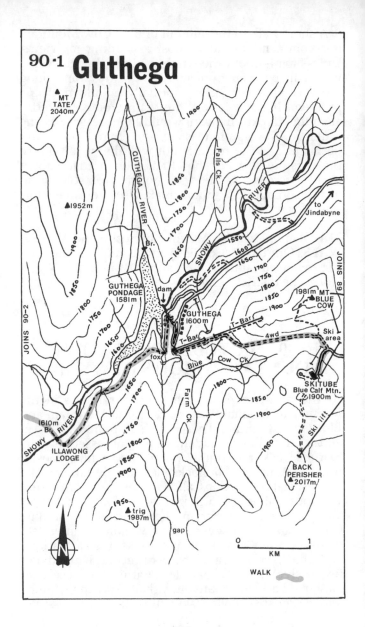

90·1 **Guthega**

MT TATE 2040m

▲1952m

GUTHEGA RIVER

Falls Ck

SNOWY RIVER

to Jindabyne

JOINS 90-2

JOINS 89

Br.

GUTHEGA PONDAGE 1581m

dam

GUTHEGA 1600m

1981m MT BLUE COW

T-Bar

T-Bar

4wd

Ski area

fox

Blue Cow Ck

SKITUBE Blue Calf Mtn. 1900m

Farm Ck

Ski lift

1610m Br. SNOWY RIVER

ILLAWONG LODGE

BACK PERISHER 2017m

▲trig 1987m

gap

N

0   1
KM

WALK

288

Dunes Myall Lakes (courtesy Sven Klinge)

Hawks Nest

Cocoparra Range

Mount Jagungal from South of Round Mountain

ridden or Blue Calf access road walked to Blue Calf station.

Mount Twynam, Australia's third highest mountain is an obvious first choice route for a walk from Blue Cow Mountain. This recommendation is for a three-day walk with two nights camped in the saddle area between Mount Twynam and Mount Little Twynam. The daily distances to be covered are short so that the second and third days could be combined if desired.

Ride the Skitube to Blue Cow Mountain station where there is a viewing platform with a broad panorama including Mount Kosciusko but dominated by Mount Twynam. To start the walk, descend the road northwards to near the adjacent saddle then turn left on to a jeep track which leads west through the saddle and down to Guthega. The latter 800 m of the jeep track is under the alignment of ski tows. The descent is through beautiful alpine vegetation. From the bottom of the ski tows turn right on to a road. This spot is 2.5 km from Blue Cow terminal. Head along the road, diverging left downhill then left again down another jeep track to the south end of the Guthega Pondage dam wall. The jeep track to the dam is near another ski tow.

The next stage requires care as the start of the walking track ahead is difficult to locate. A rough jeep track leads from the dam wall south-west not far above the high water level. Where this jeep track is reached the foot track leads off around the contour, south from the jeep tracks junction. The start is obscured by overhanging low scrub. The foot track remains on the contour for about 300 m then descends and crosses a creek which enters the pondage at the spot. There is a flying fox crossing at the creek but usually stream crossing is easy and there is no need to use the flying fox. The track continues, ascending straight up the slopes on the far side of the stream on to a ridge within 200 m. Thereafter, following the track is far easier, as it basically leads up the valley

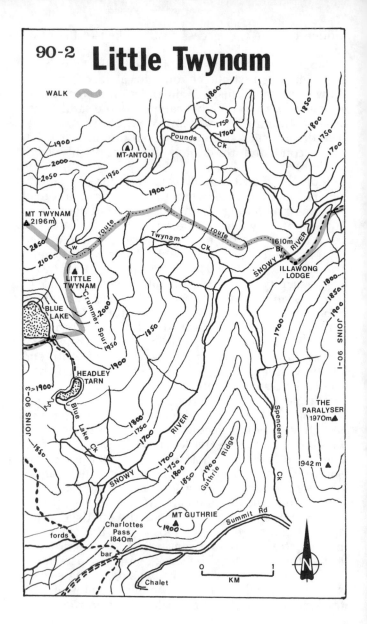

90-2 **Little Twynam**

of the Snowy River for 2 km to Illawong Lodge (a private lodge). This section of the track is over more open country, mostly 100 m to 200 m away from the river. About 1 km short of Illawong Lodge, there is a right-fork track to avoid. This pad leads to a Snowy Mountains Authority installation on the river bank. Some 200 m north-west of Illawong Lodge there is a suspension bridge across the Snowy River and the track leads from the lodge to the bridge.

Once over the bridge, the Snowy River is left and a 4 km climb rising 480 m follows. The foot track soon dissipates in the low herbage after the bridge. Climb on to the spur north-west then keep to the very crest of the spur until almost at the summit of Mount Little Twynam. The general direction of the climb is west-north-west for the first 2.5 km then south-west for 1.5 km. Most of the climb is on alpine grass and low herbage with the treeline left behind. Camp for the night is suggested in the headwaters of Pounds Creek which descends from the saddle between Mount Twynam and Mount Little Twynam. Water for camp is available there.

On the second day, an 8.5 km circuit is recommended. It includes the 2196 m high top of Mount Twynam and glacially formed Blue Lake. After the first day's climb out from Guthega, a day of relative relaxation and enjoyment of the alpine tops will no doubt be appreciated. The same camp site can then be used for the second night out.

Head off north-west for the final 600 m distance on to the rounded top of Mount Twynam. The climb from camp to the top should only be about 100 m rise and summit views are best if you wander about to get the best vantage points. About 200 m north-west of the actual top is a minor grassy jeep track which should be located. It leads 600 m west then south-west along the broad range top. After walking the 600 m, the main range is joined by the Watsons Crags Spur. There is a quite spectacular knob at 2136 m elevation 500 m north-west out on this spur.

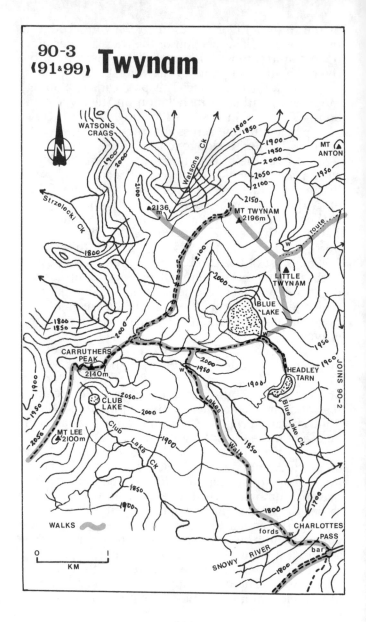

90-3
(91&99) Twynam

WATSONS CRAGS

N

Strzelecki Ck

Watsons Ck

MT ANTON

▲2136 m

MT TWYNAM 2196m

route

LITTLE TWYNAM

BLUE LAKE

CARRUTHERS PEAK
2140m

HEADLEY TARN

JOINS 90-2

Blue Lake Ck

CLUB LAKE

MT LEE 2100m

Club Lake Ck

Lakes Walk

WALKS

CHARLOTTES PASS

fords

bar

SNOWY RIVER

0 1
KM

Take the side trip to the knob for truly splendid views of the steep slopes of the Great Dividing Range.

Return to the main range to continue down the faint jeep track south then south-west for another 1.9 km to a saddle east of nearby Carruthers Peak. The Lakes Walking Track passes across this saddle.

EPACRIS

Double back east down the well defined Lakes Track for 700 m to another saddle and track junction. The right fork is the paved continuation of the Lakes Track. Take the left fork for 1 km down to the outlet of Blue Lake. The glacial features of the magnificent lake are seen to best advantage during this descent.

A small track leads down the west side of Blue Lake Creek for 500 m to Headley Tarn. Take a side trip to see this tarn before starting the 200 m elevation climb back to camp. Headley Tarn was formed by glacial moraines blocking the creek valley.

Many boulders and cliffs flank Blue Lake so once back near the lake outlet, cross the creek and sidle east about 300 m then turn north and pick a route up the main spur to Mount Little Twynam. The knob can be bypassed on its west side if desired so as to walk directly into camp.

On the third day, reverse the route of day one. Take great care, however, to correctly select the spur route down to Illawong Bridge and Lodge, especially if there is fog about. If trouble is encountered, remember that all the streams flow into Guthega Pondage, so those streams could be a rough guide. Vegetation tends to be thickest and hence progress slowest near the streams. The ridge crests tend to be far easier routes.

MAP: Lands, 1:50,000 Mount Kosciusko and Maps 90–1, 90–2 and 90–3.
WALK: Three days, 27 km (day one 9.25 km, day two 8.5 km, day three 9.25 km), medium grade, last reviewed February 1992, allow 5 hours, 3½ hours and 5 hours for each respective day.
Note: The district is snowbound in winter.
Warning: Much of the walk is over very exposed terrain above the treeline, where violent weather changes can occur at any time of the year. Be prepared for blizzard conditions even in mid summer.

91   CHARLOTTES PASS—
BLUE LAKE

Blue Lake must rate as one of the best features of the Kosciusko National Park. It is a wonderful place for seeing flowers, lazing, walking, photography and admiring the alpine scenery. It was formed by a glacier gouging out the southern slopes of Mount Twynam, one of Australia's highest mountains. As a result, the northern side of the tarn is lined with cliffs. The south-west side is grassy and relatively flat, although a certain amount of glacial moraine is present.

Travel up the main Mount Kosciusko summit road to Charlottes Pass where there is a barrier and a car park. The partly paved Lakes Track leads off from the north side of the road at the pass and should be followed. It leads west 600 m down to the youthful Snowy River, then fords it before rising gradually north-west for 3.4 km to cross a gully and reach a sharp left bend at a saddle. Turn right (east) at this bend and then it is only 1 km down to the mouth of Blue Lake via a lesser pad. Most of the route is through treeless alpine slopes which can be extremely exposed at times. But in fine weather it is really pleasant. Being in a hollow, Blue Lake is relatively sheltered. Try to time the trip for December to March when the alpine flowers are at their best.

Lunch is suggested by the lake before returning to Charlottes Pass using the same tracks.

MAP: Lands, 1:50,000 Mount Kosciusko and Map 90–3.
WALK: One day, 10 km, easy grade, last reviewed January 1992, allow 3 hours.
Note: The whole district is snowbound in winter. Camping is no longer permitted in the Blue Lake watershed.

92   MOUNT STILWELL

Charlottes Pass in the Kosciusko National Park marks the end of the road to Australia's highest mountain for ordinary vehicles. The pass is at 1840 m elevation. It is one of the points from which many walkers set off to climb Mount Kosciusko 8 km away.

Mount Stilwell, however, is right alongside the pass, rises to 2054 m and provides a quite spectacular view of all the main range and Mount Kosciusko. A foot pad leads from the pass straight up a spur to a summit trig point just 1.5 km distant. To climb this peak and return via the same pad is an excellent option if the long distance to Kosciusko is a deterrent. Mount

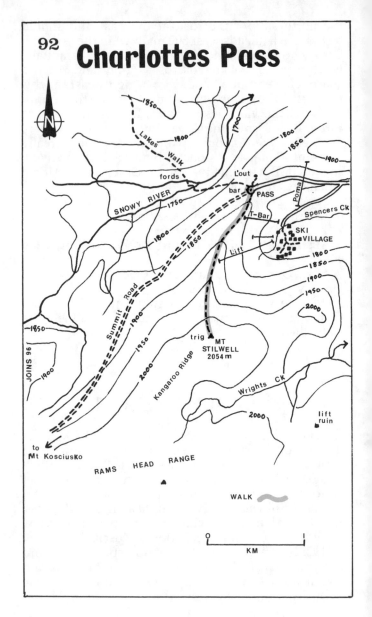

92 **Charlottes Pass**

N

1850

Lakes Walk 1800 1700

fords

1800

1850

1900

SNOWY RIVER 1750

L'out

bar PASS

T-Bar

Poma

Spencers Ck

SKI VILLAGE

1800

Lift

1850

1900

1950

2000

Summit Road

1900

1950

2000

1850

JOINS 96

1900

trig MT STILWELL 2054 m

Kangaroo Ridge

Wrights Ck

2000

lift ruin

to Mt Kosciusko

RAMS HEAD RANGE

WALK

0   1
KM

296

Stilwell's summit is rather rocky, forms part of the Ramshead Range and is well above the tree line. During the spur ascent snow gums are soon left behind and snow grass and low herbage prevails. The top stations of two ski tows are passed after leaving Charlottes Pass and for much of the distance the ski developments at Charlottes Pass are in view.

The weather in the area is notorious for sudden cold changes, so warm clothing is essential for the walk. The summit can be very cold yet the pass is quite comfortable. Do not climb the peak if fog is about as the track is very faint near the summit and there are no track markers.

MAP: Lands, 1:50,000 Mount Kosciusko and Map 92. WALK: One day, 3 km, easy grade, last reviewed January 1992, allow 1½ hours.
Note: The whole district becomes snowbound in winter.

93   CHARLOTTES PASS— KOSCIUSKO SUNRISE

As anybody in Japan will tell you, the best place from which to watch the sun rise is from the top of their country's highest mountain, Fuji San, and close to a quarter of a million persons per year make the big climb. The author was one of them. There is no day of the year when someone is not climbing Fuji, just as there are very few days when it is not snow capped. The Fuji experience gave the author the idea of seeing the sun rise from our country's highest peak, Kosciusko. What an unforgettable morning that turned out to be. The main difference from the Fuji ascent was a complete absence of any people at any stage of the walk. Even into mid-morning Australia's highest mountain was still deserted. It is high time

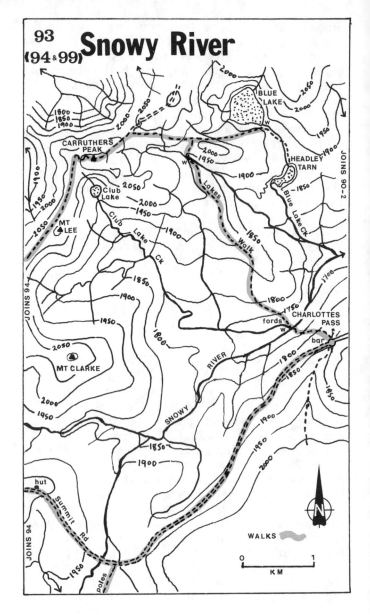

93
(94 & 99) Snowy River

BLUE LAKE

CARRUTHERS PEAK

Club Lake

MT LEE

HEADLEY TARN

JOINS 90–2

Lakes Walk

Blue Lake Ck

Club Lake Ck

JOINS 94

MT CLARKE

CHARLOTTES PASS

fords

bar

SNOWY RIVER

RIVER

hut

Summit Rd

JOINS 94

poles

WALKS

N

0   1
KM

298

Australians realised the grandeur of their own highest peak and more of them undertook the climb.

Try to pick good weather by obtaining a weather forecast the day before, and determine the time of sunrise in advance. The suggestion is to walk the now closed road from Charlottes Pass to the summit, a distance of 8.6 km each way. At least 2½ hours should be allowed prior to dawn to cover the 8.6 km and 400 m rise in elevation. The summit is 2228 m high. It is vital to carry plenty of warm waterproof clothing.

EUCALYPT

From the summit, the panorama is as if specially made for the viewer. On some fine mornings you may be above the clouds of fog in the valleys. The view includes all the main range peaks and even much of north-eastern Victoria.

The access road is easy to follow, but on some dark mornings, a torch for each walker may be advisable. Over the last 1.2 km above Rawsons Pass there are usually large drifts of near-permanent snow to cross. Seamans Hut is passed during the journey and can be useful in bad weather.

To facilitate the early morning walk start, it is worth considering motel or lodge accommodation at nearby Perisher ski village. Camping is not permitted near Charlottes Pass and off-season rates in Perisher village during summer are affordable. Some motels provide evening meals as well as breakfasts. Some walkers may even want to stay on and repeat the experience of seeing sunrise from Kosciusko.

There is a well-known saying in Japan: 'He who

climbs Fuji is a wise man; he who climbs it more than once is a fool'. Having climbed Fuji and Kosciusko the author has to admit he must be on the verge of being a fool as there is a strong urge to climb both again.

An option is to use *Walk No. 94* notes to extend this walk by returning via the lakes rather than simply making the walk back down to Charlottes Pass.

MAP: Lands, 1:50,000 Mount Kosciusko and Maps 93 and 94.
WALK: One day, 17.2 km, medium grade, last reviewed January 1992, allow 6 hours.
Note: The whole district is snowbound in winter.

94   CHARLOTTES PASS— MOUNT KOSCIUSKO— LAKES WALK

Apart from those in Tasmania, Australia has very few mountain tarns—one of the more beautiful features caused by ancient glaciers. Lake Cootapatamba, Lake Albina, Club Lake, Blue Lake and Hedley Tarn are, in fact, about the only sizeable tarns on the Australian mainland. This walk route is to Australia's highest mountain, Mount Kosciusko, then to several of the tarns via a well used track known as the Lakes Walk. The walk is best undertaken from December to March when there is the additional interest of alpine wild-flowers. In winter the whole route is quite snowbound.

Charlottes Pass marks the end of the trafficable road to Mount Kosciusko. Beyond is open to walkers only. Consequently, most people climbing Kosciusko use the Thredbo chairlift and approach the peak from the south on a shorter route than the Charlottes Pass alternative. People walking from Thredbo, however, miss the beautiful Lakes Walk.

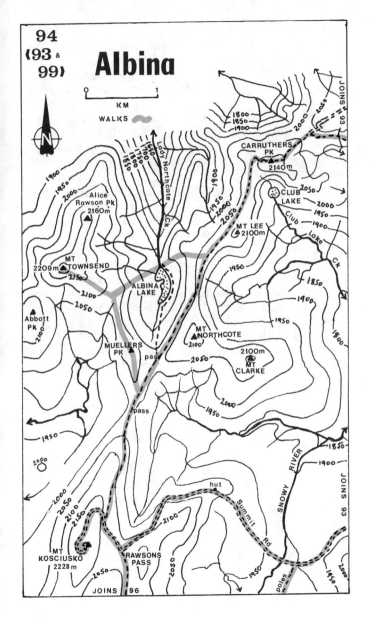

The whole area is treeless, extremely exposed and subject to sudden changes in weather. Commonsense dictates that you keep warm. There is no point in attempting the walk in fog as distant views and views of the tarns are the real feature. Be sure to make an early start.

From Charlottes Pass you should, at first, make the traditional climb to Australia's highest summit—Mount Kosciusko, 2228 m above sea level. No true walker would miss out on this goal. You need to walk up the access road for 8.6 km, including the final ascent of 1.2 km from Rawsons Pass. Above the pass the road sidles up round the northern flanks of the peak, but even in mid-summer virtually permanent snow drifts need to be crossed. Summit views are particularly good westward towards Victoria. Lake Cootapatamba is just below the peak to the south and can be seen from the Rawsons Pass area.

A foot track directly linking Rawsons Pass and the summit is now closed because of erosion problems and walkers are asked to keep to the road despite its extra length.

About midway between Rawsons Pass and the summit, via the road, a foot track leads off north, downhill along the main northern spur of Mount Kosciusko. This is the Lakes Walking Track and leads right along the tops towards Blue Lake. Follow the track down to a saddle where indistinct Hannels Spur Track joins in from the left (west) 1.5 km from the roadway.

Continue on and up the eastern slopes of Muellers Peak to another saddle between it and Mount Northcote. At this point you are some 2 km from the Summit Road and Lake Albina can be seen in the valley northwards. The main track leads up the western slopes of Mount Northcote, bypassing Lake Albina, and another track leads down to the lake. Gentians and other flowers are normally thick in summer.

The lake is in full view as you sidle Mount

Northcote and continue towards Mount Lee. The track is very close to the top of Mount Lee but bypasses it some 4 km from the Summit Road. Another 1.8 km on along the range you gain the summit of sharp Carruthers Peak, 2140 m high. In this area Club Lake can be seen down the slopes to the right. The track tends eastwards over the top, then north-east down to a saddle within 1 km. The main divide is then left at this saddle. The left fork is a minor jeep track up to the summit of Mount Twynam and the right fork is a more major route which should be followed down eastwards for 800 m where there is another track fork.

Take a side trip from this junction in a saddle down to the outlet of lovely Blue Lake. Although the lake is in view without the side trip, the 1 km descent to the outlet is most rewarding as the Blue Lake locality is one of the most scenic parts of the walk. Blue Lake clearly illustrates the effect of ice on the terrain. The scouring action here is obvious.

Camping is no longer permitted at Blue Lake nor in the watershed of each of the glacial lakes on the tops.

After the side trip head off on paved pathway towards the south for 500 m, then south-east after crossing a gully. The well defined Lakes Track continuation can then be descended another 2.9 km to the Snowy River. The stream needs to be forded on stepping stones, then a paved path can be ascended for 600 m back to Charlottes Pass road barrier and the end of the walk.

MAP: Lands, 1:50,000 Mount Kosciusko and Maps 93 and 94.
WALK: One day, 22.2 km, hard grade, last reviewed February 1992, allow 8 hours.
Note: The district is snowbound in winter.

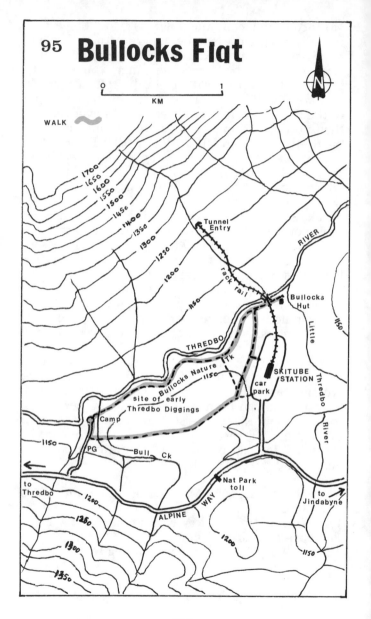

95 **Bullocks Flat**

WALK

304

95 THREDBO DIGGINGS—
BULLOCKS FLAT

Outside Jindabyne along the Alpine Way in the Snowy Mountains is the Bullocks Flat Skitube main valley terminal, surrounded by a huge car park. The terminal is outside the Kosciusko National Park and at 1140 m above sea level is normally below the winter snowline. The Skitube is a full-sized train system which operates over 8 km, mostly underground, to Perisher Valley and on to Blue Calf Mountain (Blue Cow station). It is a Swiss-style rack railway and operates year-round.

At Bullocks Flat there is an excellent circuit walking track from the car park to the old Thredbo diggings, the Thredbo River and to Bullocks Hut. There is a picnic and camping area half way along the circuit and the track picturesquely follows the riverbank of the Thredbo River for 2 km.

Cross the car park to about midway along the western edge and find the start of the walking track which leads into bushland. The track can then be followed clockwise across the former Thredbo diggings via Muzzlewood Track for 1.6 km. At the 400 m stage a track off right and an old track off left should be avoided. The way is across flats and sparse timber to Bull Creek. Over the creek is an access roadway into picnic and camp spots by the Thredbo River. Follow the road to the right for about 200 m to reach the river area and take a break.

Next, cross Bull Creek again close to the Thredbo River and continue around the walk circuit, using the Bullocks Nature Track. It leads downstream along the riverbank for 1.2 km. It is joined by a track from the right, continues by the river for 500 m then is joined by a second track from the right. This latter track marks the later return route to the Skitube station.

Continue near the river and pass under the Skitube

Thredbo River bridge. Within 300 m Bullocks Hut and its outbuildings should be reached. Hedges surround the buildings which are located at the confluence of the Thredbo and Little Thredbo Rivers. The hut dates from the 1930s when a Dr Bullock built it and spent summer holidays fishing and walking in the area.

Retrace the 300 m back under the bridge then fork left to walk the final 400 m back south in bushland to enter the car park. Recross the car park to the station to end the walk.

MAP: Lands, 1:50,000 Mount Kosciusko and Map 95. WALK: One day, 4.5 km, easy grade family suitability, last reviewed January 1992, allow 1¾ hours.

96 THREDBO— MOUNT KOSCIUSKO

Some walkers are content to wander about, simply appreciating their surroundings, while others have that extra yen for peak bagging. And, of course, no peak bagger could ever let an opportunity pass to climb Australia's highest mountain, even if the climb does involve physical effort. There is, however, one way for all walkers to reach Mount Kosciusko and be satisfied and that is to take the Crackenback chairlift from Thredbo ski village to an altitude of 1965 m. It is then a pleasant ramble to Mount Kosciusko at 2228 m.

The route is across treeless, but pleasant, grassy and flower-decked tops. Flowers are at their best from December to March. This approach to Mount Kosciusko is the most popular as well as the easiest of alternatives. In mid-summer hundreds of people make the trip each day. Fog can create danger, as can very exposed conditions. It is comforting to know that for much of the distance there is a track of mesh-

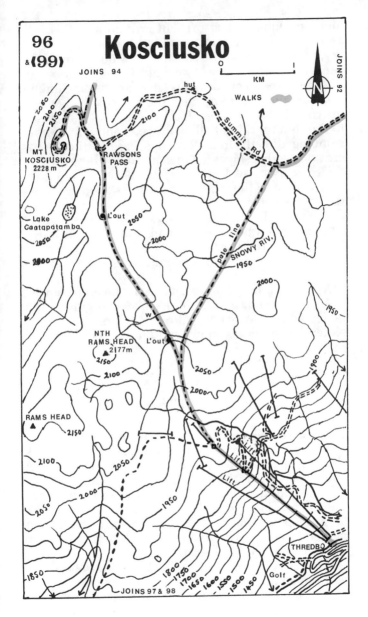

Kosciusko

JOINS 94

JOINS 92

0   KM   1

N

MT KOSCIUSKO 2228 m

2260
2100
2150

RAWSONS PASS

hut

WALKS

2100

Summit Rd

L'out

2050

2000

Lake Caatapatamba

2050

2000

pole line

SNOWY RIV.
1950

2000

1950

NTH RAMS HEAD
▲2177m
2150

w

L'out

2050

2000

1900

RAMS HEAD
▲   2150

2100

2050

2000

2050

1950

1950

Lift

Lift

Lift

THREDBO

1850

1800 1750 1700 1650 1600 1550 1500 1450

Golf

JOINS 97 & 98

metal decking laid to prevent erosion and this acts as an excellent navigation guide.

About 2 km from the top station Mount Kosciusko comes into view and at 4 km Lake Cootapatamba can be seen to the west. Rawsons Pass and the old Summit Road are reached 1 km later. The disused road curves up round the northern flanks of Mount Kosciusko to the summit cairn. Follow the road and refrain from climbing directly from Rawsons Pass to the top as erosion of the slopes has occurred in the past and a former foot pad has had to be closed. It is 1.2 km via the road to the top and snowdrifts often lie across the road even in mid-summer.

The Kosciusko summit view includes all of Australia's highest peaks and the view towards Victoria is particularly good.

For the return walk retrace the same track.

MAP: Lands, 1:50,000 Mount Kosciusko and Map 96. WALK: One day, 12.4 km, medium grade, last reviewed February 1992, allow 4½ hours.
Note: The district is snowbound in winter.

97   THREDBO—RAMSHEAD— DEAD HORSE GAP

Thredbo ski village, like other ski resorts in the Snowy Mountains has good walking areas. Crackenback chairlift at Thredbo operates during summer and it rises from 1370 m above sea level to 1965 m, so saving a lot of arduous climbing for those wanting to see the tops. It is suggested that you make use of the lift and spend time seeing the Ramshead area, then descend back to Thredbo on a track to Dead Horse Gap and along the Thredbo River.

Once at the top of the chairlift, the country becomes quite open and treeless in parts. The open places of course, are good for views and alpine flowers.

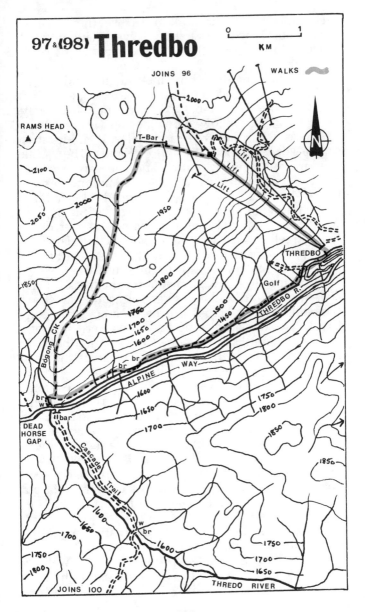

97&(98) **Thredbo**

0   1
KM

WALKS

JOINS 96

2000

RAMS HEAD

N

T-Bar

Lift

2100

Lift

2050

Lift

2000

1950

THREDBO

1800

Golf

1850

1750

THREDBO R.

1700
1650
1600

1500

1450

Bogong Ck.

br   br

ALPINE   WAY

1600

1750

1800

br
w

1650

DEAD
HORSE
GAP

bar

1700

1850

Cascade

Trail

1400

1650

w
br

1600

1750

1700

1650

1700

1800
1750

JOINS 100

THREDO RIVER

Do not attempt the walk in bad weather; it could prove most uncomfortable and even dangerous. A feature of the walk is the view so there is little point in heading off in fog.

Ride the chairlift, but instead of taking the traditional track to Mount Kosciusko, walk to the left (west) to the Basin T-bar ski lift about 300 m away. From this T-bar follow snowpoles on westwards up to Karels T-bar and to a saddle at 2019 m elevation to the left (south) of the top of Karels. The saddle is 1 km from the top station and the way becomes more defined as the track starts a 4 km long descent to the Dead Horse Gap area. Ramshead (2190 m high) is seen about 1.5 km due west. The track is marked with more snowpoles as it leads south-west down to the treeline. Views in this section include The Pilot and The Cobberas (Victoria) to the south, and many peaks in the Victorian Alps to the south-west.

Once into the snow gum country the track is fairly pronounced and walking is very pleasant. Ramshead can still be seen across the headwaters of Bogong Creek. The track sidles down the western face of a spur which marks the Bogong Creek—Thredbo River divide. The track then gains the crest of the spur and continues downhill. South Ramshead (1951 m high) is seen 2 km west as the track crosses some grassy flats on the spur crest. The pad then steepens significantly to lead south for 1 km down to the Dead Horse Gap area. Just as the grassy banks of the Thredbo River are reached there is a T junction of the track system at 1550 m altitude. The left fork is the riverside track to Thredbo. The right fork crosses Bogong Creek by foot bridge to link with the adjacent sealed Alpine Way. This area is ideal for lunch or any other break.

In returning to Thredbo an alternative would be to simply walk down the Alpine Way. The much better and recommended route is via the walking track. It keeps close by the river for most of the way. It crosses to the south bank for a short stretch then

310

resumes north bank alignment. Bridges are provided. Not much further on there is a small waterfall to enjoy. After 3.5 km, Thredbo is neared and the track divides at the western end of the golf course. Fork right to maintain riverside walking past the golf course in an area popular for trout fishing. Within 1 km, Friday Drive is reached and the river is crossed by road bridge. It is then just 400 m along Friday Drive near the river to the Crackenback chairlift terminal and walk end.

MAP: Lands, 1:50,000 Mount Kosciusko and Thredbo sheets and Map 97.
WALK: One day, 10 km, medium grade, last reviewed January 1992, allow 4 hours.
Note: The district is snowbound in winter.

98   THREDBO RIVER— DEAD HORSE GAP

Thredbo Alpine Village at 1370 m above sea level in the Kosciusko National Park is a delightful base for summer walks, either on to the main range or near the Thredbo River. One of the most pleasant walks is upstream beside the river, past the golf course and some waterfalls to Dead Horse Gap, 5.2 km distant and 1590 m above sea level. The track remains close to the river and is mostly within alpine herblands and snow gums. Dead Horse Gap marks the crest of the Dividing Range and the Alpine Way passes through it, leading to Khancoban and Victoria.

Start the walk from the car park area on Friday Drive in the ski village near the main Valley Terminal (Crackenback chairlift) and Thredbo Alpine Hotel. Walk 400 m south-west along Friday Drive, passing the village green. Cross the Thredbo River on a bridge providing access to tennis courts and the golf course. The riverside walking track then diverges off left from near the bridge and stays close to the north bank of the river thus providing good access for trout fishing enthusiasts.

After passing the golf course you reach a track junction 1 km from Friday Drive. Keep left so as to maintain the riverside track. A small waterfall is passed and then the route crosses the river on two bridges. It temporarily follows the south bank and avoids a section of steep slopes. As Dead Horse Gap is neared, a track from the main range descends steeply on a spur to link with the riverside track. The combined route then crosses Bogong Creek on a bridge and joins on to the adjacent Alpine Way. This spot is grassy and a suitable place for lunch. Follow the road 300 m west to reach Dead Horse Gap. Again, it is grassy and pleasant.

Study the map and you will note the unusual geological situation at the gap. Once the headwaters of the Thredbo River flowed north-west to the gap then through the gap down Dead Horse Creek to the Murray River. Bogong Creek also flowed into the Murray River. Erosion caused the change of stream flow towards Thredbo. Now the Thredbo River is only 300 m from the crest of the Dividing Range.

The origin of the Dead Horse Gap name is obscure but the district is steeped in the history of alpine cattle grazing. Horses used by the cattlemen for mustering were the progenitors of the now numerous wild horses (brumbies) which roam the ranges.

The rest of the walk involves retracing the river route. This is the recommended and most pleasant route. An alternative is to walk down the Alpine Way to Thredbo ski village. The road is fairly narrow, so take care and walk facing on-coming traffic.

MAP: Lands, 1:50,000 Thredbo and Map 97.
WALK: One day, 10.4 km, easy grade, last reviewed January 1992, allow 3½ hours.
Note: The whole district becomes snowbound in winter.

99 THREDBO—MAIN RANGE—
MOUNT TWYNAM

Undoubtedly the main range of the Snowy Mountains ranks as one of the best walking venues in New South Wales or, for that matter, in Australia. Every Australian peak over 2000 m high, except three, is situated in the range and the other three are all nearby. The tops are exposed and treeless with expansive views and there is a fair amount of interest caused by glacial action in the past. Apart from those in Tasmania, Australia's only tarns are here and the range is also renowned for displays of alpine flowers in summer.

A truly memorable two day walk circuit is possible, starting and finishing at Thredbo ski village on the Alpine Way, with an overnight camp near 2196 m high Mount Twynam. The route includes the highest summits in Australia. The walk grading, however, is not hard as the circuit remains high and none of the peaks involve long climbs.

Use the Crackenback chairlift from Thredbo village to save a 600 m climb in elevation.

The only major cause for concern is the weather, which can become quite foul and is apt to change dramatically. Should foggy conditions occur, extreme care should be exercised and compasses must be used. In a number of places snowpole lines can be used for guidance. The best time to visit the area is in mid-summer. In winter the whole district gets snowbound.

From the top station of the Crackenback chairlift, at 1965 m, set off north-west following a paved track up through alpine meadow for about 2 km to a point east of the peak of North Ramshead. The spot is on a spur and provides the first view of Mount Kosciusko. Long stretches of steel mesh decking cover the track in this area. It has been installed to prevent erosion as many thousands of walkers use the section to climb Mount Kosciusko. The mesh allows water to pass underneath and plants likewise can grow under the raised decking.

At 4 km there is a good view west to Lake Cootapatamba, a glacial tarn, and at 5 km Rawsons Pass and the Summit Road are reached.

Follow the old road (closed to vehicular traffic) as it curves up around the northern flanks of Mount Kosciusko to the summit cairn 1.2 km away. A direct track linking Rawsons Pass and the top is now closed due to erosion and park authorities ask walkers to refrain from climbing over the grassy slopes to short-cut the road.

Mount Kosciusko, at 2228 m, is Australia's highest mountain so that you can finally say you have reached the top of the country. The summit view includes all of Australia's highest peaks and the view west towards Victoria is particularly good.

Next, retrace 600 m down the road and double back north-north-east on to the Lakes Walking Track which is close to the crest of the range. At the first saddle down the track 1.5 km away, indistinct Hannels Spur Track enters from the left, but should be ignored. Climb up to the top of Muellers Peak 2120 m high next, which requires veering left off the main track for 500 m. Muellers provides more wonderful views including one down to Lake Albina from the north side of the peak. Go north-north-west from the top, then drop packs after 1 km in a saddle and head off north-west to scale Mount Townsend, Australia's second highest at 2210 m. Its summit is only 2 km from Muellers Peak, and views are best to the north-west.

Go back to the packs and pick a route down the very steep slopes to the outlet of Lake Albina. The descent is 1 km long and quite time-consuming because of the lack of any track, the steepness, and the rocks. There is still some 6.8 km to walk for the day so, depending upon available time, have a rest by this lovely tarn. About 100 m up the slopes on the west side of the lakes outlet there are really good views of Watsons Crags and Lady Northcote's Canyon.

Ascend the slopes steeply east from Lake Albina's northern (outlet) end to rejoin the main Lakes Track on the tops 700 m away. The climb is hard but, once on the tops, walking for the rest of the day is easier. At the track, turn left and walk over Mount Lee 2100 m high and sharp Carruthers Peak (2140 m) 1.8 km away. Thereafter, start an easterly descent for 1 km off the peak to then fork left at a saddle on to minor Mount Twynam jeep track. Club Lake is in view throughout the Carruthers Peak area and is another glacial tarn. Camping is no longer permitted in the catchment areas of the glacial tarns so the aim is to spend the night in the saddle between Mount Twynam and Mount Little Twynam.

To reach camp, follow the disused Mount Twynam jeep track for 2.5 km to a spot just 200 m north-west of the summit of Mount Twynam. The track veers off left downhill at this point. Cross the bleak grassy top and head south-east for another 600 m into the saddle area for camp. Mount Twynam is Australia's third highest peak at 2196 m. Camp water is plentiful just east of the saddle.

On the second day walk over Mount Little Twynam, then go south until 1 km from camp then turn west and pick a route down the boulder-strewn grassy slopes to the mouth of Blue Lake. This routing helps avoid awkward steep slopes verging on cliffs. Blue Lake is a beautiful glacial lake in which a rare shrimp lives. The mouth of the lake is about 1.5 km from camp.

Next climb 1 km west on a track up to a junction and in so doing achieve excellent views of Blue Lake. The Lakes Track is rejoined at this junction in a saddle. Turn left on to a paved section of path and head basically down south-east for 3.4 km to the Snowy River.

The stream needs to be forded on stepping stones, then climb the paved path to Charlottes Pass and car park 600 m away. Turn right to follow the now closed Kosciusko Summit Road south-west for 4.5 km to a creek and snowpole line off left. Broad expansive views of the main range are a feature of the road walk.

A narrow foot pad leads over snow grasses along the pole line and should be followed south-south-west across plains. Small streams on the plains need to be crossed on stepping stones in a couple of places. After 3.5 km of following the pole line rejoin the outward route. This junction occurs after the pole line has passed over a low saddle. Finally, walk the 1.5 km of the main track back to the top station and descend the Crackenback chairlift to Thredbo village to end what should have been a walk which will be remembered for life.

MAP: Lands, 1:50,000 Mount Kosciusko and Maps 96, 94, 93 and 90–3.
WALK: Two days, 35.6 km, (day one 19.6 km, day two 16 km), medium grade, last reviewed February 1992, allow 8 hours and 7 hours for each day.
Note: The whole district becomes snowbound in winter.
Warning: If fog is a possibility it would be unwise to take the option to drop packs for the Mount Townsend deviation. Much of the walk is over very exposed terrain above the treeline in an area where violent weather changes can occur and where walkers need to be prepared for blizzard conditions even in mid-summer.

100 DEAD HORSE GAP—
CASCADE HUT

The southern part of the Kosciusko National Park includes large tracts of wilderness along the Great Dividing Range. Cascade Trail, a little-used park maintenance jeep track provides access along the range through the wilderness southwards to the tin mine area and beyond. Alpine vegetation predominates throughout the whole district and there are views at the higher points along the range. Cascade Trail commences at the Alpine Way near Dead Horse Gap, leads up the Thredbo River valley, crosses the Dividing Range and then leads up Cascade Creek valley. It passes an historic cattleman's slab timber and tin hut called Cascade Hut. Brumbies are common throughout the Cascades area and are usually seen grazing near the hut. The Cascades are a series of creeks which descend the western slopes of the Dividing Range into Cascade Creek, a tributary of the Murray River.

It is an excellent plan therefore to walk from the Alpine Way near Dead Horse Gap to Cascade Hut, stay overnight and retrace the route next day. The walk start is about 4 km from Thredbo ski village and 300 m east of Dead Horse Gap. There is a road barrier across Cascade Trail at the spot beside the Thredbo River.

Note the streamflow pattern at Dead Horse Gap with the aid of a map. The headwaters of the Thredbo River flow north-west to near Dead Horse Gap where once they flowed across the gap and down Dead Horse Creek to the Murray River. Erosion has re-routed the Thredbo River (and Bogong Creek) eastwards to Thredbo.

Head off south on Cascade Trail to walk 2 km up the valley of the Thredbo River. There are snow gums and low alpine shrubs on the slopes. The valley floor is exposed and covered with alpine grasses. Cross

317

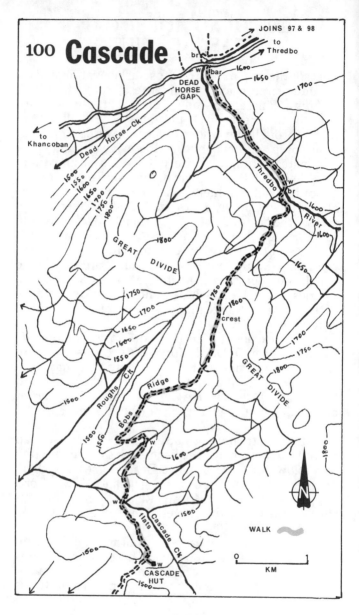

100 **Cascade**

JOINS 97 & 98

to Thredbo

br

w bar

DEAD HORSE GAP

1600

1650

1700

to Khancoban

Dead Horse Ck

1500
1550
1600
1650
1700
1750
1800

Thredbo

w bt

1600

River

1600

1650

GREAT

DIVIDE

1800

1750
1700

1650
1600
1550

1750

1800

crest

1700
1750

GREAT

DIVIDE

1800

1500

Roughs Ck

Bobs Ridge

1500
1550

w

1600

1800

w

flats

Cascade Ck

1500

WALK

N

w

CASCADE HUT

1500

0   KM

1500

the river on a bridge at 1600 m elevation then climb the Dividing Range for 2 km, ascending 180 m in the process. At the crest there are good views west and south to Victoria and the Pilot Wilderness area.

Attractive snow gums cover the range tops but are sparse and do not obscure the views much. Next, Bobs Ridge needs to be descended for 2 km south-west off the Dividing Range into forest and to a hairpin bend on the ridge. Then the track doubles back down via a side gully for 1.2 km to Cascade Creek, 320 m lower than the Dividing Range crest. Cross the creek and 800 m along the south side of the Cascade Creek plains, the jeep track turns away uphill slightly and into snow gums. Follow a 200 m long side track into Cascade Hut on the left soon after entering the snow gums. A tiny side stream joins Cascade Creek and the hut is situated in the V of the confluence but back among snow gums for shelter. This side stream provides water for the hut. There is a large tin fireplace, bunks and an exterior toilet. Replace any firewood used and leave the hut tidy. In the evening a short walk on the plain near the hut could be an enjoyable end to the day.

Next day, use the same track to retrace the 8 km back to the Alpine Way. Remember that there is a 320 m ascent up Bobs Ridge. The rest of the way is easy walking.

MAP: Lands, 1:50,000 Thredbo and Map 100.
WALK: Two days, 16 km spread over two days of 8 km, easy grade, last reviewed January 1992, allow 3½ hours each day.
Note: The whole district becomes snowbound in winter.